Who Should Read This Book?

We've all heard the scenario: the family on vacation stops at a road-side "dig your own" gem mine. Junior finds a sapphire the size of a peach and ends up on national television telling the world how he will spend his fortune.

T This book is for those who have read these stories and want their chance to find their own fortune. It is also a book for those who would enjoy the adventure of finding a few gems, getting them cut or polished, and making their own jewelry. It is a book for those people who want to plan a gem hunting vacation with their family. It is a book for those who study the metaphysical properties of gems and minerals and would like to add to their personal collections.

T This book is for those who would like to keep the art of rock-hounding alive and pass it on to their children. It is a book on where to find your own gems and minerals and on how to begin what for many is a lifelong hobby.

T This is a book for those who aren't interested in the "hidden treasure map through mosquito-infested no-man's-land" approach to treasure hunting but do want to find gems and minerals. It is for those who want to get out the pick and shovel and get a little dirty. (Although at some mines they bring the buckets of pre-dug dirt to you at an environmentally temperature controlled sluicing area.)

Many an unsuspecting tourist has stopped at a mine to try his or her luck and become a rockhound for life. Watch out! Your collection may end up taking the place of your car in your garage.

Good hunting!

This volume is one in a four-volume series.

VOLUME 1: **Northwest States**
Alaska
Idaho
Iowa
Minnesota
Montana
Nebraska
North Dakota
Oregon
South Dakota
Washington
Wyoming

VOLUME 2: **Southwest States**
Arizona
California
Colorado
Hawaii
Kansas
Nevada
New Mexico
Oklahoma
Texas
Utah

VOLUME 3: **Southeast States**
Alabama
Arkansas
Florida
Georgia
Kentucky
Louisiana
Mississippi
Missouri
North Carolina
South Carolina
Tennessee
Virginia
West Virginia

VOLUME 4: **Northeast States**
Connecticut
Delaware
District of Columbia
Illinois
Indiana
Maine
Maryland
Massachusetts
Michigan
New Hampshire
New Jersey
New York
Ohio
Pennsylvania
Rhode Island
Vermont
Wisconsin

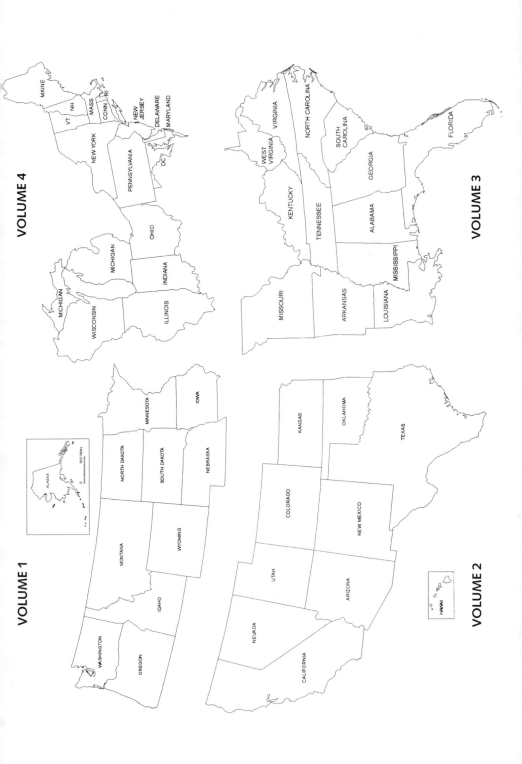

VOLUME 1

VOLUME 2

VOLUME 3

VOLUME 4

The Treasure Hunter's

GEM & MINERAL
GUIDES TO THE U.S.A.

5TH EDITION

Where & How to Dig, Pan, and Mine
Your Own Gems & Minerals

VOLUME 4: NORTHEAST STATES

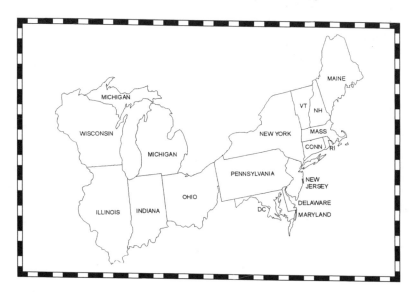

by KATHY J. RYGLE AND STEPHEN F. PEDERSEN
Preface by Antoinette Matlins, PG,
author of *Gem Identification Made Easy*

GEMSTONE PRESS
Woodstock, Vermont

The Treasure Hunter's Gem & Mineral Guides to the U.S.A.: 5th Edition
Where & How to Dig, Pan and Mine Your Own Gems & Minerals
Volume 4: Northeast States

2011 Fifth Edition, Quality Paperback, First Printing
© 2011 by Kathy J. Rygle and Stephen F. Pedersen
Preface © 2008 by Antoinette Matlins

Library of Congress Cataloging-in-Publication Data
Available upon request.

ISBNs for fifth edition:

Volume 1: 978-0-943763-74-3 (NW)
Volume 2: 978-0-943763-75-0 (SW)
Volume 3: 978-0-943763-77-4 (SE)
Volume 4: 978-0-943763-76-7 (NE)

Cover design by Bronwen Battaglia
Text design by Chelsea Dippel
10 9 8 7 6 5 4 3 2 1
Manufactured in the United States of America

Published by GemStone Press
A Division of LongHill Partners, Inc.
Sunset Farm Offices, Route 4, P.O. Box 237
Woodstock, VT 05091
Tel: (802) 457-4000   Fax: (802) 457-4004
www.gemstonepress.com

Dedications, with love, to our parents and children:

To my parents, Joe and Helen Rygle, who taught me the love of nature; my earliest remembrances of "rockhounding" are hikes with my dad in the fields, forests, and streams near our home. I also remember weekend trips with my mother to a shop that sold specimens of minerals from around the world. To my daughter, Annie Rygle, who shares with me the wonders of nature. Also, thanks to Annie for helping me sort the information for the first three editions.   —K. J. R.

To my parents, Cliff and Leone Pedersen, who taught me to value nature and to not quit. To my daughters Kristi and Debbie, who challenge me to keep growing.   —S. F. P.

To our combined families, including Georgia Pedersen, and to family no longer with us.

With special thanks:

To all the owners of fee dig mines and guide services, curators and staff of public and private museums, mine owners, miners, and fellow lapidarists. Our thanks to all those individuals both past and present who share the wonders of the earth with us.

To our agent, Barb Doyen, and her childhood rock collection.

To our publisher, Stuart M. Matlins; editors Emily Wichland, Erin Ryan, and Daniela Cockwill; Production members Tim Holtz, Gloria Todt, Kristi Menter, and Heather Pelham; and all the staff at GemStone Press for their guidance, assistance, and patience.

To Mrs. Betty Jackson for, in her own way, telling Kathy to write the books.

To God and the wonders He has given us.

And finally, to each other, with love and the perseverance to keep on trying.

Volume 4—Northeast States

CONTENTS

PREFACE
All-American Gems

by Antoinette Matlins, PG

When Americans think of costly and fabled gems, they associate them with exotic origins—Asia, South Africa or Brazil. They envision violent jungle quests or secret cellars of a sultanate, perhaps scenes from a Jorge Amado novel or from *A Thousand and One Nights*, a voluptuous Indian princess whose sari is adorned with the plentiful rubies and sapphires of her land, or a Chinese emperor sitting atop a throne flanked by dragons carved from exquisitely polished jade.

Asked what gems are mined in the United States, most Americans would probably draw a blank. We know our country is paved with one of the finest highway systems in the world, but we don't know that just below the surface, and sometimes on top of it, is a glittering pavement of gemstones that would color Old Glory. The red rubies of North Carolina, the white diamonds of Arkansas, the blue sapphires of Montana—America teems with treasures that its citizens imagine come from foreign lands. These include turquoise, tourmaline, amethyst, pearls, opals, jade, sapphires, emeralds, rubies, and even gem-quality diamonds.

Not only does America have quantity, it has quality. American gems compare very favorably with gems from other countries. In fact, fine gemstones found in the U.S. can rival specimens from anywhere else in the world. Some gems, like the luxurious emerald-green hiddenite and steely blue benitoite, are found only in America. Others, like the tourmalines of Maine and California, rival specimens found in better-known locations such as Brazil and Zambia.

The discovery of gemstones in U.S. terrain has been called a lost chapter in American history. It continues to be a saga of fashion and fable that, like the stones themselves, are a deep part of our national heritage. Appreciation of our land's generous yield of sparkling colored stones reached a zenith at the end of the nineteenth century with the art nouveau movement and its utilization of them. When the Boer Wars ended, South Africa's diamonds and platinum eclipsed many of our own then so-called semiprecious stones. Not until the 1930s, and again starting with the 1960s, did economics and the yen for color make gems more desirable again.

In the late 1800s, the nation sought out and cherished anything that was unique to the land. The search for gemstones in America coincided with the exploration of the West, and nineteenth-century mineralogists, some bonafide and others self-proclaimed, fulfilled that first call for "Made in America." Their discoveries created sensations not only throughout America but in the capitals of Europe and as far away as China. The Europeans, in fact, caught on before the Americans, exhibiting some of America's finest specimens in many of Europe's great halls.

But the search for gemstones in this country goes back even further than the nineteenth century. In 1541, the Spanish explorer Francisco Coronado trekked north from Mexico in the footsteps of Cortés and Pizarro, searching not only for gold but also for turquoise, amethyst and emeralds. In the early 1600s, when English settlers reached Virginia, they had been instructed "to searche for gold and such jeweles as ye may find."

But what eluded the Spanish explorers and early settlers was unearthed by their descendants. Benitoite, which may be our nation's most uniquely attractive gem, was discovered in 1907 in California's San Benito River headwaters. A beautiful, rare gem with the color of fine sapphire and the fire of a diamond, benitoite is currently found in gem quality only in San Benito, California.

Like many of America's finest stones discovered during the "Gem Rush" of the nineteenth century, benitoite was held in higher regard throughout the rest of the world than it was on its native U.S. soil.

The gem occurs most commonly in various shades of blue. A fine-quality blue benitoite can resemble fine blue sapphire, but it is even more brilliant. It has one weakness, however: in comparison to sapphire, it is relatively soft. It is therefore best used in pendants, brooches and earrings, or in rings with a protective setting.

While benitoite is among the rarest of our gems, our riches hardly stop there. America is the source of other unusual gems, including three even more uniquely American stones, each named after an American: kunzite, hiddenite and morganite.

The story of all-American kunzite is inseparable from the achievements of two men: Charles Lewis Tiffany, founder of Tiffany & Co., and Dr. George Frederick Kunz, world-renowned gemologist. By seeking, collecting and promoting gems found in America, these two did more for the development of native stones than anyone else during, or since, their time.

While working for Tiffany in the late 1800s, Dr. Kunz received a package in the mail containing a stone that the sender believed to be an unusual tourmaline. The stone came from an abandoned mine at Pala Mountain, California, where collectors had found traces of spodumene—a gemstone prized by the ancients but which no one had been able to find for many years. Dr. Kunz was ecstatic to find before him a specimen of "extinct spodumene of a gloriously lilac color." A fellow gemologist, Dr. Charles Baskerville, named the find "kunzite" in his honor.

Kunzite has become a favorite of such designers as Paloma Picasso, not only because of its distinctive shades—lilac, pink, and yellow-green orchid—but because it is one of a diminishing number of gems available in very large sizes at affordable prices. It is a perfect choice for the centerpiece around which to create a very bold, dramatic piece of jewelry. Designer Picasso's creations include a magnificent necklace using a 400-carat kunzite. Although it is a moderately hard stone, kunzite is easily fractured, and care must be taken to avoid any sharp blows.

Kunzite's sister gem, hiddenite, is also a truly "all-American" stone. In 1879, William Earl Hidden, an engraver and mineralogist, was sent to North Carolina on behalf of the great American inventor and prospector Thomas Alva Edison to search for platinum. Hidden found none of the precious white metal but in his pursuit unearthed a new green gemstone, which was named "hiddenite" in his honor.

Less well known than kunzite, hiddenite is an exquisite, brilliant emerald-green variety of spodumene not found anyplace else in the world. While light green and yellow-green shades have been called hiddenite, the Gemological Institute of America—this country's leading authority on gemstones—considers only the emerald-green shade of spodumene, found exclusively in the Blue Ridge Mountains of Mitchell County, North Carolina, to be true hiddenite.

The foothills of the Blue Ridge Mountains also possess America's most significant emerald deposits. While output is minimal compared to Colombia, Zambia or Pakistan, the Rist Mine in Hiddenite, North Carolina, has produced some very fine emeralds, comparable to Colombian stones. The discovery was first made by a farmer plowing his field who found them lying loose on the soil. The country folk, not knowing what they had come across, called the stones "green bolts."

In August 1970, a 26-year-old "rock hound" named Wayne Anthony found a glowing 59-carat "green bolt" at the Rist Mine only two feet from the surface. It was cut into a 13.14-carat emerald of very fine color. Tiffany & Co. later purchased the stone and called it the Carolina Emerald. "The gem is superb," said Paul E. Desautels, then the curator of mineralogy at the Smithsonian Institution. "It can stand on its own merits as a fine and lovely gem of emerald from anywhere, including Colombia." In 1973, the emerald became the official state stone of North Carolina.

A California prize, the warm peach- or pink-shaded morganite, was named by Dr. Kunz for financier John Pierpont Morgan, who purchased the Bement gem collection for donation to the American Museum of Natural History in New York, where it can be viewed today. Morganite is a member of the beryl family, which gives us aquamarine (the clear blue variety of beryl) and emerald (the deep green variety of beryl). However, morganite is available in much larger sizes than its mineralogical cousins and is much more affordable.

Many consider the core of our national treasure chest to be gems like the tourmalines of Maine and California and the sapphires of Montana, gems that are mined in commercial quantities and have earned worldwide reputations. One day in the fall of 1820, two young boys, Ezekiel Holmes and Elijah Hamlin, were rock hunting on Mount Mica in Oxford County, Maine. On the way home, one of the boys saw a flash of green light coming from underneath an uprooted tree. The find was later identified as tourmaline, and Mount Mica became the site of the first commercial gem mine in the United States. The mine was initially worked by Elijah Hamlin and his brother Hannibal, who later became Abraham Lincoln's vice president.

The colors of the rainbow meld delicately in the tourmalines of Maine, producing some of the finest specimens in the world, rivaling in quality even those from Brazil. A 150-mile strip in central Maine provides shades of apple green, burgundy red and salmon pink, to mention just a few. Some stones are bi-colored.

Miners are kept busy in the Pala district of San Diego County, California, as well. California, in fact, is North America's largest producer of gem-quality tourmaline.

The hot-pink tourmalines, for which California is famous, began to come into greater demand in 1985, as pastel-colored stones became more and more coveted by chic women around the globe. Curiously enough, over one hundred years ago the Chinese rejoiced in the fabulous colors of this fashionable stone. The Empress Dowager of the Last Chinese Imperial Dynasty sent emissaries to California in search of pink tourmalines. She garnished her robes with carved tourmaline buttons and toggles, and started a fad which overtook China. Much of the empress's collection of fine carvings was lost or stolen when the dynasty fell around 1912, but artifacts made from California's pink tourmaline can be seen today in a Beijing museum. China's fascination with pink tourmalines lasted long after the empress. In 1985, a contingent of the Chinese Geological Survey came to California with two requests: to see Disneyland and the Himalaya Mine, original site of California pink tourmaline.

While the Chinese are mesmerized by our tourmalines, Americans have always been attracted to China's jade. But perhaps we ought to take stock of our own. Wyoming, in fact, is the most important producer of the stone in the Western Hemisphere. The state produces large quantities of good-quality green nephrite jade—the type most commonly used in jewelry and carvings. California also boasts some jade, as does Alaska. Chinese immigrants panning for gold in California in the late 1800s found large boulders of nephrite and sent them back to China, where the jade was carved and sold within China and around the world.

The U.S. is also one of the largest producers of turquoise. Americans mostly associate this stone with American Indian jewelry, but its use by mainstream designers has regularly come in and out of fashion.

Some of the most prized gems of America are the stunning sapphires from Yogo Gulch, Montana. These sapphires emit a particularly pleasing shade of pale blue, and are known for their clarity and brilliance.

The Montana mine was originally owned by a gold-mining partnership. In 1895, an entire summer's work netted a total of only $700 in gold plus a cigar box full of heavy blue stones. The stones were sent to Tiffany & Co. to be identified. Tiffany then sent back a check for $3,750 for the entire box of obviously valuable stones.

Once one can conceive of gem-quality sapphires in America, it takes only a small stretch of the mind to picture the wonderful diamonds found here. A 40.23-carat white gem found in Murfreesboro, Arkansas, was cut into a 14.42-carat emerald-cut diamond named Uncle Sam. Other large diamonds include a 23.75-carat diamond found in the mid-nineteenth century in Manchester, Virginia, and a greenish 34.46-carat diamond named the Punch Jones, which was claimed to have been found in Peterstown, West Virginia.

Each year, thousands of people visit Crater of Diamonds State Park in Arkansas, where, for a fee, they can mine America's only proven location of gem-quality diamonds. Among them is a group known as "regulars" who visit the park looking for their "retirement stone."

In 1983, one of the regulars, 82-year-old Raymond Shaw, came across a 6.7-carat rough diamond. He sold it for $15,000 uncut. According to Mark Myers, assistant superintendent of the state park, the stone was cut into an exceptionally fine, 2.88-carat gem (graded E/Flawless by the Gemological Institute of America). Myers says the cut stone, later called the Shaw Diamond, was offered for sale for $58,000.

Diamonds have also been found along the shores of the Great Lakes, in many localities in California, in the Appalachian Mountains, in Illinois, Indiana, Ohio, Kentucky, New York, Idaho and Texas. Exploration for diamonds continues in Michigan, Wisconsin, Colorado and Wyoming, according to the U.S. Bureau of Mines. The discovery of gem-quality diamonds in Alaska in 1986 initiated a comprehensive search there for man's most valued gem.

Many questions concerning this country's store of gems remain unanswered. "Numerous domestic deposits of semiprecious gem stones are known and have been mined for many years," wrote the Bureau of Mines in a 1985 report. "However, no systematic evaluations of the magnitude of these deposits have been made and no positive statements can be made about them." Even as the United States continues to offer up its kaleidoscopic range of gems, our American soil may hold a still greater variety and quantity of gems yet to be unearthed.

And here, with the help of these down-to-earth (in the best possible way!)

guides, you can experience America's gem and mineral riches for yourself. In these pages rockhounds, gemologists, vacationers, and families alike will find a hands-on introduction to the fascinating world of gems and minerals . . . and a treasure map to a sparkling side of America. Happy digging!

T

Antoinette Matlins, PG, is the most widely read author in the world on the subject of jewelry and gems (*Jewelry & Gems: The Buying Guide* alone has over 400,000 copies in print). Her books are published in six languages and are widely used throughout the world by consumers and professionals in the gem and jewelry fields. An internationally respected gem and jewelry expert and a popular media guest, she is frequently quoted as an expert source in print media and is seen on ABC, CBS, NBC, and CNN, educating the public about gems and jewelry and exposing fraud. In addition, Matlins is active in the gem trade. Her books include *Jewelry & Gems: The Buying Guide; Jewelry & Gems at Auction: The Definitive Guide to Buying & Selling at the Auction House & on Internet Auction Sites; Colored Gemstones: The Antoinette Matlins Buying Guide—How to Select, Buy, Care for & Enjoy Sapphires, Emeralds, Rubies and Other Colored Gems with Confidence and Knowledge; Diamonds: The Antoinette Matlins Buying Guide—How to Select, Buy, Care for & Enjoy Diamonds with Confidence and Knowledge; Engagement & Wedding Rings: The Definitive Buying Guide for People in Love; The Pearl Book: The Definitive Buying Guide;* and *Gem Identification Made Easy: A Hands-On Guide to More Confident Buying & Selling* (all GemStone Press).

Introduction

This is a guide to commercially operated gem and mineral mines (fee dig mines) within the United States that offer would-be treasure hunters the chance to "dig their own," from diamonds to thundereggs.

For simplicity, the term *fee dig site* is used to represent all types of fee-based mines or collection sites. However, for liability reasons, many mines no longer let collectors dig their own dirt, but rather dig it for them and provide it in buckets or bags. Some fee-based sites involve surface collection.

This book got its start when the authors, both environmental scientists, decided to make their own wedding rings. Having heard stories about digging your own gems, they decided to dig their own stones for their rings. So off to Idaho and Montana they went, taking their three children, ages 8, 13, and 15 at the time, in search of opals and garnets, their birthstones. They got a little vague information before and during the trip on where to find gem mines and in the process got lost in some of those "mosquito-infested lands." But when they did find actual "dig your own" mines (the kind outlined in this book), they found opals, garnets, and even sapphires. They have since made other trips to fee dig mines and each time have come home with treasures and some incredible memories.

Upon making their second collecting trip out west, the authors purchased some lapidary equipment, i.e. rock saw and rock polisher. They first used them to cut thundereggs collected from a mine in Oregon. The next project was to trim the many pounds of fossil fish rocks they acquired at a fee dig fossil site. A sequel to this guide series is proposed to cover authorized fossil collecting sites and educational digs, as well as museums on fossils and dinosaurs. It will include such topics as where to view and even make plaster casts of actual dinosaur tracks. There are even museums where kids of all ages can dig up a full-sized model of a dinosaur!

Types of Sites

The purpose of this book is principally to guide the reader to fee dig mine sites. These are gem or mineral mines where you hunt for the gem or mineral in ore at or from the mine. At fee dig sites where you are actually permitted to go into the field and dig for yourself, you will normally be shown what the gem or mineral you are seeking looks like in its natural state (much different from the polished or cut stone). Often someone is available to go out in the field with you and show you where to dig. At sites where you purchase gem- or mineral-bearing ore (either native or enriched) for washing in a flume, the process is the same: there will usually be examples of rough stones for comparison, and help in identifying your finds.

Also included are a few areas that are not fee dig sites but that are well-defined collecting sites, usually parks or beaches.

Guided field trips are a little different. Here the guide may or may not have examples of what you are looking for, but he or she will be with you in the field to help in identifying finds.

For the more experienced collector, there are field collecting areas where you are on your own in identifying what you have found. Several fee areas and guided field trips appropriate for the experienced collector are available. Check out the listings for Ruggles Mine (Grafton, NH, volume 4); Harding Mine (Dixon, NM, volume 2); Poland Mining Camps (Poland, ME, volume 4); Perham's (West Paris, ME, volume 4); and Gem Mountain Quarry Trips (Spruce Pine, NC, volume 3).

Knowing What You're Looking For

Before you go out into the field, it is a good idea to know what you are looking for. Most of the fee dig mines listed in this guide will show you specimens before you set out to find your own. If you are using a guide service, you have the added bonus of having a knowledgeable person with you while you search to help you find the best place to look and help you identify your finds.

Included in this guide is a listing of museums that contain rock and gem exhibits. A visit to these museums will help prepare you for your search. You may find examples of gems in the rough and examples of mineral specimens similar to the ones you will be looking for. Museums will most likely have displays of gems or minerals native to the local area. Some of the gems and minerals listed in this guide are of significant interest, and specimens of them can be found in museums around the country. Displays accompanying the exhibits might tell you how the gems and minerals were found, and their place in our nation's history. Many museums also hold collecting field trips or geology programs, or may be able to put you in touch with local rock and lapidary clubs.

For more information on learning how to identify your finds yourself— and even how to put together a basic portable "lab" to use at the sites—the book *Gem Identification Made Easy* by Antoinette Matlins and A. C. Bonanno (GemStone Press) is a good resource.

Rock shops are another excellent place to view gem and mineral specimens before going out to dig your own. A listing of rock shops would be too extensive to include in a book such as this. A good place to get information on rock shops in the area you plan to visit is to contact the chamber of commerce for that area. Rock shops may be able to provide information not only on rockhounding field trips but also on local rock clubs that sponsor trips. There are numerous listings on the Internet of rock and mineral clubs. Among these are the American Federation of Mineralogical Societies (www.amfed.org), which lists member clubs, and Bob's Rock Shop (www.rockhounds.com), which has a U.S. club directory (supplied information).

Through mine tours you can see how minerals and gems were and are taken from the earth. On these tours, visitors learn what miners go through to remove the ores from the earth. This will give you a better appreciation for those sparkly gems you see in the showroom windows, and for many of the items we all take for granted in daily use.

You will meet other rockhounds at the mine. Attending one of the yearly events listed in the guide will also give you the chance to meet people who share your interest in gems and minerals and exchange ideas, stories, and knowledge of the hobby.

How to Use This Guide

To use this book, you can pick a state and determine what mining is available there, or pick a gem or mineral and determine where to go to "mine" it.

In this guide are indexes that will make the guide simple to use. If you are interested in finding a particular gem or mineral, go to the Index by Gem or Mineral in the back of the book. In this index, gems and minerals are listed in alphabetical order with the states and cities where fee dig sites for that gem or mineral may be found.

If you are interested in learning of sites near where you live, or in the area where you are planning a vacation, or if you simply want to know whether there are gems and minerals in a particular location, go to the Index by State, located in the back of the guide. The state index entries are broken down into three categories: Fee Dig Sites/Guide Services, Museums and Mine Tours, and Special Events and Tourist Information. Please note that the information provided in each individual listing is subject to availability.

There are also several special indexes for use in finding your birthstone, anniversary stone, or zodiac stone.

Site Listings

The first section of each chapter lists fee dig sites and guide services that are available in each state. Included with the location of each site (if available) is a description of the site, directions to find it, what equipment is provided, and what you must supply. Costs are listed, along with specific policies of the site. Also included are other services available at the site and information on camping, lodging, etc. in the area of the site. Included in the section with fee dig sites are guide services for collecting gems and minerals.

In the second section of each chapter, museums of special interest to the gem/mineral collector and mine tours available to the public are listed. Besides being wonderful ways to learn about earth science, geology, and mining history (many museums and tours also offer child-friendly exhibits), museums are particularly useful for viewing gems and minerals in their rough or natural states before going out in the field to search for them.

The third section of each chapter lists special events involving gems and minerals, and resources for general tourist information.

A sample of the listings for fee dig mines and guide services (Section 1 in the guides) is on the next page.

Tips for mining:

1. Learn what gems or minerals can be found at the mine you are going to visit.

2. Know what the gem or mineral that you're hunting looks like in the rough before you begin mining.

Visiting local rock shops and museums will help in this effort.

3. When in doubt, save any stone that you are unsure about. Have an expert at the mine or at a local rock shop help you identify your find.

Sample Fee Dig Site Listing

TOWN in which the site is located / *Native or enriched[1]* • *Easy, moderate, difficult[2]*

Dig your own T
The following gems may be found:
• List of gems and minerals found at the mine

Mine name
Owner or contact (where available)
Address
Phone number
Fax
E-mail address
Website address

Open: months, hours, days
Info: Descriptive text regarding the site, including whether equipment is provided
Admission: Fee to dig; costs for predug dirt
Other services available
Other area attractions (at times)
Information on lodging or camp-ground facilities (where available)
Directions

Map (where available)

Notes:

1. Native or enriched. *Native* refers to gems or minerals found in the ground at the site, put there by nature. *Enriched* means that gems and minerals from an outside source have been brought in and added to the soil. Enriching is also called "salting"—it is a guaranteed return. Whatever is added in a salted mine is generally the product of some commercial mine elsewhere. Thus, it is an opportunity to "find" gemstones from around the world the easy way, instead of traveling to jungles and climbing mountains in remote areas of the globe. Salted mines are particularly nice for giving children the opportunity to find a wide variety of gems and become involved in gem identification. The authors have tried to indicate if a mine is enriched, but to be sure, ask at the mine beforehand. If the status could not be determined, this designation was left out.

2. Sites are designated as easy, moderate, or difficult. This was done to give

you a feel for what a site may be like. You should contact the site and make a determination for yourself if you have any doubts.

Easy: This might be a site where the gem hunter simply purchases bags or buckets of predug dirt, washes the ore in a flume or screens the gem-bearing gravel to concentrate the gems, and flips the screen. The gems or minerals are then picked out of the material remaining in the screen. A mine which has set aside a pile of mine material for people to pick through would be another type of site designated as "Easy."

Moderate: Mining at a "Moderate" site might mean digging with a shovel, then loading the dirt into buckets, followed by sifting and sluicing. Depending on your knowledge of mineral identification, work at a "Moderate" site might include searching the surface of the ground at an unsupervised area for a gem or mineral you are not familiar with (this could also be considered difficult).

Difficult: This might be a site requiring tools such as picks and shovels, or sledgehammers and chisels. The site may be out of the way and/or difficult to get to. Mining might involve heavy digging with the pick and shovel or breaking gems or minerals out of base rock using a sledge or chisel.

Maps

Maps are included to help you locate the sites in the guide. At the beginning of each state, there is a state map showing the general location of towns where sites are located.

Local maps are included in a listing when the information was available. *These maps are not drawn to scale!* These maps provide information to help you get to the site but are not intended to be a substitute for a road map. Please check directly with the site you are interested in for more detailed directions.

Special Note:

Although most museums and many fee dig sites are handicapped accessible, please check with the listing directly.

Fees

Fees listed in these guides were obtained when the book was updated, and may have changed. They are included to give you at least a general idea of the costs you will be dealing with. Please contact the site directly to confirm charges.

Many museums have discounts for members and for groups, as well as special programs for school groups. Please check directly with the institution for information. Many smaller and/or private institutions have no fee, but do appreciate donations to help meet the costs of staying open.

Many sites accept credit cards; some may not. Please check ahead for payment options if this is important.

Requesting Information by Mail

When requesting information by mail, it is always appreciated if you send a SASE (self-addressed stamped envelope) along with your request. Doing this will often speed up the return of information.

Equipment and Safety Precautions

Equipment

The individual sites listed in these guides often provide equipment at the mine. Please note that some fee dig sites place limitations on the equipment you can use at their site. Those limitations will be noted where the information was available. Always abide by the limitations; remember that you are a guest at the site.

On the following pages are figures showing equipment for rockhounding. Figures A and B identify some of the equipment you may be told you need at a site. Figure C shows material needed to collect, package, transport, and record your findings. Figure D illustrates typical safety equipment.

Always use safety glasses with side shields or goggles when you are hammering or chiseling. Chips of rock or metal from your tools can fly off at great speed in any direction when hammering. Use gloves to protect your hands as well.

Other useful tools not shown include an ultraviolet hand lamp, and a hand magnifier.

Not pictured, but something you don't want to forget, is your camera. You may also want to bring along your video camera to record that "big" find, no matter what it might be.

Not pictured, but to be considered: knee pads and seat cushions.

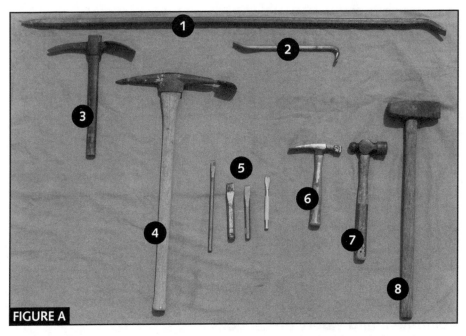

FIGURE A

1. Crowbar
2. Pry bar
3. Smaller pick
4. Rock pick
5. Various-sized chisels (*Note:* When working with a hammer and chisel, you may want to use a chisel holder, not shown, for protecting your hand if you miss. Always use eye protection with side shields and gloves!)
6. Rock hammer (*Note:* Always use eye protection.)
7. 3-pound hammer (*Note:* Always use eye protection.)
8. Sledgehammer (*Note:* When working with a sledgehammer, wear hard-toed boots along with eye protection.)

Other Safety Precautions

- Never go into the field or on an unsupervised site alone. With protective clothing, reasonable care, proper use of equipment, and common sense, accidents should be avoided, but in the event of an illness or accident, you always want to have someone with you who can administer first aid and seek help.
- Always keep children under your supervision.
- Never enter old abandoned mines or underground diggings!
- Never break or hammer rocks close to another person!

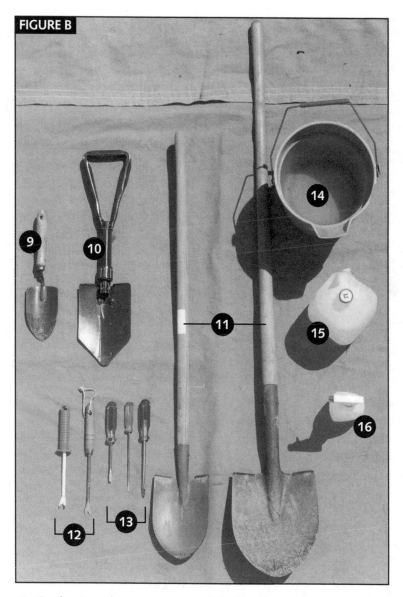

FIGURE B

9. Garden trowel
10. Camp shovel
11. Long-handled shovels
12. Garden cultivators
13. Screwdrivers
14. Bucket of water
15. (Plastic) jug of water
16. Squirt bottle of water; comes in handy at many of the mines to wash off rocks so you can see if they are or contain gem material

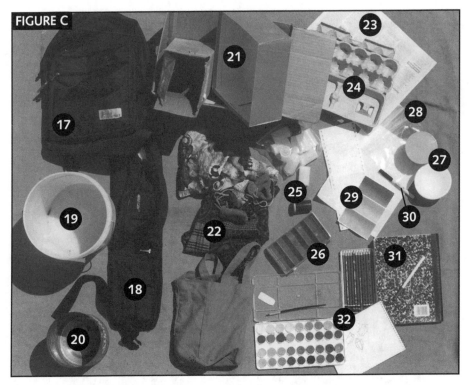

FIGURE C

17. Backpack
18. Waist pack to hold specimens
19. Bucket to hold specimens
20. Coffee can to hold specimens
21. Boxes to pack, transport, and ship specimens
22. Bags—various sized bags to carry collected specimens in the field
23. Newspaper to wrap specimens for transport
24. Egg cartons to transport delicate specimens
25. Empty film canisters to hold small specimens
26. Plastic box with dividers to hold small specimens
27. Margarine containers to hold small specimens
28. Reclosable plastic bags to hold small specimens
29. Gummed labels to label specimens (Whether you are at a fee dig site or with a guide, usually there will be someone to help you identify your find. It is a good idea to label the find when it is identified so that when you reach home, you won't have boxes of unknown rocks.)
30. Waterproof marker for labeling
31. Field log book to make notes on where specimens were found
32. Sketching pencils, sketchbook (waterproof notebooks are available), paint to record your finds and the surrounding scenery

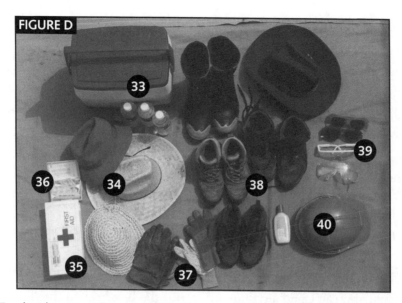

FIGURE D

33. Food and water—always carry plenty of drinking water. (*Note:* many sites tell you in advance if they have food and water available or if you should bring some; however, it is always a good idea to bring extra drinking water. Remember—if you bring it in, pack it back out.)

34. Hats. Many of the sites are in the open, and the summer sun can be hot and dangerous to unprotected skin. Check with the site to see if they have any recommendations for protective clothing. Also, don't forget sunscreen.

35. First aid/safety kit

36. Snakebite kit. If the area is known to have snakes, be alert and take appropriate safety measures, such as boots and long pants. (*Note:* while planning our first gem-hunting trip, we read that the first aid kit should contain a snakebite kit. Just like rockhounds, snakes seem to love rocky areas!) In most cases, if you visit sites in the book, you will be either at a

flume provided by the facility, or with an experienced guide. At the first, you will most likely never see a snake; at the second, your guide will fill you in on precautions. For listings where you will be searching on a ranch or state park, ask about special safety concerns such as snakes and insects when you pay your fee. These sites may not be for everyone.

37. Gloves to protect your hands when you are working with sharp rock or using a hammer or chisel

38. Boots—particularly important at sites where you will be doing a lot of walking, or walking on rocks

39. Safety glasses with side shields, or goggles. Particularly important at hard rock sites or any site where you or others may be hitting rocks. Safety glasses are available with tinted lenses for protection from the sun.

40. Hard hats—may be mandatory if you are visiting an active quarry or mine; suggested near cliffs

Mining Techniques

How to Sluice for Gems

This is the most common technique used at fee dig mines where you buy a bucket of gem ore (gem dirt) and wash it at a flume.

1. Place a quantity of the gem ore in the screen box, and place the screen box in the water. Use enough gem ore to fill the box about a third.

2. Place the box in the water, and shake it back and forth, raising one side, then the other, so that the material in the box moves back and forth. What you are doing is making the stones move around in the screen box, while washing dirt and sand out of the mixture.

3. After a minute or two of washing, take the screen box out of the flume, and let it drain. Look through the stones remaining in the screen box for your treasure. If you're not sure about something, ask one of the attendants.

4. When you can't find anything more, put the box back in the flume and wash it some more, then take it out and search again.

Clockwise from top: Gold pan; screen box used for sluicing; screen box used for screening.

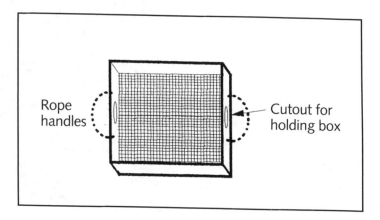

Rope handles

Cutout for holding box

How to Build a Screen Box

1. A screen box that is easy to handle is generally built from 1" x 4" lumber and window screening.

2. Decide on the dimensions of the screen box you want, and cut the wood accordingly. Dimensions generally run from 12" x 12" up to 18" x 18". Remember that the end pieces will overlap the side pieces, so cut the end pieces 1½" longer.

3. There are two alternative methods of construction. In one, drill pilot holes in the end pieces, and use wood screws to fasten the end pieces to the side pieces. In the other, use angle irons and screws to attach the ends and sides.

4. Cut the screening to be ¼" smaller than the outside dimensions of the screen box, and use staples to attach the screen to the bottom of the box. Use metal screening rather than plastic if possible. For a stronger box, cut ¼" or ⅜" hardware cloth to the same dimensions as the screening, and staple the hardware cloth over the screening. The hardware cloth will provide support for the screening.

5. Cut ¼" wood trim to fit, and attach it to the bottom of the box to cover the edges of the screening and hardware cloth and staples.

6. If you like, add rope handles or cut handholds in the side pieces for easier handling.

5. If possible, move your screen box into bright light while you are searching, since the gems and minerals often show up better in bright light.

How to Screen for Gems

This is another common technique used at fee dig mines where you buy a bucket of gem ore and screen it for gems. (The authors used this technique for garnets and sapphires in Montana.)

1. Place a quantity of the gem ore in the screen box, and place the screen box in the water. Use enough gem dirt to fill the box about a third.

2. Place the box in the water, and begin tipping it back and forth, raising one side, then the other, so that the material in the box moves back and forth. What you are doing is making the gemstones, which are heavier than the rock and dirt, move into the bottom center of the screen box while at the same time washing dirt and sand out of the mixture.

3. After a minute or two, change the direction of movement to front and back.

4. Repeat these two movements (Steps 2 and 3) three or four times.

5. Take the box out of the water and let it drain, then place a board on top and carefully flip the box over onto the sorting table. It may be helpful to put a foam pad in the box, then put the board over it. This helps keep the stones in place when you flip the box. If you have done it right, the gemstones will be found in the center of the rocks dumped onto the board. Use tweezers to pick the rough gemstones out of the rocks, and place them in a small container.

How to Pan for Gold

The technique for panning for gold is based on the fact that gold is much heavier than rock or soil. Gently washing and swirling the gold-bearing soil in a pan causes the gold to settle to the bottom of the pan. A gold pan has a flat

bottom and gently slanting sides. Some modern pans also have small ridges or rings around the inside of the pan on these slanting sides. As the soil is washed out of the pan, the gold will slide down the sides, or be caught on the ridges and stay in the pan. Here's how:

1. Begin by filling the pan with ore, about ⅔ to ¾ full.

2. Put your pan in the water, let it gently fill with water, then put the pan under the water surface. Leave the pan in the water, and mix the dirt around in the pan, cleaning and removing any large rocks.

3. Lift the pan out of the water, then gently shake the pan from side to side while swirling it at the same time. Do this for 20–30 seconds to get the gold settled to the bottom of the pan.

4. Still holding the pan out of the water, continue these motions while tilting the pan so that the dirt begins to wash out. Keep the angle of the pan so that the crease (where the bottom and sides meet) is the lowest point.

5. When there is only about a tablespoon of material left in the pan, put about ½ inch of water in the pan, and swirl the water over the remaining material. As the top material is moved off, you should see gold underneath.

6. No luck? Try again at a different spot.

Notes on Gem Faceting, Cabbing, and Mounting Your Finds

Many of the fee dig sites offer services to cut and mount your finds. Quality and costs vary. Trade journals such as *Lapidary Journal Jewelry Artist* and *Rock & Gem* (available at most large bookstores or by subscription) list suppliers of these services, both in the United States and overseas. Again, quality and cost vary. Local rock and gem shops in your area may offer these services, or it may be possible to work with a local jeweler. Your local rock club may be able to provide these services or make recommendations.

After their first gem-hunting trip, the authors had some of their finds faceted and cabochoned. They then designed rings and had them made using these stones, as shown in the photos below.

After saying for years that they would like to learn to cabochon and facet (and in the process learn how better to collect "usable" material), the authors were fortunate enough to meet a local gemologist at a gem and mineral show who taught classes in the lapidary arts. They have since cut their own cabo-

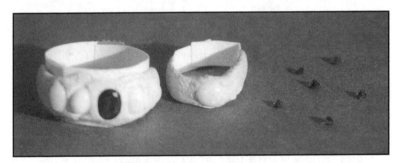

The authors sent their rough gems away for faceting. Using the faceted gems, they made crude mock-ups and sketches of the rings they wanted; then they sent the mock-ups, sketches, and gems to be made into rings.

The finished rings.

chons and faceted gemstones, getting a true appreciation for the art and knowledge of what to look for when field collecting.

Cutting your own finds can be a very rewarding hobby, and this hobby works two ways. You can cabochon, facet, and carve your special finds to your specifications, then make or have them made into jewelry. A cabochon is a highly polished convex-cut, but unfaceted gem. Facets are flat faces on geometric shapes which are cut into a rough gemstone in order to improve their appearance. The angles used for each facet affect the appearance of the gemstone. In learning the lapidary procedures, you also gain knowledge of what is a good find. You can look at a stone in the field and see if it is facetable, or if the pattern would make a spectacular cabochon.

Understanding what beautiful pieces you can make from your discoveries will amaze you, be they dug from a native mine, sluiced at a salted site, purchased from a local rock shop, or traded at a club meeting.

The first step to learning the lapidary arts is to do some research to see if it is for you. Search out books and articles on the topic and contact local clubs or rock shops to see if there are any classes near you.

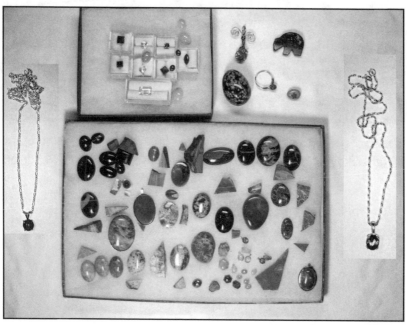

A sample of the authors' lapidary work.

Taking sifted gravel to the jig at a sapphire mine in Montana. Pictured from left to right: Steve, Kathy, Annie Rygle, Debra Pedersen, Kristin Pedersen.

CONNECTICUT

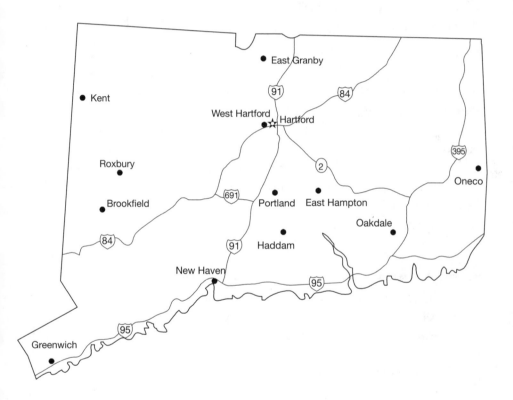

State Gemstone: Garnet (1977)*

*Dates refer to when stones and minerals were adopted by the state legislature.

ROXBURY / *Native • Easy*

Find Your Own Garnets T

The following gems or minerals can be found:

• Garnets (May not be gem-quality, but many nice specimens ½- to 1-inch long, dark red to black in color)

Green's Farm Garnet Mine
Perkins Road
Roxbury, CT 06783

Open: All year, weather permitting.
Info: This is an unattended fee dig site. You leave your fee at the green house (leave the fee under the mat if no one is home). There is a parking area near the house; search for garnets in the old mine workings north of the parking area. His-torically, garnets were mined, in this area of Connecticut, for making sandpaper.
Admission: $5.00 parking fee.
Directions: Take I-84 east to Route 7 north. Take Route 7 north to Route 25 south. Take Route 25 south for a mile, and take Route 133 north for 6 miles, then look for Stuart Road on the right. Turn right on Stuart Road, and follow it (names may change) through Rox-bury Falls. Another road branches to the right at Roxbury Falls; stay left, and look for Perkins Road on the left. Take Perkins Road; it will bend to the left, then go into an old farm, where there will be a newer house on the right, with a small parking area in front. Trail is next to the garage. Pay the fee at the newer house.

The Connecticut Department of Environmental Protection has a program of educational mineral collecting at three different quarries for schools, mineral clubs, nature centers, and museums. Mineral collecting field days can be scheduled at Case Quarries, in Meshomasic State Forest, Portland, CT; Clark Hill Quarries, in Meshomasic State Forest, East Hampton, CT; and CCC Quarry, Cockaponset State Forest, Haddam, CT. Only one group will be scheduled at a site on any given day, the sites will be open for col-lecting from 8:00 A.M. to 4:00 P.M., and only small hand tools may be used. Applications are accepted after January 1 for days during a year; additional information may be obtained from the DEP website, www.ct.gov/dep (click on "Natural Resources," then "Geology") or by contacting Margaret Thomas by e-mail at margaret.thomas@ct.gov or by phone at (860) 424-3583.

There are family/children educational activities at the following locations:

Brookfield
Mother Earth Gallery & Mining Co.
806 Federal Road
Brookfield, CT 06804
Phone: (203) 775-6272
Fax: (203) 775-5620
www.motherearthcrystals.com
Kids can don a miner's helmet with a light, grab a glow-in-the-dark bucket, and dig for gemstones such as amethyst and pyrite, arrowheads, and more in a re-created mine. Many crystals, minerals, and other objects are available in the gift shop.

Hartford
The Children's Museum
950 Trout Brook Drive
West Hartford, CT 06119
Phone: (860) 231-2824
Fax: (860) 232-0705
www.thechildrensmuseumct.org
Sift sand and gravel in a sluice with running water to find gems and min-erals, using a process often used by early pioneers.

Oakdale
The Dinosaur Place™ at Nature's Art
1650 Hartford-New London Turn-pike
Oakdale, CT 06370
Phone: (860) 443-4367
www.thedinosaurplace.com
Dig in "gem dirt" in a candlelit silver mine to look for gems or minerals, or learn to pan for gold in Thunder Creek and find your own nuggets of pyrite.

Oneco
River Bend Campground
Route 14A, Box 23
Oneco, CT 06373
Phone: (860) 564-3440
www.riverbendcamp.com
Grab a helmet and bucket, and go into a recreated mine to hunt for gems and minerals.

EAST GRANBY

Mine Tour/Museum

Old New-Gate Prison and
Copper Mine
National Historic Landmark and State
Archaeological Preserve
115 Newgate Road
East Granby, CT 06026
Phone: (860) 653-3563
Off-season: (860) 256-2800
Fax: (860) 256-2811
www.cultureandtourism.org
(Click on "Museums" at top of page.)

Open: Check website for current days
and hours.

Info: The Old New-Gate Prison and
Copper Mine, formerly the Simsbury
Copper Mine, was the first American
copper mine, chartered in 1707. Ore
from the Simsbury Copper Mine aver-
aged about 12% copper and in some
cases ran as high as 50% copper. In the
1750s, work at the mine ceased
because of several factors, including the
expense of shipping ore to England for
smelting.

In December 1773, the mine became
a prison. Other copper mines existed
near New-Gate, one of which was the

Higley Mine. Between 1729 and 1737,
Dr. Samuel Higley designed the first
copper coins used for trading purposes
in the country.

Miners followed the ore-bearing strata, which tipped twenty-two percent to
the east, so at the lowest point of the
tour, visitors are seventy feet underground. Tours at the mine tunnels are
self-guided. When in the mine tunnels,
be aware that the ceilings are sometimes low. The temperature stays in the
low-50s, and a sweater is recommended, along with good walking shoes.

Admission: Adults $10.00, seniors
(60+) $8.00, youth (6–17) $6.00, children 5 and under free. Special arrangements for groups, by appointment only.

Other services available: Picnic area,
gift shop, and ample free parking.

Directions: From exit 40 on I-91, take

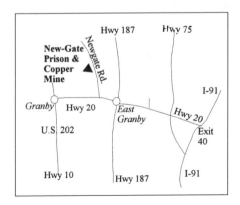

Route 20W through East Granby Center to traffic light at Newgate Road. Turn right on Newgate, and drive 1 mile to mine. From Routes 10/202, take Route 20E from Granby Center for 2.8 miles to the light at Newgate Road in East Granby. Turn left on Newgate, and drive 1 mile to the mine.

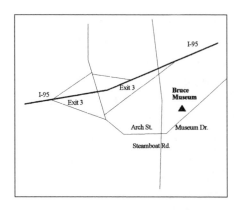

GREENWICH

Museum

Bruce Museum
1 Museum Drive
Greenwich, CT 06830-7157
Phone: (203) 869-0376
www.brucemuseum.org

Open: All year, 10:00 A.M.–5:00 P.M. Tuesday–Saturday. Sunday 1:00 P.M.–5:00 P.M. Closed Mondays and major holidays.

Info: Exhibits of minerals and rocks are on display, including iron meteorites and mineral species and gem-quality specimens.

Admission: Adults $7.00, seniors (65+) and students (5–22) $6.00. On Tuesdays, admission is free.

Directions: Take exit 3 off I-95. At the end of the ramp, turn east on Arch Street, and drive to the intersection with Steamboat Road. Go straight across to Museum Drive, and the museum will be 500 feet on the left. The museum is also easily accessible via the Greenwich train station on Metro North's New Haven Line.

KENT

Museum

Connecticut Museum of Mining and Mineral Science
Connecticut Antique Machinery Association (CAMA)
P.O. Box 425
Kent, CT 06757
Phone: (860) 927-0050
www.ctamachinery.com

Open: May–end of October, 10:00 A.M.–4:00 P.M., Wednesday–Sunday, or by appointment.

Info: Connecticut had deposits of iron, copper, garnet, marble limestone, and other rocks, which drove the early industrial activities in the state. The museum is located in an old iron-making area, with a historic iron furnace (Kent Furnace) located nearby. The museum has a collection of Connecticut minerals, displays on geology, and on how the local Native American population used the local mineral resources.

Admission: Adults $3.00, children under 12 free.

Directions: Located in Kent on Highway U.S. Route 7. Shares a common driveway with the Sloane-Stanley Museum.

NEW HAVEN

Museum

Yale Peabody Museum of
Natural History
P.O. Box 208118
170 Whitney Avenue
New Haven, CT 06520-8118
Phone: (203) 432-5050
Fax: (203) 432-6342
www.peabody.yale.edu

Open: All year except major holidays, 10:00 A.M.–5:00 P.M. Monday–Saturday, 12:00–5:00 P.M. Sunday. Groups must register in advance.

Info: The new permanent Hall of Minerals, Earth, and Space explores Earth's vast mineral resources. The new permanent mineral exhibit highlights Connecticut geology and the diversity of minerals, ores, fluorescent minerals, and gemstones. This exhibit showcases Peabody's specimens, many of which have not been on display for decades. The study of minerals at Yale began with Benjamin Silliman and was carried on by luminaries such as James Dwight Dana, the Yale professor generally acknowledged as the founder of modern mineralogy. Exhibits show how minerals form and grow, why crystals have such alluring shapes and colors, and how to use practices of mineral identification. A special feature of the new gallery is a display of spectacular gemstones and jewelry, including objects from the Benjamin Zucker and Barbara Zucker Family Collection.

Admission: Adults $9.00, seniors (65+) $8.00, and children (3–18) $5.00.

Directions: For directions, call (203) 432-5050.

SECTION 3: Special Events and Tourist Information

TOURIST INFORMATION

State Tourist Agency

Connecticut Office of Tourism
Connecticut Commission
on Culture and Tourism
One Constitution Plaza, 2nd Fl.
Hartford, CT 06103

Phone: (888) CTVISIT;
(888)-288-4748
Fax: (860) 270-8077
www.ctvisit.com

DELAWARE

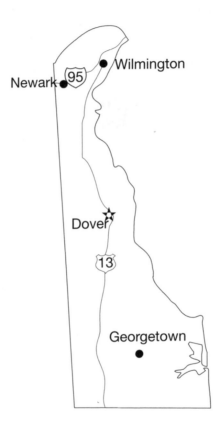

State Mineral: Sillimanite (1977)

WILMINGTON / *Native • Easy to Moderate*

Collect Common Minerals from Tailings Piles *T*

The following gems and minerals may be found:

- Feldspar, quartz, mica, garnet, and beryl

Woodlawn Quarry
Woodlawn Trustees, Inc.
1020 N. Bancroft Parkway
Wilmington, DE 19805
Phone: (302) 655-6209
www.dgs.udel.edu/delaware-geology/woodlawn-quarry-geoadventure-delaware-piedmont

Open: Generally open during daylight hours.

Info: The quarry is located in a wildlife preserve owned and managed by the Woodlawn Trustees. You must obtain permission from the trustees before visiting this site. You cannot dig at this site, but you are allowed to look through the two tailings piles at the old quarry and pick up specimens. The quarry was active from 1850–1920 for quarrying feldspar.

Rates: Free. Suitable for ages 10–adult.

Directions: Off Ramsey Road, near Brandywine Creek State Park. A map can be found at the website.

The Delaware Geological Survey has a series of Geo Adventures, which are designed to allow one to learn about a particular geologic point of interest in Delaware's Piedmont or Coastal Plain provinces and then take a short field trip to that area. You can find information on these Geo Adventures on the Survey's website: http://www.dgs.udel.edu/delaware-geology/what-are-geoadventures.

SECTION 2: **Museums and Mine Tours**

NEWARK

Museum

Iron Hill Museum
1355 Old Baltimore Pike
Newark, DE 19702
Phone: (302) 368-5703
Fax: (302) 369-4287
E-mail: info@ironhill-museum.org
www.ironhill-museum.org

Open: 9:00 A.M.–2:00 P.M. Tuesday–Friday, noon–4:00 P.M. Saturday, closed Sunday and Monday.

Info: The Iron Hill Museum specializes in the natural history of Delaware. The rock and mineral collection includes many Delaware specimens as well as a small portion of the Irenée du Pont collection, which was donated many years ago. (The bulk of the Irenée du Pont collection is at Penny Hall on the University of Delaware Campus. This Mineral Museum in Penny Hall is also open to the public. See entry on University of Delaware Mineralogical Museum.)

The museum also has an excellent display of fluorescent minerals (not from Delaware). Group programs and school field trips include a walk to the old iron mines and sometimes rock collection at the top of Iron Hill and at other sites.

The Iron Mountain area was mined for iron ore for approximately 200 years. An original open-pit iron mine exists along the museum trail, as well as spoils piles resulting from mining activity.

Before iron ore was mined, large outcrops of jasper at the site brought Native Americans to the area in search of this valuable stone (lithic) resource for making the tools necessary for survival. Evidence gathered as a result of archeological excavation indicates that the site was used as both a procurement area and a workshop complex, since both finished projectile points and late-stage rejected stone material have been recovered. Jasper, along with chert and chalcedony, is restricted to a small region called the Delaware Chalcedony Complex. Iron Hill was the only jasper source in the area and was geographically the southernmost point of access for this important resource.

Admission: General admission $2.00, seniors and children under 6 free.

Directions: The Iron Hill Museum is located on Old Baltimore Pike, just south of the Newark, Delaware, city limits. Call or check website for directions.

Info: For information on other Native American stone quarries, see listings in Calumet and Copper Harbor, MI: copper (Vol. 4); Pipestone, MN: pipestone quarries (Vol.1); Hopewell and Brownsville, OH: flint quarries (Vol. 4); and Fritch, TX: flint quarries (Vol. 2).

NEWARK

Museum

University of Delaware
Mineralogical Museum
Penny Hall
Academy Street
Newark, DE 19716-2544
Phone: (302) 831-6557
www.museums.udel.edu

Open: Noon–5:00 P.M. Wednesday–Sunday (open until 8:00 P.M. Thursday); closed Mondays, Tuesdays, and university breaks and holidays.

Info: The museum's collection includes approximately 10,000 specimens, about 450 of which are on display. The collection of the late Irenée du Pont served as the foundation for the University Mineralogical Museum. Mr. du Pont had been interested in minerals for several years and in 1919 purchased the mineral collection assembled by George Kunz, which Tiffany & Co. had on display in its Fifth Avenue showroom in New York City.

The collection has been expanded by other donors. The museum's focus is on individual displays that illustrate particular mineralogical concepts or themes. Among those exhibits are the Irenée du Pont exhibit, the Crystal System exhibit, the United States–Canada Exhibit, and the Pseudomorphs and other Growth Phenomena exhibit. Newly installed display cabinets with fiber-optic lighting present accurate color balance for specimens.

Admission: Free.

Directions: In Penny Hall on the university campus. Parking is in the Perkins Garage location on Academy Street.

The Treasures of the Sea Exhibit in the Stephen J. Betze Library of Delaware Technical and Community College (Seashore Highway, Route 18/404, Georgetown, DE) displays jewels, notably emeralds, and gold and silver ingots, coins, and jewelry recovered from the wreck of the Spanish galleon Atocha. (See www.treasuresofthesea.org.)

SECTION 3: Special Events and Tourist Information

TOURIST INFORMATION

State Tourist Agency

Delaware Tourism Office
99 Kings Highway
Wilmington, DE 19901

Phone: (302) 739-4271;
(866) 284-7483
www.visitdelaware.com

DISTRICT OF COLUMBIA

SECTION 1: Fee Dig Sites and Guide Services

No information available.

SECTION 2: Museums and Mine Tours

Museum

Smithsonian Institution
National Museum of Natural History
10th Street and
Constitution Avenue NW
Washington, D.C. 20560-0119
Phone: (202) 633-1000
www.mnh.si.edu
(Click on "Research and Collections,"
then go to "Mineral Sciences.")

Open: All year, 10:00 A.M.–5:30 P.M. 7 days/week. Closed December 25.
Info: Renovated in 1997, the Janet Annenberg Hooker Hall of Gems and Minerals contains nearly 3,500 gems, minerals, rocks, and meteorites from the museum's unparalleled collections. The collection includes both cut and uncut stones, including many world-famous gems. The more impressive items are housed in individual cases. The Carmen Lúcia Ruby—a 23.1-carat Burmese ruby of exceptional color and transparency—is a recent addition.

Many gems and minerals from locales listed in this book are a part of the Smithsonian collection.

The National Gem and Mineral Collection contains over 375,000 individual specimens, including the Hope Diamond and the Star of Asia Sapphire. It also contains a research mineral collection used by scientists all over the world. The National Meteorite Collection is one of the three largest meteorite collections in the world, consisting of over 4,000 specimens. The National Rock and Ore Collection contains over 235,000 specimens.
Admission: Free.
Directions: Located at the corner of 10th Street and Constitution Avenue; reachable by Metro.

SECTION 3: Special Events and Tourist Information

TOURIST INFORMATION

State Tourist Agency

Destination D.C.
901 7th Street NW, 4th Floor
Washington, DC 20001
Phone: (202) 789-7000
Fax: (202) 789-7037
www.washington.org

ILLINOIS

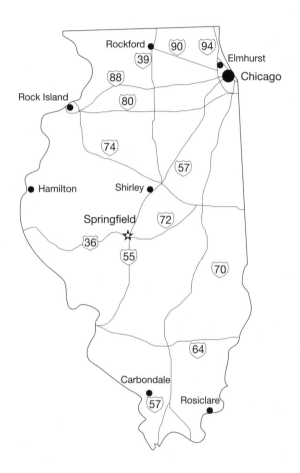

State Mineral: Fluorite (1965)

HAMILTON / *Native • Easy to Moderate*

Hunt for Geodes *T*

The following gems or minerals may be found:

▪ **Geodes**

Jacobs Geodes

Gary Jacobs

823 E. County Road 1220

Hamilton, IL 62341

Phone: (217) 847-3509

Open: All year, weather permitting, 8:00 A.M.–dusk.

Info: Dig geodes from a pit, or hunt them in the creek. Some have calcite, pyrite, barite, quartz, or kaolinite inside; a few have water inside.

Rates: $18.00 per 5-gallon bucket.

Other services available: Mr. Jacobs sometimes has whole and cracked geodes for sale.

Directions: In Hamilton, take Highway 96S south for 1.1 miles from the intersection with Highway 136, and look for signs for the Geode Shop and Mine.

HAMILTON / *Native • Easy to Moderate*

Hunt for Geodes *T*

The following gems or minerals may be found:

▪ **Geodes**

Nick's Geodes (aka Evans Property)

251 North 7th Street

Hamilton, IL 62341

Phone: (217) 357-5384

Open: Call for days and hours of operation. Generally closed on Sundays.

Info: Dig for geodes.

Rates: $16.00 per 5-gallon bucket; $8.00 for a half-bucket.

Directions: Call for directions.

HAMILTON / *Native • Easy to Moderate*

Hunt for Geodes *T*

The following gems or minerals may be found:

▪ **Geodes**

Dennis Stevenson Geodes

625 18th Street

Hamilton, IL 62341

Phone: (217) 847-2952 or (309) 337-3089

Open: By appointment only.

Info: Dig for geodes in and along a creek.

Rates: $20.00 for the first 5-gallon bucket, $10.00 for the second, $15.00 for each additional bucket.

Directions: Call for directions.

ROSICLARE / *Native • Easy*

Dig for Fluorite in Mine Ore *T*

The following gems or minerals may be found:

▪ **Fluorite**

American Fluorite Museum

Main Street

P.O. Box 755

Rosiclare, IL 62982

Phone: (618) 285-3513

Open: Beginning of April–end of October; 1:00 P.M.–4:00 P.M. Thursday, Friday, Sunday; 10:00 A.M.–4:00 P.M. Saturday.
Info: Ore from the closed mine has been piled at the museum for collectors to dig for fluorite and other minerals.

Admission: See entry in Section 2 for museum prices; $1.00/pound for collected material.
Other services available: Gift shop. (Do not need to pay museum admission to enter gift shop.)

SECTION 2: Museums and Mine Tours

CARBONDALE

Museum

University Museum
1000 Faner Drive, Mail Code 4508
Southern Illinois University
Carbondale, IL 62901
Phone: (618) 453-5388
www.museum.siu.edu

Open: 10:00 A.M.–4:00 P.M. Tuesday–Friday, 1:00–4:00 P.M. Saturday, when school is open.
Info: The museum maintains a collection of over 26,000 geological specimens, mostly reflecting a Midwestern locale. The collection was amassed by the museum's late Adjunct Curator of Geology Dr. George Fraunfelter.
Admission: Free, donations welcome.
Directions: In the center of the university campus. Call for specific directions and for information on parking.

CHICAGO

Museum

The Field Museum
1400 S. Lake Shore Drive
Chicago, IL 60605-2496
Phone: (312) 922-9410
Fax: (312) 665-7101
www.fieldmuseum.org

Open: All year, except Christmas, 9:00 A.M.–5:00 P.M. 7 days/week. Dates of early and/or late closings are listed on the website.
Info: Beginning with a donated collection from the Tiffany & Company exhibit at the 1893 World's Fair, the gem exhibition at the Field Museum has over 500 pieces on display. The Museum's Grainger Hall of Gems has been recently renovated, and features a new interpretation of the gems, focusing on their origins and relationships by showing various gemstones in the matrix, as cut gems, and as jewelry pieces. The gems are arranged according to type—from organic gems such as amber, coral, and pearls, to gems made of one element, such as

diamonds, to gems made of various minerals (oxides, silicates, phosphates).

Admission: Basic admission to the museum: Adults $15.00, children (3-11) $10.00, students and seniors (65+) $12.00 (Chicago residents receive a discount). Check website or call for a list of 52 days with free basic admission.

Directions: Roosevelt Road at Lakeshore Drive in downtown Chicago.

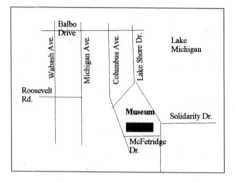

CHICAGO

Museum

Museum of Science and Industry
57th Street and Lake Shore Drive
Chicago, IL 60637
Phone: (773) 684-1414
E-mail: msi@msichicago.org
www.msichicago.org

Open: 9:30 A.M.–4:00 P.M. daily. Check with museum for dates with extended hours.

Info: Take a narrated ride to the bottom of a mine shaft in the *Coal Mine* exhibit. You'll examine the evolution of technology used in mining coal, and

experience first-hand the work environment of the U.S. mining industry.

Rates: Adults $15.00, seniors (65+) $14.00, children (3–11) $10.00, Chicago residents slightly less. Call or check the website for free admission days.

Other services available: Gift shop.

Directions: On Lake Shore Drive. Call or check the website for specific directions and information on parking.

ELMHURST

Museum 🏛

Lizzadro Museum of Lapidary Art
Wilder Park
220 Cottage Hill Ave.
Elmhurst, IL 60126
Phone: (630) 833-1616
Fax: (630) 833-1225
www.lizzadromuseum.org

Open: All year, 10:00 A.M.–5:00 P.M. Tuesday–Saturday, 1:00–5:00 P.M. Sunday. Closed Mondays and major holidays. Groups should call for reservations.

Info: Joseph F. Lizzadro, Sr., gained a first-hand appreciation for the unique characteristics of the mineral world through working with rough gem material as a hobbyist and collector. The museum opened on November 4, 1962, with this statement of purpose by the Lizzadro family: "To share with others our enjoyment of the eternal beauty in gemstones and promote the study of earth science."

The museum displays over 1,300 pieces of cut and polished gems and minerals. Displays include masterpieces of lapidary work from European countries, including Germany and Italy. Fine Chinese jadeite carvings are also displayed. Visitors can see fluorescent rocks, a birthstone display, fossils, unusual or noteworthy rocks, meteorites, and micromounts.

Admission: Adults $4.00, seniors $3.00, students and teens $2.00, children (7–12) $1.00, children under 7 free. Admission free on Fridays.

Other services available: Gift shop and educational programs on select Saturdays. Every Sunday afternoon a 50-minute video is shown which discusses how to start a mineral collection, where to search for specimens, and how to cut and polish stones.

Directions: Take St. Charles Road east from Highway 83 in Elmhurst. Turn left on Prospect to the Wilder Park entrance. An alternative route is to take York Avenue to Church Street, and turn west on Church to Prospect and turn right to Wilder Park.

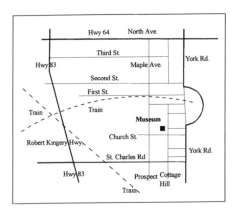

ROCKFORD

Museum

Burpee Museum of Natural History
737 N. Main Street
Rockford, IL 61103
Phone: (815) 965-3433
Fax: (815) 965-2703
E-mail: info@burpee.org
www.burpee.org

Open: 10:00 A.M.–5:00 P.M.

Info: Displays of rocks, minerals, gems, and exhibits on geological forces shaping our world. Extensive exhibit on local geology, updated in spring 2007.

Admission: Adults $7.00, children (3–17) $7.00, children under 3 free.

Other services available: Gift shop.

Directions: Located on the northern edge of downtown Rockford. Call or check the website for directions.

ROCK ISLAND

Museum

Augustana Fryxell Geology Museum
Augustana College
38th Street
Rock Island, IL 61201
Phone: (309) 794-7318
www.augustana.edu/x11053.xml

Open: During the academic school year, 8:00 A.M.–4:30 P.M. Monday–Friday; 1:00 P.M.–4:00 P.M. Saturday and Sunday.

Info: The Fryxell Museum has become one of the largest and finest rock and mineral collections in the Midwest. All types of minerals are displayed including a fine collection of Illinois minerals as well as a state-of-the-art fluorescent display.

Admission: Free.

Directions: Located in the Swenson Hall of Geosciences on the Augustana College campus, on 38th Street in Rock Island.

ROSICLARE

Museum

The American Fluorite Museum
Main Street
P.O. Box 755
Rosiclare, IL 62982
Phone: (618) 215-3513
http://kcminerals.com/american.htm

Open: Beginning of April–end of October, 1:00 P.M.–4:00 P.M. Thursday, Friday, Sunday; 10:00 A.M.–4:00 P.M. Saturday.

Info: The museum is located in the former Rosiclare Lead and Fluorspar Mining Company office building. Displays tell the story of the fluorspar mining industry using ore specimens, mining equipment, and photographs. There is also a display of mineral specimens, including many fluorite specimens.

Admission: Adults $3.00, children (6–12) $1.00, children under 6 free.

Other services available: Gift shop. (Do not need to pay museum admission to enter gift shop.)

Directions: Call for directions.

SHIRLEY

Museum

The Funk Gem and Mineral Museum
10875 Prairie Home Lane
Shirley, IL 61772
Phone: (309) 827-6792

Open: Tours by reservation only. 9:00 A.M.–4:00 P.M. Tuesday–Saturday.

Info: The museum is located on the same site as the Prairie Home. The museum displays part of the Funk gem and mineral collection, called the biggest one-man mineral collection in the world. Displays include one gem case and 50 mineral cases with specimens from around the world (including fluorescent minerals). Petrified wood is displayed outside and in the museum's fossil room.

Admission: Free.

Directions: Call for directions when making reservations.

SPRINGFIELD

Museum

Illinois State Museum
502 S. Spring Street
Springfield, IL 62706-5000
Phone: (217) 782-7386
Fax: (217) 782-1254
www.museum.state.il.us

Open: All year, 8:30 A.M.–5:00 P.M. 6 days/week, noon–5:00 P.M. Sunday; closed on Thanksgiving, Christmas, and New Year's Day.

Info: Rock collections at the museum contain representative samples of most rock types, including the major formations in Illinois. Touch one of the largest masses of copper, and see dioramas presenting environmental change over the last 500 million years based on geological specimens and evidence.

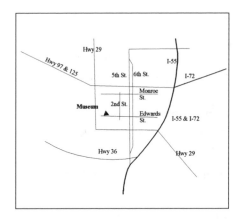

Admission: Free, donations appreciated.

Other services available: Gift shop.

Directions: The museum is located on the southwest corner of the state capitol grounds, at the intersection of Spring and Edwards Streets. Free parking is available nearby.

SECTION 3: Special Events and Tourist Information

ANNUAL EVENT

Geode Fest, Hamilton, IL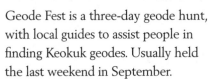

Geode Fest is a three-day geode hunt, with local guides to assist people in finding Keokuk geodes. Usually held the last weekend in September.

For more information, contact:
Geode Fest
c/o Mike Shumate
709 East County Road 1720
Nauvoo, IL 62354
(573) 518-4739
or TJ Ramsey (319) 325-5860, or
geodefest@gmail.com
www.firstcrackgeodes.com
(Click on the "Geode Fest" link.)

TOURIST INFORMATION

State Tourist Agency

Illinois Department of Commerce and Economic Opportunity
100 W. Randolph Street
Suite 3–400
Chicago, IL 60601
Phone: (800) 226-6632
www.enjoyillinois.com
For information on Keokuk geode collecting sites in Illinois, contact:
Keokuk Area Convention and Tourism Bureau
Phone: (800) 383-1219 or (319) 524-5599
info@keokukiowatourism.org

INDIANA

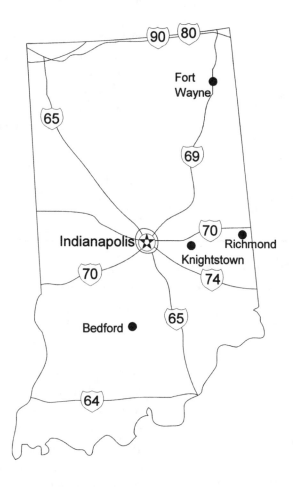

State Stone/Rock: Salem Limestone (1971)

SECTION 1: Fee Dig Sites and Guide Services

KNIGHTSTOWN / *Native* ▪
Moderate

Midwestern Gold Prospecting *T*

The following gems or minerals may be found:
▪ Gold

Yogi Bear's Jellystone Park Camping Resort
5964 South State Road 109
Knightstown, IN 46148
Phone: (800) IGO-YOGI or
(800) 446-9644
www.jellystoneindy.com

Open: Call for hours for panning.
Info: Pan, sluice, or dredge in a creek bed, or glacial sand and gravel deposits. The resort also has special weekend events such as Old Prospectors Weekend in August.
Fee: $5.00/person if you are not camping. 10% discount on camping fees for GPAA members. Must stop in the office to fill out DNR permission slip before prospecting.
Other services available: Camping cabins; fishing; camping store; showers; playground; swimming pool; paddleboats.
Directions: State Highway 109 and Interstate 70 (exit 115), 25 miles east of Indianapolis, at Knightstown.

SECTION 2: Museums and Mine Tours

BEDFORD

Museum

Land of Limestone Exhibit
Bedford Campus-Oakland City University
405 I Street
Bedford, IN 47421
Phone: (812) 279-8126
E-mail: limestonecountry@frontier.com
www.limestonecountry.com
(Click on "attractions.")

For information, write:
Lawrence County Tourism Commission
533 W. Main Street

Mitchell, IN 47446
Phone: (812) 849-1090; (800) 798-0769
Fax: (812) 849-0168

Open: All year, 8:30 A.M.–4:30 P.M. Monday–Friday.
Info: Limestone has been quarried in this part of southern Indiana since the mid-19th century and used to build and embellish America's most distinguished architectural landmarks, including Washington's National Cathedral, the Empire State Building, Rockefeller Center, the United States Archives, and Grand Central Station. The Land of Limestone exhibit takes you to the sources of lime-

stone, to the quarries and mills, and commemorates the distinguished legacy of Indiana limestone. The exhibit brings to life the people, events, and history surrounding Lawrence County's famous natural resources, Salem limestone.

Admission: Free.

Directions: Just north of the Courthouse Square Historic District.

BEDFORD

Museum

Lawrence County Museum of History
929 15th Street
Bedford, IN 47421
Phone: (812) 278-8575
Fax: (812) 278-8583
www.lawrencecountyhistory.org

Open: All year. 9:00 A.M.–4:00 P.M. Tuesday–Friday; 9:00 A.M.–3:00 P.M. Saturday.

Info: Exhibits on limestone and many other geological specimens from Lawrence County.

Directions: For more information, contact the Lawrence County Tourism Commission.

FORT WAYNE

Geosciences/Museum

Indiana Purdue University Fort Wayne
Fort Wayne, IN 46805
www.geosci.ipfw.edu

Open: 7:00 A.M.–10:00 P.M. Closed July 4.

Info: Hallway displays feature 285 mineral specimens, 19 meteorite specimens, and 113 rock specimens, as well as various maps and other exhibits around the halls, including a computer that shows information about earthquakes. There is also a Geogarden consisting of a number of large boulder-sized local specimens on display located outside in a garden setting.

Admission: Free.

Directions: Call (260) 481-6249, or go to http://www.ipfw.edu/campus/maps.

INDIANAPOLIS

Museum

Indiana State Museum
650 W. Washington Street
Indianapolis, IN 46204
Phone: (317) 232-1637
Fax: (317) 234-2447
www.indianamuseum.org

Open: All year, 9:00 A.M.–5:00 P.M. Tuesday–Saturday, 11:00 A.M–5:00 P.M. Sunday. Closed Thanksgiving, Christmas, and most Mondays.

Info: The Indiana State Museum in White River State Park is Indiana's museum for science and culture. The building construction included Indiana stones such as limestone and sandstone.

The museum now displays mineral suites that present minerals from Indiana and the surrounding regions. Galleries tell the story of Indiana's natural history, and hands-on activities teach geologic processes. The museum's annual GeoFest is held in October.

Admission: Adults $7.00, seniors (above 60) $6.50, children (3–12) $4.00.

Directions: Just west of the corner of West and Washington Streets in downtown Indianapolis, in White River State Park. Parking is available in the underground garage off Washington Street.

RICHMOND

Museum 🏛

Joseph Moore Museum of Natural History
Earlham College
Drawer 68
Richmond, IN 47374
Phone: (765) 983-1303
www.earlham.edu/museum

Open: All year: 1:00 P.M.–5:00 P.M. Sunday; Academic year: 1:00 P.M.–5:00 P.M. Monday, Wednesday, Friday.

Info: The museum was established in 1847 as a teaching collection. The geology exhibit displays geological specimens from the local Ordovician limestone.

As a college program, the museum hours reflect the academic schedule. The museum is staffed almost entirely by students, who design exhibits, maintain collections, and lead tours.

Admission: Free; donations welcome.

Directions: The museum is located on the Earlham College campus in Richmond on U.S. 40, west of the river. From I-70, take the U.S. 35 exit, drive south until you come to U.S. 40, then turn right.

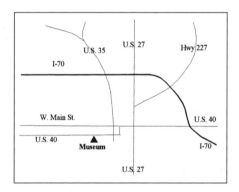

SECTION 3: Special Events and Tourist Information

TOURIST INFORMATION

State Tourist Agency 🐾

Indiana Department of Tourism Development
One North Capitol, Suite 600
Indianapolis, IN 46204-2288
Phone: (800) 677-9800
Fax: (317) 233-6887
www.enjoyindiana.com

MAINE

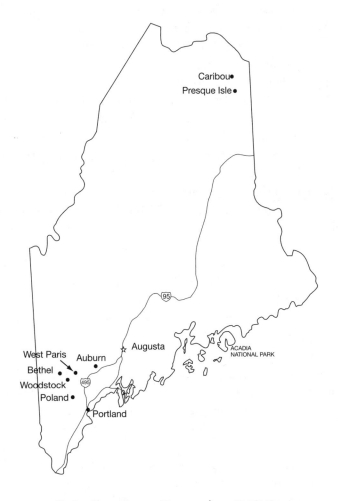

Caribou●
Presque Isle●

🛡95

West Paris
Bethel ● ● Auburn
Woodstock ●   🛡495
Poland ●

☆ Augusta

ACADIA
NATIONAL PARK

● Portland

State Gemstone: Tourmaline (1971)

The Story of Maine Tourmaline

A band of mineralization runs from the Maine coast at Brunswick through Auburn and Newry and into New Hampshire. In this area or band are found Maine tourmaline and other gems and minerals. This band of mineralization was formed 300 million years ago when intense volcanic activity resulted in lava flowing into cracks in the existing granite rock. As the lava and surrounding rock cooled, gems and mineral crystals formed in voids in the rock. Over the intervening time, rain and glaciers have eroded the overlying rock, bringing the crystal-bearing voids near or to the surface. In some instances, the rock was so eroded that the crystals were released into the soil and washed down the slope. Thus, the crystals are found in both soil and rock.

Maine tourmaline was first discovered in 1820 by two students who spent much of their leisure time hunting gems in the area around Paris, Maine. Late that year, while exploring Mt. Mica, one of the students found an intense green crystal—a tourmaline—in the soil. When the students returned the next spring, they found more crystals and crystal fragments. Crystals were found in a multitude of colors, including green, red, yellow, and white. Tourmaline

has been mined from Mt. Mica for over 175 years; major finds are still being made. A crystal found in 1978 yielded several cut gems, including a blue-green 256-carat stone.

Other major finds have also been made in this band of mineralization. Tourmaline has been found on Mt. Apatite, in Auburn, since 1839, and tourmaline has been mined there sporadically since 1883. The Plumbago Mining Company was established in 1972 following the discovery of tourmaline on Plumbago Mountain. In the following year and a half, over 1 metric ton of tourmaline, much of it gem quality, was recovered.

One unique type of tourmaline found in Maine is watermelon tourmaline, which has a deep red center and a green outer layer. Another type of tourmaline found in Maine, but in few other locations, is bicolor tourmaline, in which the crystals have one color at one end and a different color at the other. A few tricolor crystals have even been found. Most of the quarries are closed or private, but some collecting can be done.

(Portions of this text are excerpted from "The History of Maine Tourmaline" with permission from Cross Jewelers, Portland, ME.)

AUBURN / *Native · Moderate*

Hunt for Gems and Minerals *T*

*The following gems and minerals
may be found:*

- **Apatite, tourmaline, quartz**

Mt. Apatite Quarry
c/o Auburn Parks & Recreation Dept.
48 Pettengill Park Road
Auburn, ME 04210
Phone: (207) 333-6601 x 2108
www.maine.gov/doc/nrimc/mgs/
explore/minerals/sites/apatite.htm

Open: Dawn–dusk. Dept. hours: open
8:00 A.M.–4:30 P.M. Monday–Friday.
Info: Rock hunting and mining has
occurred in the park area for over 150
years. No pneumatic tools or motorized
vehicles allowed. Contact the Auburn
Recreation Department for park rules
and guidelines.
Admission: Free.
Directions: The quarry is located in
Auburn, Maine, off of Garfield Road, by
passing through the Auburn Suburban
Little League complex to the entrance
gate. Maps available at the recreation
department office at 48 Pettengill Park
Road, or call (207) 333-6601 x 2108 to
have one mailed.

AUBURN / *Native · Moderate*

Hunt for Gems and Minerals *T*

*The following gems and minerals
may be found:*

- Tourmaline, black tourmaline, garnet,
graphic granite, clevelandite, autunite,
mica, beryl, purple and blue apatite—
rubalite, smoky black quartz crystals

Mount Apatite Farm/Hatch Ledge
171 Hatch Road
Auburn, ME 04210
Phone: (207) 795-6376; (207) 650-1573
E-mail: cookincarol@roadrunner.com
www.cookincarol.com

Open: May–October; call for hours and
reservations.
Info: This is one of several old feldspar and
gem quarries on Mt. Apatite. The farm has
organic vegetable and flower gardens, and
a catering business; and the owner allows
collecting in the quarry. Read about the
2008 Halloween Pocket, a sizable gemstone discovery at the quarry, on the website. (Go to "Introduction" and then scroll
down to "Mining/Mineral links.")
Admission: Adults $5.00, under 18 free.
Directions: Get directions when you
make a reservation.

BETHEL / *Native · Easy*

Collect Your Own
Gems and Minerals *T*

*The following gems and minerals
may be found:*

- Albite, almandine garnet, beryl, rose
and other varieties of quartz, black tourmaline, biotite, autunite, zircon, and
many others

Maine Mineralogy Expeditions
c/o Bethel Outdoor Adventure
121 Mayville Road
Bethel, ME 04217
Phone: (207) 824-4224;
(800) 533-3607
Fax: (207) 824-8511
E-mail: info@betheloutdooradventure.com
www.rocksme.biz

Open: May–September, subject to weather. Call in advance for reservations.

Info: Two collecting options available. **Option 1:** Weekly educational/collecting tours leave from Bethel Outdoor Adventure at noon and go to the Bumpus Mine, a feldspar and beryl mine last operated in 1967. After a presentation and guided tour you may dig in mine dumps for specimens. Keep what you find. **Option 2:** Tailings from Mt. Mica are trucked to the Sluice at Bethel Outdoor Adventure, where a sluice and sorting benches are provided. Pay at the office, then dig and sluice pails of mine dirt. Keep all you find. See www.rocksme.biz for details and guidelines.

Admission: Call or see website for schedule and fees.

BETHEL / *Native • Moderate to Difficult*

Collect Minerals at a Working Aquamarine Mine T

The following gems or minerals may be found (these have been observed to date):

• Beryl (aquamarine variety), quartz (smoky and milky), albite feldspar, black tourmaline, garnet, mica, pyrite, amethyst (rare), zircon, biotite mica, hydroxyl herderite, columbite, rutile, apatite, siderite, and hyalite opal

Songo Pond Mine
Jan Neal Brownstein
40 South Shore Lane
P.O. Box 864
Bethel, ME 04217
Phone: (207) 824-3898
www.songopondmine.com

Open: Late spring until snow (November) 9:00 A.M.– 5:00 P.M. Daily admissions are limited. Call ahead—advance reservations required.

Site may be closed to visitors during certain mining operations or inclement weather.

Info: The mine is open to the public on a seasonal basis and gives a chance to collect minerals from the mine tailings (dump area) and observe a small-scale mining operation at the same time. Bring your own equipment (hammer, chisel, scraper, shovel, screen, etc.). Boots, safety glasses, gloves, and hats are recommended for protective clothing, along with sunscreen. Also, bring something to drink and whatever you will need to eat.

Admission: Adults full day $25.00, up to 4 hours $15.00; children under 12 full day $7.50, 4 hour pass $5.00; children under 6 free. Collection limit: one 5-gallon pail. Groups call ahead for a discount.

Other services available: New "off-the-grid" shop 800 feet from mine sells jewelry, gemstones, and mineral specimens. Gem cutting is available. Tools also for sale. A portable toilet is provided at the mine.

Directions: From Route 26 or Route 2, travel to the town of Bethel; you will see a sign for Route 5 south. Travel 4 miles south to the south shore of Songo Pond, then look for a highway sign for South Shore Lane, which is a dirt road on the left. Take South Shore Lane, and the mine parking lot is ¼ mile on the right.

The parking lot is a 5–10-minute walk from the mine. Handicapped and elderly persons may use limited parking at the top of the hill, 150 feet from the mine. Others may drive up and leave passengers and tools at the mine, then drive back down to the parking lot at the bottom.

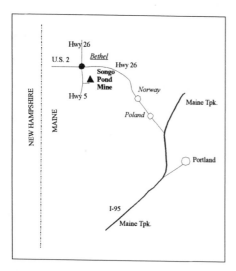

POLAND / *Native • Moderate to Difficult*

Camp and Collect Minerals in Maine *T*

The following gems or minerals may be found:

• **Tourmaline, beryl, garnet, mica, quartz, albite, columbite, rutile, apatite, and other Maine gems and minerals** (See complete list on page 66)

Poland Mining Camps
Mary Groves
P.O. Box 26
Poland, ME 04274
Phone: (207) 998-2350
http://polandminingcamps.com

Open: June 1–September 30 by reservation only.

Info: Check the website for upcoming special events. Collect minerals at pegmatite quarries closed to the public. Poland Mining Camps have collection access at Mount Mica Quarry, Emmons Quarry, Mount Apatite, Pulsifer Quarry, Keith Quarry, Wade Quarry, Hole-in-the-Ground Quarry, Dionne Quarry, Marie Luise Hopfe Quarry, Newry Mine, G. E. Mine, and others.

This is a unique vacation opportunity. Fee includes lodging, all meals, mine fees, and a guide to famous and active quarries. Lodging is in cabins with two private bedrooms, living room with fireplace (only heat for the cabin), ½ kitchen with fridge, etc., and bath with flush facilities and shower (hot and cold). All linens, bedding, and towels are provided. At the center of the camp complex is a pavilion, which is the hub of activity at the camp. It is used for meals, functions, and general socializing with other campers. Minerals are displayed from the various quarries where you hunt for gems, and lectures and

Minerals List
(Some of the More Common Minerals That May Be Found)

Albite	Cassiterite	Petalite
Albite (cleavelandite var.)	Columbite	Pollucite
	Gahnite (spinel)	Pyrite
Almandine garnet	Herderite-Hydroxyl	Quartz
Apatite (fluor-)	Kaolinite	Rhodochrosite
Apatite (hydroxyl-)	Lepidolite mica	Spodumene
Arsenopyrite	Lithiophilite	Topaz
Autunite	Lollingite	Tourmaline (elbaite)
Beryl (aquamarine, morganite, goshenite)	Microcline/orthoclase (feldspar)	Tourmaline (schorl)
		Triphyllite
Beryllonite	Montebrasite	Uranite
Bertrandite	Montmorillonite	Zircon
Biotite mica	Muscovite mica	

Phosphate Species Minerals
(That May Be Found in Addition to the Ones Listed Above)

Augelite	Hureaulite	Reddingite
Beraumite	Jahnsite	Rochbridgeite
Bermanite	Kosnarite	Stewartite
Brazilianite	Landsite	Strunzite
Childrenite	Laueite	Switzerite (and metaswitzerite)
Diadochite	Ludlamite	
Dickinsonite	McCrillisite	Torberite
Earlshannonite	Mitridatite	Triplite
Eosphorite	Monzaite	Uralolite
Farifieldite	Moraesite	Vivianite
Gainsite	Perhamite	Wardite
Goyazite	Phosphosiderite	Whitlockite
Graftonite	Phosphouranylite	Whitmoreite
Heterosite	Purpurite	Wodginite

demonstrations by local craftsmen and miners are presented there.

The late Dudy Groves had over 30 years of experience in mining and collecting gemstones and minerals in the local quarries. He worked for and/or mined in many of the historically important mining operations, including Mount Apatite and Mount Mica. Mary Groves is in charge of the large organic garden, which supplies much of the food for the camp. She is famous for her down-home cooking and will cater to any special dietary needs. Mary is continuing mining at Mt. Apatite with the help of many wonderful people.

Fee: $650.00 per person per week for cabins, $125.00 per person per day for a 3-day stay (minimum length of stay). Must provide your own equipment, protective clothing, and transportation. Reservations and a nonrefundable 50% deposit required. Walk-ins will be accommodated only if space is available.

Serious mineral collectors who can't stay at Poland Mining Camps may still join the resident clients on selected days and collect at the Quarry-of-the-Day, selected by Poland Mining Camps. The Tag-a-long Package includes quarry access, quarry fees, up to 7 hours of collecting time (dependent on travel times and other variables), liability coverage, and the services of the guide. It does not include food, lodging, transportation, or other services of the Camps. With the Tag-a-long Package, which requires a reservation, you must join the caravan leaving Poland Mining Camps at 8:00 A.M. and leave the quarry when the guide leaves. Tag-a-long customers must follow all rules and restrictions of Poland Mining Camps and must stay with and follow directions of the Poland Mining Camps guide. You may not enter or return to the Quarry-of-the-Day on your own at any time.

Poland Mining Camps is now offering night trips for collecting fluorescent minerals. The trips begin with a weenie roast at the collecting location, followed by collecting using UV lights, and are being offered as part of the week's stay. Tag-a-Long rate for night trips is $25.00 and includes supper.

Tag-a-Long Rates: $60.00 per person per day; 10% discount for 3 consecutive days. Prices subject to change.

Note: All prices are subject to change and to sales tax.

Other services available: Poland Mining Camps has opened Oma's Attic, a store offering mineral specimens from local mines as well as from locations around the world. They are also selling fine jewelry, including jewelry made by local craftspeople. Mineral specimens from many Maine localities are displayed at the camp's Pavilion. There is also an area set aside for microscope work, and one scope equipped with a video monitor for group study. References on minerals and literature for the area are also available. The camp has laundry facilities, pay phone and other services on site,

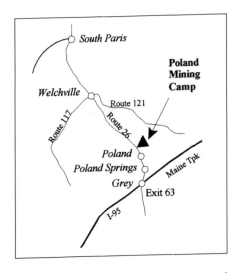

including a mineral washing station and wrapping supplies.

Directions: From I-95 take exit 63, Gray. Go north on Route 26 to Poland. Continue north for a couple of miles. Poland Mining Camps is on the right, just before the junction of Route 26 and Route 11.

WEST PARIS / *Native • Moderate to Difficult*

Collect Minerals in Maine *T*

The following gems or minerals may be found:

• Tourmaline (including green and black); beryl; scheelite; quartz crystals; albite; columbite; apatite; amethyst; spodumene; zircon; petalite; cookeite; and other Maine gems and minerals

Perham's of West Paris
West Paris, ME

Open: Quarries are available for collect-

ing during daylight hours. Sites may be closed to visitors during occasional mining operations.

Info: The Perham jewelry shop is now closed. Three quarries owned by Frank Perham are open for collecting. These are Harvard Quarry, Tamminen Quarry, and Waisanen Quarry. Their locations are shown on the map on the right, above. Bring your own equipment and protective clothing. Keep what you find in your collecting venture.

Note: Mr. Perham is allowing collecting in these quarries, but the collecting is at your own risk. No liability is assumed by the owners. No camping and no open fires are allowed at the sites.

Rates: May visit quarries free of charge.
Directions: Take exit 63 on the Maine Turnpike; then Maine Route 26 north to West Paris.

Important Note: During late October and November, hunting season is open. The land owned by Perham's is *not* posted, so it is advisable to wear blaze orange when visiting the quarries during this time.

Perham's Quarries

Local quarries are all open pits, and collecting usually takes place in the surrounding dump areas, or tailings. Actual mining is sporadic, but mineral collecting is an ongoing activity taking place when weather permits. Common-sense safety guidelines offer adequate protection. What you find will depend upon your persistence—and your luck.

Harvard Quarry

This renowned locale was initially developed about 1870 by George "Shavey" Noyes. Harvard University conducted a mining operation here in 1917, and the quarry was mined by Arthur Valley in 1942. Since 1958 this locale, owned by the Perham family, has been explored sporadically by Frank Perham. The Harvard is noted for fine crystals of purple apatite as well as for green tourmaline, black tourmaline, garnet, beryl, quartz, and cookeite. Amethyst, cassiterite, zircon, petalite, columbite, gahnite, spodumene, scheelite, vesuvianite, and lepidolite are also found here.

Tamminen Quarry

Mining here began about 1930, and the quarry has since been explored by several mining firms. Owned by Nestor Tamminen for many years, this site was a valued source of feldspar. Among the minerals found here are amblygonite, pollucite, cleavelandite, montmorillonite, and altered spodumene. This locale is renowned for especially fine pseudocubic quartz crystals.

Waisanen Quarry

Mining here began in 1931 when Matti Waisanen conducted an exploration directed at the recovery of mica. The quarry has since been mined extensively for mica and feldspar, both commercially valuable materials. Frank Perham's 1963 mining endeavor produced superb specimens of hydroxyl-herderite, bertrandite, purple apatite, and superb parallel-growth quartz crystals. Other mineral varieties found here include gem tourmaline, spodumene, triphylite, and columbite.

WOODSTOCK / *Native • Easy to Moderate*

Collect Minerals in Maine *T*

The following gems or minerals may be found:

- Quartz crystals (clear, smoky, rose, and clusters), tourmaline, aquamarine, golden beryl (rare), lepidolite and other Lithia accessory minerals, cassiterite, montebrasite, spodumene, pollucite, lollingite.

Maine Mineral Adventures
1148 S. Main Street
Woodstock, ME 04219
Phone: (207) 674-3440
Cell: (207) 890-9753
www.digmainegems.com

Open: For screening: mid-April–mid-November. Summer hours: 10:00 A.M.–5:00 P.M., 7 days/week; Fall hours: 10:00 A.M.–3:00 P.M. Thursday–Sunday. For field trips: mid-April–December (weather permitting).

Info: Two gem mining activities are available. A screening area offers the opportunity to buy and search through a bucket of mine run gravel with material from local gem and mineral deposits, or attend a field collecting trip to one of the local Maine mines, such as Mt. Mica, the Bennett Quarry, the Orchard Pit, the Intergalactic Mine on Deer Hill, or other closed Maine mines. Prior reservations are recommended for field trips; reservations required for trips to Mt. Mica (the owners of Mt. Mica have requested that children under 8 not be allowed in the mine).

Rates: Screen your own bucket of Maine minerals: $10.00 per bucket; specialty buckets: $25.00 up to $100.00 per bucket. Educational bag for children: $5.00; contains material from Mt. Mica and from around the world.

Field trips: $60.00/day or $25.00/hr. per adult, plus any fees to enter private locations. Two-person minimum; children under 12 free when accompanied by an adult. Group rates are available.

Other services available: Rock and mineral shop. Food and lodging packages are available at the motel next to the screening area.

Directions: Take I-95 to Gray (exit 63). Follow Route 26 north for approximately 35 miles. Facility is located next to the Mollyockett Motel on Route 26.

SECTION 2: Museums and Mine Tours

AUGUSTA

Museum

Maine State Museum
83 State House Station
Augusta, ME 04333-0083
Phone: (207) 287-2301
Fax: (207) 287-6633
www.mainestatemuseum.org

Open: All year; closed major holidays. 9:00 A.M.–5:00 P.M. Tuesday–Friday, 10:00 A.M.–4:00 P.M. Saturday.

Info: Gem and mineral cases present a display of Maine gemstones, including smoky quartz, milky quartz, rose quartz, amethyst, garnet, beryl, and gold. Various types of the Maine state mineral, tourmaline, are on display. The Peary necklace, which Arctic explorer Robert Peary gave to his wife for a birthday present in 1913, is on display. It is made from gold collected from the Swift River in western Maine, and Maine tourmaline.

Admission: Adults $2.00, seniors $1.00, students (6–18) $1.00, children under 6 free. $6.00 maximum/family.

Directions: Take Interstate I-95, exit 109 to route 202 (Western Avenue). Take Western Avenue to rotary. At the rotary take RT 201 South (State Street). The state capitol will be on your right. The museum is located past the capitol on your right.

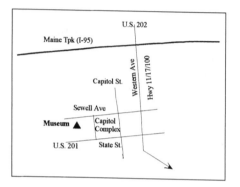

BETHEL

Museum

Maine Mineral Museum
Mt. Mann Jeweler's Gallery
57 Main Street
Bethel, ME 04217
Phone: (207) 824-3030
mtmann@megalink.net
www.mtmann.com

Open: 9:00 A.M.–5:00 P.M. Tuesday–Friday; 10:00 A.M.–5:00 P.M. Saturday.

Info: Tour the Maine Mineral Museum and the Crystal Cave for Kids. The museum presents examples of gems from both local and world-wide sources. The Crystal Cave provides kids an opportunity to see and collect local minerals in the rough.

Admission: Free.

Directions: On Main Street in Bethel.

CARIBOU

Museum

Nylander Museum of Natural History
657 Main Street
Caribou, ME 04736
Phone: (207) 493-4209
E-mail: nylander@maine.rr.com
www.nylandermuseum.org

Open: Call or check website for current hours.

Info: Contains a collection of minerals from northern Maine, as well as rocks and lithic artifacts (stone tools). Handicapped accessible.

Admission: Free; donations appreciated.

Directions: On Main Street in Caribou.

PRESQUE ISLE

Museum

The Northern Maine Museum of Science
Folsom Hall
University of Maine at Presque Isle
181 Main Street
Presque Isle, ME 04769
Phone: (207) 768-9400
www.umpi.maine.edu/info/nmms/museum.htm

Open: When the campus is open. Call

or check website for details or e-mail Kevin at kevin.mccartney@umpi.edu.

Info: This museum formally opened in 1996, and contains displays in hallways on several floors, and in the entrances to Folsom Hall. Rotating displays include minerals of Maine, Earth history, tourmaline, Maine slate, fluorescent minerals, and crystals and their atomic structure.

Admission: Free.

Directions: On the University of Maine campus at Presque Isle, on Route One. Call, e-mail, or check website for specific directions.

SECTION 3: Special Events and Tourist Information

ANNUAL EVENT

Maine Mineral Symposium, Augusta, Maine

The symposium includes lectures, exhibits, displays, and dealers. Several mineral localities are available for field collecting. Held the second full weekend (Friday–Sunday) in May.

For registration or more information on the symposium, visit:
www.maine.gov/doc/nrimc/mgs/explore/minerals/symposium.htm

ANNUAL EVENT

Maine Pegmatite Workshop, Poland, Maine

One week at the end of May or beginning of June, held at Poland Mining Camp. A Saturday–Friday program, generally with classroom activities in the morning and field trips in the afternoon. Includes a textbook on pegmatites and a faculty ranging from college professors to local miners.

See contact information under Poland Mining Camps.

TOURIST INFORMATION

State Tourist Agency

Maine Office of Tourism
#59 State House Station

Augusta, ME 04333-0059
Phone: (888) 624-6345
www.visitmaine.com

MARYLAND

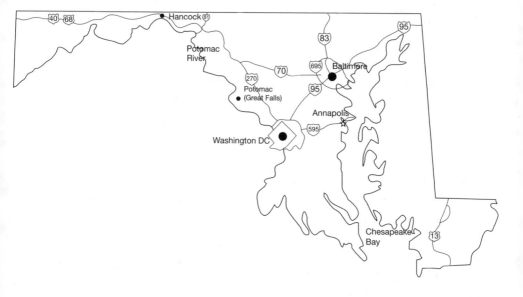

State Gemstone: Patuxent River Stone (2004)

No information available.

HANCOCK

Museum 🏛

Hancock–Sideling Hill Geological
Museum
42 W. Main Street
Hancock, MD 21750
Phone: (301) 678-6236
www.hancockmd.com/
HancockMuseum.htm

Open: 10:00 A.M.–5:00 P.M. Monday,
Tuesday, Thursday, Friday, Saturday;
10:00 A.M.–4:00 P.M. Sunday. Closed
Wednesdays.

Info: One of the best rock exposures in
Maryland is located approximately 6
miles west of Hancock in Washington
County, where Interstate 68 cuts
through Sideling Hill. Almost 810 feet of
strata in a tightly folded syncline are
exposed in this road cut. The state exhibit center at the road cut was closed, and
the exhibits moved to the Hancock
Museum. The parking lot, paved walk-
ways, observation bridge and restrooms
at the road cut remain open.

Admission: Free.

Directions: Call for directions to the
museum. The rock cut is located on
I-68, 6 miles west of Hancock.

POTOMAC

Gold Mine Trail 🏛

C & O Canal National Historical Park
Great Falls Visitor's Center
11710 MacArthur Boulevard
Potomac, MD 20854
Phone: (301) 767-3714

Open: During daylight hours.

Info: The Maryland Mine produced
gold from 1867–1939. A 3.2-mile, moderate hiking trail goes past the old mine
workings. Guided tours are scheduled
periodically for up to 25 people; reservations are required.

Admission: Park entrance fee is $5.00
per vehicle.

Other services available: Geology
hikes are also conducted periodically;
call ahead.

Directions: I-495 to the Clara Barton

Parkway. Turn left at the intersection with MacArthur Boulevard, and continue 2.2 miles to the park entrance. Turn left into the park, continue to the admission booth, then to the Great Falls Tavern Visitor's Center. The trail begins behind the Center.

SECTION 3: Special Events and Tourist Information

TOURIST INFORMATION

State Tourist Agency

Maryland Office of Tourism
Development
104 East Pratt Street, 14th Fl.
Baltimore, MD 21202
Phone: (866) 639-3526
info@visitmaryland.org
www.visitmaryland.org

MASSACHUSETTS

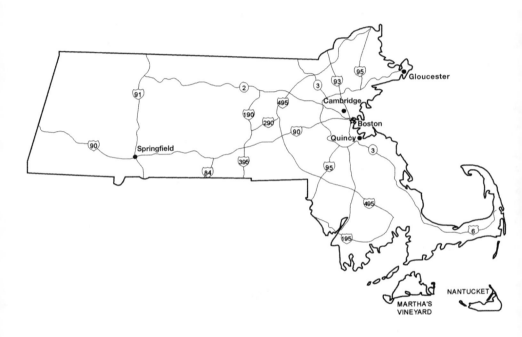

State Gemstone: Rhodonite (1979)
State Mineral: Babingtonite (1971)
State Stone/Rock: Plymouth Rock; Dighton Rock;
Roxbury Conglomerate; Granite (1983)

No information available.

CAMBRIDGE

Museum

Harvard Museum of Natural History
Harvard University
26 Oxford Street
Cambridge, MA 02138
Phone: (617) 495-3045
www.hmnh.harvard.edu

Open: All year, 9:00 A.M.–5:00 P.M. daily. Closed Thanksgiving, December 24-25, and January 1. Open for the majority of holidays.

Info: The exhibits feature a comprehensive collection of some 3,000 gems, minerals, ores, and meteorites drawn from the Harvard Mineralogical Museum's collections. Begun in 1784, the university's collections cover virtually the entire scope of the mineral sciences, with 50,000 specimens.

The petrology collection and economic geology collection, comprising suites of igneous, sedimentary, and metamorphic rocks and ores (75,000+ specimens), are an impressive sampling of the Earth's crust.

Meteorites provide insight into the origin of the solar system and the universe. In 1883 the museum augmented its holdings by the acquisition of the J. Lawrence Smith Collection. The museum has a broadly representative collection of over 514 meteorites, many of which are on display in a new exhibit called *Impact*.

Admission: Adults $9.00, non-Harvard students with ID and seniors $7.00, children (3–18) $6.00. Group rates available.

Directions: The museum is a 7-minute walk across the campus from the Harvard Square Red Line T. See the museum's website for map, directions, and info on pre-reserving parking.

GLOUCESTER

Museum

Cape Ann Historical Museum
27 Pleasant Street
Gloucester, MA 01930
Phone: (978) 283-0455
www.capeannmuseum.org

Open: 10:00 A.M.–5:00 P.M.
Tuesday–Saturday; 1:00 P.M.–4:00 P.M.
Sunday. Closed Mondays, major holidays, and during the month of February.

Info: The museum has exhibits of local granite, tools, equipment, photographs, paintings, and sculpture that illustrate the region's granite quarrying history.

Admission: Adults $8.00; Cape Ann residents, seniors, students $6.00. Group rates are available.

Directions: Call for directions.

QUINCY

Museum

Quincy Historical Society Museum
8 Adams Street
Adams Academy Bldg.
Quincy, MA 02169
Phone: (617) 773-1144
http://quincyhistory.org

Open: Year round, 9:00 A.M.–4:00 P.M.
Monday-Friday; April 14 through November 10, noon–3:00 P.M. Saturdays. Closed holidays.

Info: The museum has exhibits on the granite industry in Quincy.

Admission: Suggested donations: Adults $3.00; seniors and students $1.50; children free.

Other services available: Museum shop.

Directions: Quincy Historical Society is housed in the landmark Adams Academy Building, at 8 Adams Street, at the junction of Adams, Hancock, and Dimmock Streets. There is parking in the rear of the building.

SPRINGFIELD

Museum

Springfield Science Museum
21 Edwards Street
Springfield, MA 01103
Phone: (413) 263-6800;
(800) 625-7738
www.springfieldmuseums.org/
the_museums/science

Open: All year, 10:00 A.M.–5:00 P.M.
Tuesday–Saturday; 11:00 A.M.–5:00 P.M.
Sunday. Closed major holidays.

Info: Mineral Hall displays minerals from around the world, including a collection made by two local jewelers. It also has a fluorescent mineral display, specimens of local minerals, and a meteorite from Arizona.

Admission: Adults $12.50, seniors $9.00, college students $9.00, children (3–17) $6.50, children under 3 free.

Directions: The museum is located on 21 Edwards Street. Free on-site parking.

SECTION 3: Special Events and Tourist Information

TOURIST INFORMATION

State Tourist Agency

Massachusetts Office of Travel and
Tourism
10 Park Plaza, Suite 4510
Boston, MA 02116

Phone: (617) 973-8500;
(800) 227-MASS or (800) 227-6277
Fax: (617) 973-8525
E-mail: vacationinfo@state.ma.us
www.mass-vacation.com

MICHIGAN

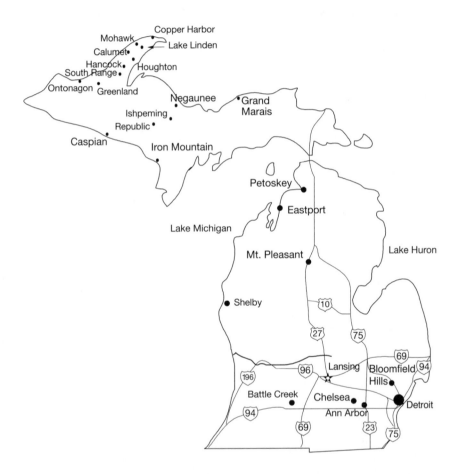

State Gemstone: Isle Royal Greenstone (Chlorostrolite) (1973)
State Stone/Rock: Petoskey Stone (1965)

GRAND MARAIS / *Native • Easy*

Collect Agates along the Beach *T*

The following gems or minerals may be found:

- Agates

Woodland Park Campground
P.O. Box 430
Grand Marais, MI 49839
Park phone (April-October):
(906) 494-2613
Burt Township office phone (all year):
(906) 494-2381
www.grandmaraismichigan.com/
WoodlandPark/index.html

Open: April–October.

Info: This is a campground on the shores of Lake Superior; the beach is accessible for agate collecting.
Note: The campground is located next to the Pictured Rocks National Lakeshore. Collecting agates is prohibited on the National Lakeshore. Check to be sure that you are not collecting on the National Lakeshore.

Rates: Call or check the website for rates. Full hook up or primitive sites are available. First come, first served basis; reservations are not accepted.

Other services available: Camping, recreational facilities.

Directions: On Brazel Street in Grand Marais. Call for directions.

MOHAWK / *Native • Easy*

Find Your Own Copper *T*

The following gems or minerals may be found:

- Copper

Delaware Copper Mine
HCI, Box 102
Mohawk, MI 49950
Phone: (906) 289-4688
www.delawarecopperminetours.com

Open: Seven days a week. 10:00 A.M.–6:00 P.M. June, July, August; 10:00 A.M.–5:00 P.M. September–October.

Info: Search for souvenir copper at an authentic copper mine dating back to 1847–1887.

Admission: For further information on the mine tour, see listing under Section 2.

Directions: Located in the historic ghost town of Delaware, 12 miles south of Copper Harbor and 38 miles north of Houghton on U.S. 41.

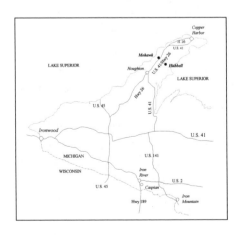

ONTONAGON / *Native · Easy*

Collect Your Own Copper and Minerals *T*

The following gems or minerals may be found:

- Native pure copper, silver, epidote, feldspar, calcite, datolite, quartz

The Caledonia Copper Mine
Red Metal Minerals
202 Ontonagon Street
Ontonagon, MI 49953
Phone: (906) 884-6618
Fax: (906) 884-6753
E-mail: caledoniamine@charter.net
www.caledoniamine.com

Open: Advance registrations required. Morning events: Registration is at 8:30 A.M., and digging is from 9:00 A.M.–noon. Afternoon events: Registration is at 12:30 P.M., digging is from 1:00 P.M.–4:00 P.M.

Info: Dig in your own private ore pile or datolite pile, or search the Caledonia Mine Rock Dump left by commercial mining from the mid-1860s through the 1950s. You may bring your own collecting equipment if you desire. The mine will provide the use of a bucket and digging tools for the ore and datolite pile options. Metal detectors and tools are also available for rental. Safety glasses and proper footgear and clothing are required, and gloves are strongly recommended.

Rates: Private Ore Pile (2–4 adults per pile) $80.00, Datolite Pile (1–2 adults only) $100.00, Rock Dump: Adults $15.00, youth (6–13) $5.00.

Directions: The mine is located about 14 miles from Ontonagon, MI, 41 miles from Houghton, and 62 miles from Ironwood. Get specific directions when you make a reservation.

PETOSKEY / *Native · Moderate*

Collect Your Own Copper and Minerals *T*

The following gems or minerals may be found:

- Petoskey Stones

Petoskey State Park
2475 M-119 Highway
Petoskey, MI 19770
Phone: (231) 347-2311
www.mi.gov/dnr (Click on "Recreation & Camping.")

Open: Call for days and hours of operation.

Info: Hunt for Petoskey Stones, fossilized coral often found on the shores along Little Traverse Bay on Lake Michigan. Some areas of the park are also designated for metal detecting activities.

Rates: Admission fees for entry into the park.

Other services available: Camping.

Directions: The park is located north of Petoskey, MI, on MI Route 119, at the northwestern tip of the lower peninsula.

ANN ARBOR

Museum

Exhibit Museum of Natural History
University of Michigan
1109 Geddes Avenue
Ann Arbor, MI 48019-1079
Phone: (734) 764-0478
Fax: (734) 647-2767
www.lsa.umich.edu/exhibitmuseum

Open: All year, 9:00 A.M.–5:00 P.M. Monday–Saturday, noon–5:00 P.M. Sunday. Closed major holidays.
Info: The museum has geology displays of rocks and minerals.
Admission: Free.
Directions: On Geddes Avenue at Washtenaw Avenue in Ann Arbor.

BATTLE CREEK

Museum

Kingman Museum
175 Limit Street
Battle Creek, MI 49037
Phone: (269) 965-5117
Fax: (269) 965-3330
www.kingmanmuseum.org

Open: 11:00 A.M.–4:30 P.M. Tuesday–Thursday, 11:00 A.M.–6:00 P.M. Friday, 1:00 P.M.–5:00 P.M. Saturday. Closed Sundays and Mondays, and some holidays.

Info: The museum has a gem and mineral display.
Admission: Weekdays: Adults $6.00, veterans and seniors $5.00, students (3-18) $4.00, children under 3 free, family up to 6 members $18.00. Fridays from 1:00 p.m.–6:00 p.m. and Saturdays (planetarium show hours): Adults $7.00, veterans and seniors $6.00, students (3-18) $5.00, children under 3 free, family up to 6 members $20.00. Member adults $1.00 for planetarium.
Other services available: Gift shop.
Directions: Located on the grounds of Leila Arboretum. Call for specific directions.

BLOOMFIELD HILLS

Museum

Cranbrook Institute of Science
39221 Woodward Avenue
Bloomfield Hills, MI 48303-0801
Phone: (248) 645-3200
http://science.cranbrook.edu

Open: All year, 10:00 A.M.–5:00 P.M. Tuesday–Saturday (Friday until 10:00 P.M.), noon–4:00 P.M. Sunday.
Info: Mineral Hall contains numerous cases displaying approximately 5,000 minerals from all over the world. This prize collection of minerals and crystals includes what has been described as an almost perfect hiddenite crystal and what is per-

haps the finest gold specimen in the world.

Admission: Adults $12.50, children (2–12) and seniors $9.50, children under 2 free. Call for special Friday admission prices. Parking is free.

Directions: Located at 39221 Woodward Avenue in Bloomfield Hills. Cranbrook is located on the west side of Woodward Avenue between Long Lake and Lone Pine Roads. From I-75, exit Big Beaver (west) to Woodward Avenue (north). From I-696; exit Woodward Avenue (north). From Telegraph: Long Lake Road (east) to Woodward Avenue (south).

CALUMET

Mining Museum

Summer:
Coppertown, U.S.A.
25815 Red Jacket Road
Calumet, MI 49913
Phone: (906) 337-4354
www.uppermichigan.com/coppertown

Off-season:
Coppertown, U.S.A.
56638 Calumet Avenue
Calumet, MI 49913
Phone: (800) 338-7982

Open: early June–late-September, 11:00 A.M.–5:00 P.M. Monday–Saturday.

Info: Coppertown is a Heritage Site of the Keweenaw National Historical Park. The mining museum is an introduction to the story of the copper country and Keweenaw Peninsula, and America's first real mining boom. Michigan's copper industry began thousands of years ago when ancient miners attacked exposed veins of pure copper with huge hammer-stones. The tools and techniques of mining advanced considerably

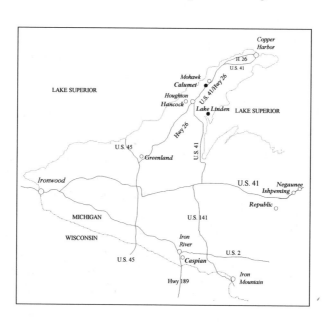

in the centuries that followed, and Coppertown's mining museum traces this evolution of mines and mining people with a series of exhibits designed for the family visitor.

Admission: Adults $4.00, children $2.00, children under 6 free.

Other services: Gift shop.

Directions: Turn west off U.S. 41 (Calumet Avenue) onto Red Jacket Road, and travel 1½ blocks to the museum on the left.

For information on other Native American stone quarries, see listings in Newark, DE: jasper quarries (Vol. 4); Copper Harbor, MI: copper (Vol. 4); Pipestone, MN: pipestone quarries (Vol.1); Hopewell, OH: flint quarries (Vol. 4); and Fritch, TX: flint quarries (Vol. 2).

CASPIAN

Museum

Iron County Museum and Park
P.O. Box 272
Caspian, MI 49915
Phone: (906) 265-2617
www.ironcountymuseum.com

Open: May by appointment only; Memorial Day–Labor Day, 10:00 A.M.–4:00 P.M. Monday–Saturday, 1:00 P.M.–4:00 P.M. Sunday; September, noon–4:00 P.M. Tuesday–Saturday, closed Sundays.

Info: Sample over 110 years of history at a park and museum with 21 buildings moved to the site of the head frame and engine house of the Caspian Mine. This mine was originally opened in 1903, and shipped over 6.6 million tons of iron ore before it was shut down in 1937. Besides the head frame and engine house (on the

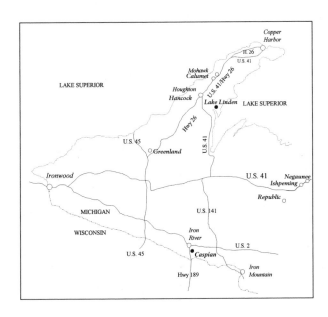

National Registry of Historic Places), the park contains a diamond drill rig (reported to be one of only three existing in the world), a simulated scraper drift, a mine ore rail car, and two mining halls containing artifacts, displays, and models telling the story of iron ore mining in Michigan over the last century.

Admission: Adults $8.00, seniors (65+) $7.00, youth $5.00, under 5 free.

Other services available: Gift shop.

Directions: Brady at Museum Road in Caspian, off M-189, or 2 miles off U.S. 2 at Iron River.

CHELSEA

Discovery Center

Gerald E. Eddy Discovery Center
Waterloo Recreation Area
17030 Bush Road
Chelsea, MI 48118
Phone: (734) 475-3170

Open: January–Easter Sunday, Tuesday–Saturday, 10:00 A.M.–5:00 P.M.; Sunday after Easter until Thanksgiving, Tuesday–Saturday, 10:00 A.M.–5:00 P.M., Sunday noon–5:00 P.M. Closed Thanksgiving Day through December. Closed state holidays and Mondays but open Memorial Day, July 4th, and Labor Day.

Info: The center introduces the world of geology with a focus on Michigan rocks, minerals, crystals, and mining from prehistoric times through the 20th century. Visitors can see displays, exhibits, and a

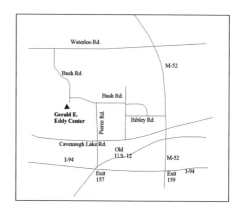

multiprojector slide show. There is also an easy geology walking trail, ⅛ mile long.

Admission: A Recreation Passport is required to enter all Michigan state parks. No charge to enter the Discovery Center.

Other services available: Gift shop.

The center is part of the 20,000-acre Waterloo Recreation Area, which features four campgrounds, a swimming beach, picnic sites, hiking, skiing, and horse trails.

Directions: From I-94, take exit 157, then take Pierce Road north to Bush Road. When Pierce Road ends, turn left to Bush Road, then left again to the Discovery Center.

COPPER HARBOR

Mine Tour

Fort Wilkins Historic State Park
P.O. Box 71
Copper Harbor, MI 49918
Phone: (906) 289-4215
www.michigan.gov/ftwilkins

Open: Early May–early October, daily 8:00 A.M.–dusk.

Info: The interpretation of copper mining in the Copper Harbor region in the mid-1800s takes place in three locations at the State Park. One is within the fort, showing all phases of mining, beginning with the initial discovery and including Native American artifacts. A map shows the underlying geography and location of several old mine shafts. An interpretive walking trail at the lighthouse complex takes the visitor to the still-visible remains of a copper silicate vein (which gave Copper Harbor its name) and to the site of the first commercial copper mine in Michigan. Finally, there are several other mining pits located within the grounds of the fort, some of which have interpretive information.

Admission: Michigan residents: A Recreation Passport is required to enter all Michigan state parks. Nonresidents: $8.00/day per vehicle; $29.00 annual pass for entry into any Michigan state park.

Directions: Take U.S. 45 north from the Michigan-Wisconsin border to State Highway 26/U.S. 41. After you pass through Houghton and the highway splits, either continue on U.S. 41 or take U.S. 26 to Copper Harbor.

GRAND MARAIS

Museum 🏛

Gitche Gumee Agate and History Museum
E21739 Brazel Street
P.O. Box 308
Grand Marais, MI 49839

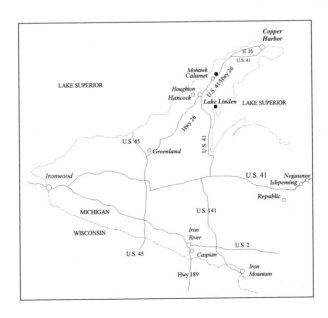

Phone: (906) 494-3000
Office phone: (906) 494-2590
E-mail: karen@agatelady.com
karen@agatelady.blogspot.com
www.agatelady.com

Open: July–August: noon–7:00 P.M. Monday–Saturday, noon–5:00 P.M. Sunday; June, September: 2:00 P.M.–5:00 P.M. Sunday–Friday, noon–7:00 P.M. Saturday; January–May by appointment; open specific hours last two weeks in May—check website.

Info: Displays a large variety of agates, also beach rocks, crystals, and fluorescent rocks. Historical displays present information on iron and copper mining.

Admission: Adults (18 and over) $1.00; under 18 free.

Other services available: Evening lectures in July and August; kids' science classes in July and August; rock cutting and polishing; rock collecting classes.

Directions: The museum is located in Grand Marais, MI. Take Main Street (M 77) past the only gas station (Bayshore Market), and turn left (west) at the next street (Brazel Street). The museum is on the south side of the second block. Look for the green and yellow building and the fish tug.

GREENLAND

Mine Tour

Adventure Copper Mine
Matthew & Victoria Portfleet
Greenland, MI 49929
Phone: (906) 883-3371

E-mail: info@adventureminetours.com

Open: Late May to mid-October; 9:00 A.M.–6:00 P.M. daily, 11:00 A.M.–6:00 P.M. Sunday. After Labor Day closed Wednesdays.

Info: Take a guided tour of an underground copper mine. Tours range from a historic surface tour to an underground walking tour, and even an underground cliff climb to lower mine levels. See website for age limitations and safety discussions.

Admission:

- Surface tour or trammer tour—adults $12.50, children (6–12) $7.00, under 6 free.
- Prospector's underground tour—adults $23.50, children $13.50.
- Miners underground tour—adults $55.00.

Other services available: Hiking trails, gift shop.

Directions: Off M-28, 12 miles east of Ontonagon. Call for directions or see website.

HANCOCK

Museum/Mine Tour

The Quincy Mine Hoist Association
49750 U.S. Highway 41
Hancock, MI 49930
Phone: (906) 482-3101
www.quincymine.com

Open: Summer season: 9:30 A.M.–5:00 P.M. daily; spring and fall, limited hours, call ahead.

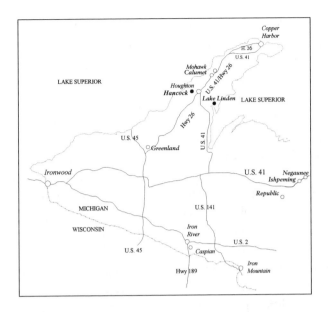

Info: First-hand glimpse of what our nation's first mineral boom was like. Visitors will experience a total copper mining experience, including visits to the steam hoist buildings, the Number Two Shafthouse, and the underground copper mine. The Quincy Steam Hoist is the world's largest steam-driven hoist and was first operational in 1920. The underground mine tour includes a scenic cogwheel tram ride and a guided tour ½ mile into the mine at the seventh level.
Admission: Full mine tour and surface tour: Adults (13-54) $18.00, seniors (55+) $15.00, youth (6–12) $8.00, children under 6 free. Surface mine tour and train ride: Adults and seniors $12.50, youth $5.00. AAA discount available.
Other services available: Gift shop.
Directions: Located on Route U.S. 41 North in Hancock.

HOUGHTON

Museum

The A. E. Seaman Mineral Museum
Michigan Technological University
1404 E. Sharon Avenue
Houghton, MI 49931-1295
Phone: (906) 487-2572
Fax: (906) 487-3027
www.museum.mtu.edu

Open: Portions of the museum are being updated and renovated throughout 2011-2012. New galleries will open as completed. Check website for progress and hours of visitation.
Info: Michigan Technological University's A. E. Seaman Mineral Museum (SMM), one of North America's finest mineral museums, is recognized worldwide for having one of the premier natural crystal

collections in North America. Founded in 1902 by pioneer Lake Superior geologist Arthur Edmund Seaman, the SMM collection today totals more than 30,000 mineral specimens, of which some 5,000 are currently on exhibit. The museum's collections include an irreplaceable heritage of minerals from the great copper-mining days of Michigan's Keweenaw Peninsula, from Upper Peninsula iron mines, and Lower Peninsula dolostone and limestone quarries. Also displayed are minerals from other parts of North America, as well as Europe, China, Russia, and other worldwide mineral localities. The museum is the official "Mineralogical Museum of Michigan," and a charter Heritage Site for the Keweenaw National Historical Park. The museum's mission is to preserve minerals to educate and inspire people about minerals and their relevance to society. The vision of the A. E. Seaman mineral museum is to be a dynamic museum of national and international prominence.

Admission: Check website. Donations appreciated.

Other services available: Mineral identification by prior arrangement. Museum gift shop.

IRON MOUNTAIN

Mine Tour

Iron Mountain Iron Mine
P.O. Box 177
Iron Mountain, MI 49801

Phone: (906) 563-8077
Off-season: (906) 774-7914
E-mail: ironmine@uplogon.com
www.ironmountainironmine.com

Open: Daily, June 1–October 15, 9:00 A.M.–5:00 P.M. Special arrangements can be made for groups.

Info: This is the largest public tour iron mine. Ride an underground mine train through 2,600 feet of underground drifts and tunnels to a depth of 400 feet below the earth's surface. Watch expert miners operate modern mining equipment. Get a free iron ore sample.

Admission: Adults $9.00, children (6–12) $7.00, children under 6 free.

Other services: Large and well-stocked rock and mineral gift shop, historical equipment display.

Directions: Located on U.S. 2 in Vulcan, 9 miles east of Iron Mountain.

IRON MOUNTAIN

Museum

Iron Mining Museum and Gift Shop
Cornish Pumping Engine
Kent Street
Iron Mountain MI, 49801
Phone: (906) 774-1086

Open: Memorial Day–Labor Day, 9:00 A.M.–5:00 P.M. Monday–Saturday, noon–4:00 P.M. Sunday.

Info: The museum has the largest collection of underground mining equipment on display in the state of Michigan; these are displayed both inside and outside of

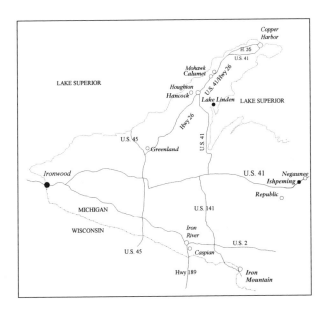

the museum. The Cornish Pumping Station was used to de-water the Chapin iron ore mine, pumping 5 million gallons a day from a depth of 1,500 feet.

Admission: Call for rates.

Other services available: Gift shop.

Directions: Call for directions.

ISHPEMING

Mine Tour and Museum

Cliffs Shaft Mine Museum
501 W. Euclid Street
Ishpeming, MI 49849
Phone: (906) 485-1882

Open: Memorial Day to September, noon–5:00 P.M. Tuesday–Saturday. Take a guided tour of the iron mine tunnels that the miners walked and listen to the history of mining from those who

worked the mines. Displays include mining-related artifacts and rocks, gems, and minerals.

Admission: Adults $5.00, youth (13-18) $3.00, children 12 and under free.

Directions: From U.S. 41, turn south onto Lake Shore at the stoplight by McDonald's, and turn left onto Euclid just past the lake. From downtown Ishpeming, take Division west to Lake Shore, go north to Euclid just south of the lake, turn right and park.

LAKE LINDEN

Museum

Houghton County Historical Museum
P.O. Box 127
53102 Highway M-26
Lake Linden, MI 49945

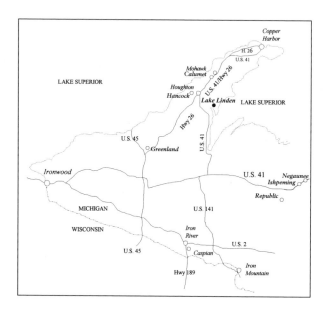

Phone: (906) 296-4121

www.houghtonhistory.org

Open: June–September, variable hours; staff is all volunteer. Please call for times. Special arrangements can be made for groups.

Info: The museum is located in the former main mill office of the Calumet & Hecla Mining Company, built in 1917. Displays include mining equipment and copper refining equipment.

Admission: Adults (17-61) $5.00, seniors (62+) $3.00, students (6-16) $3.00, children under 6 free.

Other services available: The Historical Museum Complex includes eight historic buildings, on 15 acres of land, which depict life in the early days in the upper Michigan peninsula's copper country.

Directions: Located on Highway M-26 north from the Portage Lake Lift Bridge or south from Laurium.

MOHAWK

Mine Tour 🏛

Delaware Copper Mine
HCI, Box 102
Mohawk, MI 49950
Phone: (906) 289-4688
www.delawarecopperminetours.com

Open: June–October. June, July, August 10:00 A.M.–6:00 P.M., last tour at 5:15 P.M. September, October 10:00 A.M.–5:00 P.M., last tour at 4:15 P.M. Special arrangements can be made for groups.

Info: Tour an authentic copper mine that dates back to 1847. Two tours are

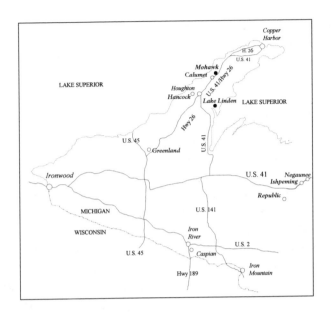

available. (1) The self-guided tour, where you can take your time and examine the shafts and tunnels, runs from mid-May through June and from September through mid-October. (2) The guided tour goes down Shaft #1 to the first level at a depth of 110 feet, lasts about 45 minutes, and is followed by an above-ground walk through the mine site. The guided tour is offered in July and August.

Jackets and walking shoes are recommended, as it is 45°F in the mine. Searching for souvenir copper is allowed (no metal detectors).

Admission: Adults $8.00, children (6-12) $4.00, under 6 free.

Other services available: Rock and mineral displays, refreshments, copper souvenirs, mini-zoo, mining displays, copper art, walking trails, antique engines, gift shop.

Directions: The mine is located in the historic ghost town of Delaware, which is 12 miles south of Copper Harbor and 38 miles north of Houghton on U.S. 41.

MOUNT PLEASANT

Museum

The Museum of Cultural and Natural History
Central Michigan University
103 Rowe Hall
Mount Pleasant, MI 48859
Phone: (989) 774-3829
E-mail: cmuseum@cmich.edu
www.museum.cmich.edu

Open: 8:00 A.M.–5:00 P.M. Monday– Friday, 1:00 P.M.–5:00 P.M. Saturday– Sunday, closed holidays and school breaks.
Info: The museum has a small collection of rocks and minerals and includes a display of rocks and minerals of Michigan, as well as what is believed to be the largest Petoskey Stone ever found (420 pounds).
Admission: Free.
Directions: The museum is located in Rowe Hall, on Bellows Street just west of Business Route U.S. 27 (Mission Street). Park free in Lot 14 with a permit from the campus Department of Public Safety.

NEGAUNEE

Museum

Michigan Iron Industry Museum
73 Forge Road
Negaunee, MI 49866-9532
Phone: (906) 475-7857
www.michigan.gov/ironindustrymuseum

Open: All year. June 1–September 30: 9:30 A.M.–4:30 P.M., 7 days/week; October and May: 9:30 A.M.–4:00 P.M., 7 days/week; November 1–April 30: Call ahead for museum hours.
Info: Dedicated to the story of Michigan's iron industry, which began in 1848 and continues today, the museum interprets Michigan's three iron ranges and the people who worked them. The museum overlooks the Carp River and the site of the first iron forge in the Lake Superior region. The museum features

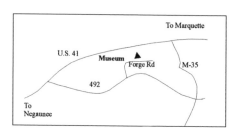

many exhibits, outdoor interpretive paths, and the video "Iron Spirits: Life on the Michigan Iron Ranges," which is shown in the auditorium. The Michigan Iron Industry Museum is part of the Michigan Historical Museum System.
Admission: Free.
Directions: The museum is located just off U.S. 41, 8 miles west of Marquette.

REPUBLIC

Mineview

Republic Iron Mine
M-95
Republic, MI 49879

The open-pit hard-rock Republic Iron Mine closed in 1981, and has gradually filled with water. A viewing stand has been erected for this pit just off MI Route M-95, south of the Michigamme River Bridge.

SHELBY

Factory Tour

Shelby Man-Made Gemstones
1330 Industrial Drive
Shelby, MI 49455

> A monument in Negaunee commemorates the location where iron ore was discovered in 1845. This monument has been constructed using every kind of rock, ore, or mineral found in Iron County.

Phone: (231) 861-2165
Fax: (231) 861-6458
www.shelbygemfactory.com

Open: All year, 9:00 A.M.–5:30 P.M. Monday–Friday; noon– 4:00 P.M. Saturday.

Info: Visit a gemstone factory where artificial diamonds are created at an intense heat of 5040°F. Rubies, emeralds, and sapphires in various colors are also made here. Exhibits and shows in a 50-seat theatre present the story of artificial gemstones.

Admission: Free.

Other services available: Gift shop with a complete line of jewelry.

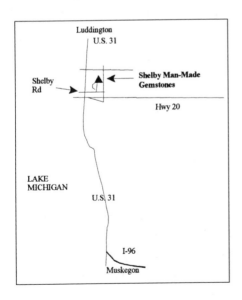

Directions: Shelby Man-Made Gemstones is located on Industrial Drive in Shelby. Take U.S. 31 north from Muskegon to the Shelby Road exit, then turn east on Shelby Road, then north onto 72nd Avenue. Turn east onto Woodrow Road, then north onto Industrial Park Drive.

SOUTH RANGE

Museum 🏛

The Copper Range Historical Museum
44 Trimountain Ave.
South Range, MI 49963
Phone: (906) 482-6125

Open: June, September, and October: noon–3:00 P.M. Tuesday–Saturday; July and August: noon–3:00 P.M. Monday–Saturday.

Info: Exhibits focus on the miners' lives and families and on the copper mining industry.

Admission: Adults $1.00 donation, children free.

Directions: Located two blocks off of MI Route M-26 on the main street of South Range (Trimountain Avenue).

ANNUAL EVENT

Antrim County Petoskey Stone Festival ☜

Barnes Park
P.O. Box 504
Eastport, MI 49627
www.petoskeystonefestival.com

The Petoskey Stone Festival is a one-day festival held during the early summer, and includes a Petoskey Stone hunting contest.

For more information, contact:

Antrim County Conservation District
Christy Roman
Phone: (231) 533-8363
Fax: (231) 533-6388
Email: christy.roman@macd.org

ANNUAL EVENT

Copper Country Mineral Retreat ☜

The retreat during August offers collecting opportunities at a number of mines in the Copper Country. This area is notable for native copper mines, and the rock piles used for the retreat are waste rock from these old copper mines. At all of the localities it is possible to find native copper either in mass or crystallized form. Massive is much, much more common than crystallized, and virtually everyone will find native copper at a locality notable for native copper. Native silver accompanies native copper, and it, too, can be found at all localities, but much less frequently. There are over 130 different minerals found in the mines of the Copper Country. You can find many of these at every site.

Retreat Contact:
A. E. Seaman Mineral Museum
Phone: (906) 487-2437
dmcomfor@mtu.edu
www.museum.mtu.edu

Other sponsors include Copper Country Rock and Mineral Club and Red Metal Minerals (Caledonia Mines).

TOURIST INFORMATION

State Tourist Agency ☜

Travel Michigan
P.O. Box 30226
Lansing, MI 48909
Phone: (888) 784-7328;
(866) 644-2489
www.michigan.org

Michigan State Recreation Passport
Michigan residents can obtain this passport for $10.00 when renewing their vehicle plates. Passports purchased at state parks may cost up to three times as much. Non-residents may purchase a $29.00 annual pass, or pay an $8.00 daily fee.

NEW HAMPSHIRE

Stoneham, ME •
Stow, ME •
93
Conway
•
Rumney
•
Grafton   Laconia
•   •
89
Contoocook ☆ Concord   Dover
•   •
95
3 93

State Gemstone: Smoky Quartz (1985)
State Mineral: Beryl (1985)
State Stone/Rock: Granite (1985)

SECTION 1: Fee Dig Sites and Guide Services

CONWAY / *Native ▪ Moderate*

Collect Your Own Minerals *T*

The following gems or minerals may be found:

▪ Quartz, amethyst, smoky quartz, feldspar, topaz, phenakite, muscovite (mica), garnet, zircon, triplite, uranite, vivianite, gahnite, fluorapatite, bertrandite

White Mountain National Forest
Saco Ranger District
33 Kancamagus Highway
Conway, NH 03818
Phone: (603) 447-5448
TTY: (603) 447-3121
www.fs.fed.us/r9/forests/white_mountain

Open: All year, weather permitting.

Info: There are three collecting sites in the White Mountain National Forest that are managed by the Saco Ranger District: Deer Hill, Moat Mountain, and Lord Hill. Recreational rock collecting is allowed in the National Forest. General guidelines for collection are: bring bags to hold your specimens, or old newspaper to wrap the specimens. Other recommended items include safety glasses, gloves, geologist's hammer and cold chisel, a field guide to rocks and minerals, and in sunny weather, a hat, sunblock, and water.

Only small hand tools are permitted. The use of power, mechanized equipment, or explosives is prohibited.

Maximum excavation at any one site is limited to one cubic yard. Only one site may be disturbed at a time.

Excavated holes must not be dug deeper than three feet as measured from the bottom of the hole to a projected horizontal line drawn between the bases of trees or plants adjoining the hole. In areas where the entire site is already disturbed and the original ground level altered, an estimated projection will be made of the earth's surface for the purposes of monitoring or enforcement.

Prior to leaving the site, restore the disturbed area similar to the condition you found it in.

No collecting activities are allowed within developed recreation areas, immediately adjacent to roads, trails, other facilities, in streambanks, wetlands, shores, designated rock climbing areas, or cultural or historic features.

Digging under trees or severing roots greater than ½ inch in diameter is not permitted.

Surface disturbance that creates or contributes to a safety hazard is not allowed.

Rock and mineral collecting is not permitted on, in, or adjacent to existing safety hazards, such as overhanging ledges, deep tunnels, and unstable slopes.

A rock and mineral collecting use permit is being developed that will allow Forest Service managers to monitor collecting activities and associated impacts. The permit requirements are based on the Forest Plan standards and guidelines. There will be no charge for the permit, and the public will be notified when it is available.

Specific information on the sites:
Deer Hill Mineral Site: Permit required for any collector 18 or older (three permits available—daily: $3.00, available at the trailhead; 10–day: $10.00, available at Saco Ranger Station; 20–day: $20.00, available at Saco Ranger Station). Collect amethyst, smoky quartz, quartz, mica.

Moat Mountain Smoky Quartz Collecting Site: Information sheet available at Saco Ranger Station. This is a well-known collecting site for smoky quartz.

Lord Hill collection site: This is a long-closed feldspar open pit mine covered with small pieces of rock. Collect quartz, feldspar, topaz, phenakite, muscovite (mica), garnet, zircon, triplite, uranite, vivianite, gahnite, fluorapatite, and betrandite.

Gold panning is allowed in the National Forest mainly on the Pemigewasset and Ammonoosuc Ranger districts. There is a history of gold recovery in the Ammonoosuc River, Tunnel Brook, Little Ammonoosuc River, Baker River, Wild Ammonoosuc River, plus other drainages on the west side.

Rates: Fee charged for Deer Hill Mineral Site only.

Directions: Deer Hill Mineral Site is located in Stow, ME. Follow Route 113 to Deer Hill Road in N. Chatham, NH. Follow Deer Hill Road 2.2 miles to the Deer Hill Mineral Collecting Area trail-head and self-service pay station. Follow the yellow blazed hiking trail for 0.1 miles to a fork in the trail. Bear right for 0.4 miles to permit area 1, left for 0.4 miles to permit areas 2 and 3. Hobby mineral collecting is only allowed in these designated areas marked by a blue painted boundary.

Moat Mountain Smoky Quartz Collecting Site: From West Side Road in Conway, turn onto Passaconaway Road, travel 1.2 miles, and turn right on High Street (dirt). The road leads into the White Mountain National Forest, passing a gate at 1.4 miles. At 1.7 miles, bear left at the sign pointing to the mineral site and drive 0.7 miles to the parking area. Hike 0.9 miles to the Moat Mountain Smoky Quartz Collecting area.

Lord Hill is located in Stoneham, ME. Follow Deer Hill Road (FR 9) 4.7 miles from NH 113 to the Horseshoe Pond Trail, a small parking area at a curve in the road. From Deer Hill Road, the trail descends moderately past the Styles grave, which is on the right of the trail, then enters a gravel road and turns right onto it. The trail follows this road, keeping straight at a junction in 100 yds. At 0.3 miles, just before the gravel road ends, the trail turns right onto a grassy road. The trail is a gradual uphill climb to the intersection with the Conant Trail. Go left onto the Conant Trail and follow the trail for 0.3 miles to the Lord Hill summit. At the summit, go left for a great view of Horseshoe Pond. Take the Mine Trail to your right to the abandoned mine.

GRAFTON / *Native • Moderate to Difficult*

Collect up to 150 Different Minerals *T*

The following gems or minerals may be found:

• Mica, topaz, aquamarine, feldspar, beryl, chrysoberyl, amethyst and other quartz minerals, garnet, uranium minerals, tourmaline, columbite, molybdenite, pyrite, purpurite, zircon, and many others

(See complete list below)

Ruggles Mine
Geraldine Searles
Off Rt. 4 at the Village Green
Grafton, NH 03240
Phone: (603) 523-4275
www.rugglesmine.com

Open: Weekends, mid-May–June; daily, mid-June–mid-October, 9:00 A.M.– 5:00 P.M. Last ticket sold 1 hour before closing.

Info: Commercial production of mica

Some of the Minerals Found at Ruggles Mine

Albite	Dendrite	Pyrrhotite
Amethyst	Feldspar	Quartz (rose, smoky,
Amphibolite	Fluorapatite	white)
Apatite	Garnet	Reddingite
Aplite	Graftonite	Safflorite
Aquamarine	Gummite	Sillimanite
Autunite	Kasolite	Soddylite (pseudo-
Bertrandite	Lepidolite (lemon yel-	uranite, dense yellow)
Beryl (golden, blue,	low)	Staurolite
aqua)	Lepidomelane	Tobernite
Beta-uranophane	Lithiophilite	Topaz crystals
Biotite	Marcasite	Tourmaline (black)
Bornite	Manganapatite	Triphyllite
Calcite	Montmorillonite	Uranite (species with
Chrysoberyl	Molybdenite	gummite, world
Clarkite	Muscovite	famous)
Clevelandite	Parsonite	Uranium
Columbite	Phosphyanylite	Uranophane
Compotite	Psilomelane	Vandendriesscheite
Cryolite	Purpurite	Vivianite
Cymatolite	Pyrite	Voelerkenite
		Zircon crystals

Secret of Ruggles Mine

It all began in 1803, back in the days of the whale oil lamp, when Sam Ruggles not only discovered mica on his land but knew what to do about it. Mica was in keen demand, for use in lamp chimneys and stove windows.

A shrewd hard-working farmer, he set his large family to working it out, and hauled it to Portsmouth by ox team along with his farm products. There it was consigned and shipped to relatives in England to be sold. (Ruggles was too shrewd to sell to American buyers lest they learn the secret of his mine.) Soon, however, the demand for his fine product became so great that special trips to the port were necessary. These were made in the dead of night by horse and buggy, or sleigh, according to season. This continued for several years.

The mine is famous for its huge books of mica, measuring 3–4 feet across and weighing over 100 pounds. General Electric once worked this mine and others in the area for mica. The Bon Ami Company operated the mine from 1932 to 1959 for feldspar, mica, and beryl. Feldspar production during this period ran about 10,000 tons per year. During this time, one mass of beryl was found that filled three freight cars and paid for an entire year's operation.

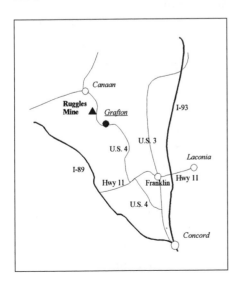

began in 1803 at the Ruggles Mine. It also is known for the production of beryl and feldspar. Located on the top of Isinglass Mountain, the mine now consists of open pits, giant rooms, and up to $1/3$ mile of tunnels with arched ceilings. Its uranium minerals, such as gummite and autunite are prized by collectors and museums all over the world. Bring a camera—a vast panorama of valleys, forest, and surrounding mountains can be seen from the top of the Isinglass Mountain. Unsurpassed fall foliage! Periodic blasting is done to reveal newly exposed minerals.

Admission: Adults $25.00/day, children (4–11) $13.00, children under 4 free with a paid adult.

Other services available: Snack bar, gift and mineral shop, restrooms.

Note: Knowledge of mineral identification is a plus at this mine.

Directions: See website or call for directions.

There are family/children educational activities at the following location:

Polar Caves Park
705 Rumney Route 25
Rumney, NH 03266
Phone: (603) 536-1888
www.polarcaves.com

Grab a lamp and bucket and go into a re-created mine to hunt for gems and minerals, or sift sand and gravel in a sluice with running water to find gems and minerals using a process often used by early pioneers.

SECTION 2: Museums and Mine Tours

CONTOOCOOK

Museum

The Little Nature Museum
Gould Hill Farm
656 Gould Hill Road
Contoocook, NH 03229
Phone: (603) 746-6121
E-mail: info@littlenaturemuseum.org
www.littlenaturemuseum.org

Open: End of June–end of October on weekends and holidays; call for hours. Other times by appointment.

Info: The museum's collection includes rocks, ores, minerals, and fluorescent minerals.

Admission: A donation of $2.00 is appreciated.

Directions: From I-89, go through Hopkinton Village, and take Route 103 toward Contoocook. After 1½ miles, turn right on Gould Hill Road, and follow the signs.

DOVER

Museum 🏛

The Woodman Institute
182 Central Avenue
Dover, NH 03820
Phone: (603) 742-1038
www.woodmaninstitutemuseum.com

Open: 12:30–4:30 P.M. Wednesday–Sunday (except holidays); closed December 1–March 31 and Memorial Day.

Info: The museum has over 1,500 specimens displayed in 1930s science lab cabinets, including local minerals and a large piece of the Nantan Meteorite, which fell in China in 1516.

Admission: Adults $6.00, students and seniors (65+) $5.00, children (6–15) $3.00, children 5 and under free.

Directions: Take I-95 to Spaulding Turnpike, then take exit 7 to Central Avenue.

SECTION 3: Special Events and Tourist Information

TOURIST INFORMATION

State Tourist Agency

New Hampshire Division of Travel & Tourism Development
P.O. Box 1856
1172 Pembroke Road
Concord, NH 03302-1856

Phone: (603) 271-2665
Fax: (603) 271-6870
www.visitnh.gov

NEW JERSEY

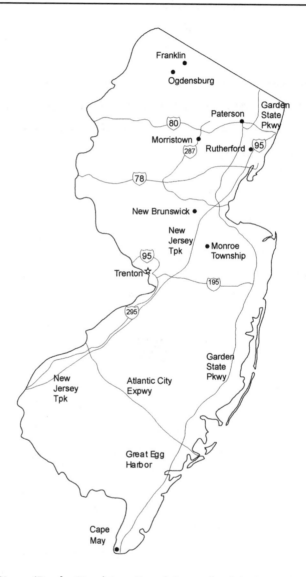

- Franklin
- Ogdensburg
- Paterson
- Garden State Pkwy
- 80
- Morristown
- 287
- Rutherford
- 95
- 78
- New Brunswick
- New Jersey Tpk
- Monroe Township
- 95
- Trenton ☆
- 195
- 295
- New Jersey Tpk
- Atlantic City Expwy
- Garden State Pkwy
- Great Egg Harbor
- Cape May

State Stone/Rock: Stockton Sandstone (legislation pending)

CAPE MAY / *Native*

Hunt for Cape May "Diamonds" on the Beach *T*

The following gems or minerals may be found:

- Cape May "diamonds"

Cape May Welcome Center
Transportation Center
609 Lafayette Street
Cape May, NJ 08204
Phone: (609) 884-9562

Open: All year, dawn–dusk.

Info: Cape May "diamonds" are pure quartz crystals. Their source is the upper reaches of the Delaware River. Some 200 miles upstream from Cape May, pockets and veins of quartz have been eroded. During the thousands of years it takes for these pieces of quartz to make their way down the Delaware to the bay, they are worn smooth. The stones eventually find their way to the mouth of the bay, where strong currents move them along the shores. Eventually some of them wash ashore. The larger stones come ashore mostly in the winter months, particularly during storms, when the currents and waves are stronger. They can be found in abundance on Sunset Beach in historic Cape May Point; currents encounter the concrete ship *Atlantus* here, and the resulting eddies wash the "diamonds" ashore. When polished or cut and faceted, they are said to have the appearance of diamonds. Many people mount them into jewelry items.

Admission: Free.

Other attractions: Dolphin watching, concrete ship *Atlantus*, evening flag ceremony, spectacular sunsets, walking distance to lighthouse and state park.

Cape May "Diamonds" *

The gems are found in limited areas on the beaches along Delaware Bay. They are said to have first been found by the Kechmeche Indians. The Indians attached mystical powers to the stones and believed that these stones possessed supernatural powers, influencing the well-being, success, and good fortunes of the possessor. They often sealed bonds of friendship and goodwill with the gift of these stones.

For other areas where quartz "diamonds" can be found, see entries under Lucerne, CA, and Herkimer, Middleville, and St. Johnsville, NY.

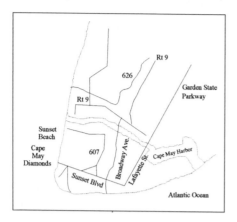

Directions: Sunset Beach in Cape May. Information and directions may be obtained by calling the Sunset Beach Gift Shops (800) 757-6468.

FRANKLIN / *Native • Easy*

Tailings Digging for Fluorescent Minerals

The following gems or minerals may be found:

• Fluorescent minerals, franklinite

Franklin Mineral Museum and
Buckwheat Dump
32 Evans Street
Franklin, NJ 07416
Phone: (973) 827-3481
www.franklinmineralmuseum.com

Open: April–November, 10:00 A.M.–4:00 P.M. Monday–Friday; 10:00 A.M.–5:00 P.M. Saturday; 11:00 A.M.– 5:00 P.M. Sunday. Open to all visitors on March weekends and weekdays for groups by appointment. Collecting is available daily during operating hours. Special night digs are held the first Saturday of June and November.

Info: The "Buckwheat Dump" is located in "the fluorescent mineral capital of the world!" Collect rocks and minerals characteristic of the area. Find specimens and fluorescent minerals unique to the area on the mine waste pile, which dates back to the 1870s. Facilities are available for testing specimens under ultraviolet light. Abundant specimens are available without the use of tools. A specimen exhibit in the testing facility and museum shows what to look for. Ultraviolet mineral lamps and other related items are for sale at the museum gift shop. See the listing in Section 2 for details on the Franklin Mineral Museum.

Admission: Combination museum and rock collecting: Adults $12.00, children (3–12) $8.00, seniors $9.00; includes collecting bag and 2 pounds per paid admission. Additional pounds $1.50/lb.

Directions: 32 Evans Street off Route 23. Follow blue signs from Route 23 to Evans Street (between Main Street and Buckwheat Road).

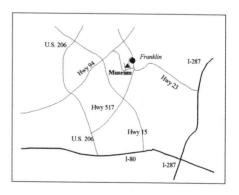

OGDENSBURG / *Native • Moderate*

Collect Your Own Fluorescent Minerals

The following gems or minerals may be found:

- Fluorescent minerals

Sterling Hill Mining Museum
30 Plant Street
Ogdensburg, NJ 07439
Phone: (973) 209-7212
www.sterlinghillminingmuseum.org

Open: Mine dump collection area is open any day the museum is open. See the museum listing under section 2. Collection is from 10:00 A.M. to 3:30 P.M. on mine dumps. The fill quarry and Passaic Pit areas are only open the last Sunday of the month.

Rates: $5.00 admission; $1.50 per pound collected. Not recommended for children under 8 years old.

Other services: See Ogdensburg entry in "Museums and Mine Tours" section.

SECTION 2: Museums and Mine Tours

FRANKLIN

Museum 🏛

Franklin Mineral Museum
32 Evans Street
Franklin, NJ 07416
Phone: (973) 827-3481
www.franklinmineralmuseum.com

Open: April–November, 10:00 A.M.– 4:00 P.M. Monday–Friday, 10:00 A.M.–5:00 P.M. Saturday, 11:00 A.M.– 5:00 P.M. Sunday. Closed Easter, Thanksgiving. Open to all visitors weekends in March, and weekdays for groups by appointment. Reservations are not required for visitors other than groups. Guided tours are offered hourly. Times adjusted during April through June and then again in September through November due to morning groups. Visitors are welcome to go through the museum exhibits on their own.

Info: The museum features minerals, rocks, geology, and replicas of mine workings. The specimens come from local and worldwide sources. The museum features a 33-foot-long fluorescent room, where various ores and minerals from the Franklin area are displayed under long-wave and short-wave ultraviolet light. Other displays feature specimens unique to the area and include gemstones and colorful crystals. The museum displays over 4,000 local specimens, some exclusive to the area, and over 5,000 worldwide minerals. The Jensen wing contains the Welsh natural history collection. The mine replica is two levels containing mining artifacts. Items are featured throughout the museum regarding the mining history and mineralogy of the local area. The displays are impressive as well as educational.

The Franklin area was the site of iron

and zinc mining from 1854 to 1954. Fluorescent minerals from the Franklin area are said to be the world's most brilliant, and specimens from this area are in museum collections all over the world. Franklin has been named "the fluorescent mineral capital of the world" by the state's legislature. The Franklin area has produced a tenth of all known species of minerals. (Species are still being identified today.) All displayed specimens are identified.

Admission: Museum only: Adults $7.00, seniors $6.00, children (3–12) $5.00.

Directions: 32 Evans Street off Route 23. Follow blue signs from Route 23 to Evans Street (between Main Street and Buckwheat Road).

MONROE TOWNSHIP

Museum

Displayworld's Stone Museum
Displayworld, Inc.
608 Spotswood-Englishtown Road
(Route 613)
Monroe Township, NJ 08831
Phone: (732) 521-2232
Fax: (732) 521-3388
www.displayworld.com
(click on The Stone Museum)

Open: April 1–December 23, 7 days/week. 8:00 A.M.–5:00 P.M. Monday–Saturday, 10:00 A.M.–5:00 P.M. Sunday. Closed Memorial Day, July 4, Labor Day.

Info: Museum of minerals (and fossils) with a host of indoor and outdoor displays that are "hands-on" so that visitors can actually touch specimens from 80 countries. Recent additions include an exhibit of fluorescent minerals from central New Jersey. Wander through the grounds and enjoy the lake and six stone waterfalls.

The museum is also a showcase of practical masonry. This 5-acre outdoor showroom has hundreds of full-size samples of every type of stone and stone product. Material on display is available for purchase.

The rock and gift shop contains a wide variety of polished gemstones, jewelry, fossils, collectibles, and carved products.

Admission: Free.

Directions: Garden State Parkway from the north: Take second exit south of Raritan toll plaza (exit 123—Route 9S); follow Route 9 south until you pass under Route 18 overpass, then take first right onto Texas Road (Route 520 West). Follow Route 520 to end, then turn left onto Route 613S; follow 2 miles to Displayworld on right.

From Turnpike exit 8A: Take Route 32 east to Jamesburg (Forsgate Drive), go about 2 miles to end, then right on Route 522E for 2 miles. Pass water tower on left, then drive 2 miles and

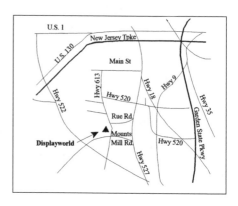

turn left onto Route 613N. Follow Route 613N 2 miles to Displayworld.

From Turnpike exit 9: Take Route 18S, go about 9 miles to Route 9S. Take first right off Route 9 onto Texas Road (Route 520W), to end. Follow Route 520 to end, then turn left onto Route 613S; follow 2 miles to Displayworld on right.

MORRISTOWN

Museum

The Morris Museum
6 Normandy Heights Road
Morristown, NJ 07960
Phone: (973) 971-3700
www.morrismuseum.org

Open: All year, 11:00 A.M.–5:00 P.M. Wednesday–Saturday (open until 8:00 P.M. Thursday), 1:00–5:00 P.M. Sunday.
Info: The Rock and Mineral Gallery features specimens from five continents, and includes a calcite specimen weighing 258 pounds, and a giant amethyst. Exhibits explore the five geographic areas of the U.S., with emphasis on New Jersey. Another traces the path of a gem from raw material to precious stone. There is also a fluorescent mineral display.
Admission: Adults $10.00, children (3+) and seniors $7.00. Children under 3 free. Admission is free to general public every Thursday between the hours of 5:00 P.M. and 8:00 P.M.
Directions: At 6 Normandy Heights Road, at the intersection with Columbia Turnpike in Morristown, NJ.

NEW BRUNSWICK

Museum

Rutgers Geology Museum
Geology Building
College Avenue Campus
New Brunswick, NJ 08901
Phone: (848) 932-7243
http://www.geologymuseum.rutgers.edu

Open: 9:00 A.M.–6:00 P.M. Monday–Thursday, 9:00 A.M.–4:00 P.M. Friday, 10:00 A.M.–4:00 P.M. Saturday. Closed during the month of August.
Info: The Rutgers University Geology Museum features collections that date from 1836 and include a variety of minerals and geologic specimens and emphasize the geology of New Jersey and surrounding states.
Admission: Free.
Other services available: Gift shop, pre-arranged tours available for groups of 10 to 50 people, and special late-night and weekend events offered throughout the year. Check website for more information.
Directions: From the NJ Turnpike, take exit 9 and follow signs for Route 18 North—New Brunswick. Follow Route 18 for about 3 miles. Take the Route 27 South—Princeton exit onto Albany Street. At the third traffic light, turn right onto George Street. Proceed one block on George, pass through the railroad underpass, and proceed through the large iron gates on the corner of George and Somerset Streets. Parking is available in Lot 1.

If traveling from the south, take the Parkway north to exit 105 and follow

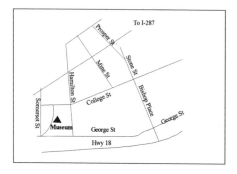

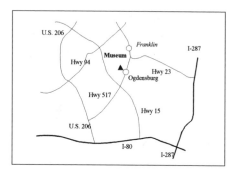

the signs to Route 18—North, and follow as above.

If traveling from Route 287, take exit 9, Highland Park River Road. At the fifth light, in about 3 miles, at Metlars Lane, turn right and cross the Raritan River to New Brunswick on Route 18. Take the first exit, George Street. Proceed on George Street to the point where you pass under the railroad underpass, and follow as above.

OGDENSBURG

Museum/Mining Tour

Sterling Hill Mining Museum
30 Plant Street
Ogdensburg, NJ 07439
Phone: (973) 209-7212
www.sterlinghillminingmuseum.org

Open: 7 days/week, April 1–November 30; weekends, January–February, weather permitting; 7 days/week in December and March, weather permitting. Call ahead to inquire. Closed Easter, Thanksgiving, Christmas, and New Year's Day.

Info: Tour ¼ mile of mine tunnels in the last underground mine to operate in New Jersey. Mine passages contain equipment used in the mine, and the tour includes rooms used by the miners and the Rainbow Room, a chamber lit with UV light to cause the ores to fluoresce. There are both indoor and outdoor exhibits of minerals and artifacts. The Thomas S. Warren Museum of Fluorescence includes four rooms devoted to displays of fluorescent minerals, gemstones, and carvings. The museum includes more than two dozen exhibits, nearly all of which explore a theme of fluorescence. The Rock Discovery Center is a large outdoor area where visitors learn about the various rock types that are quarried in the northeastern United States. Each visitor collects six specimens to take home. For each rock type, instruction is provided in how to recognize it, where it is obtained, and how it is used in society today. Participants are given a partitioned cardboard box in which to place their samples. The rocks are already broken to sizes that fit in the boxes provided, so no tools are necessary.

Admission: Tours: Adults $10.00, seniors $9.00, children under 12 $7.50. The Rock Discovery Center is an add-on option to the mine tour and is open to all visitors, provided a minimum of 10 people elect to participate. This option costs $3.50 per person.

Other services available: Picnic area, snack bar, modern restrooms.

Directions: From Route 23 in Franklin, take Route 517 south to Ogdensburg. Turn right on Passaic Avenue and drive to the mine. From Route 15 in Sparta, take Route 517 north to Ogdensburg, then turn left onto Passaic Avenue, and drive to the mine.

Note: See information under Section one for fee dig at this site.

PATERSON

Museum

The Paterson Museum
Thomas Rogers Building
2 Market Street
Paterson, NJ 07501
Phone: (973) 321-1260

Open: 10:00 A.M.– 4:00 P.M. Tuesday–Friday, 12:30 – 4:30 P.M. Saturday–Sunday, closed Mondays and holidays.

Info: There are two major mineralized basalt flows in the world: one in the Deccan plateau of India, and one in Paterson. The minerals found in both locations have much in common, but there are also significant differences. Many of the best and rarest Paterson specimens ever found are exhibited in the museum, along with many fine examples from the Poona region of India.

The museum's mineral collection is one of the finest exhibited collections in the state of New Jersey, with mineral specimens from the state and from around the world.

Admission: Suggested donation: Adults $2.00, children 18 and under free.

Directions: The museum is located in the Thomas Rogers Locomotive Erecting Building, the focal point of the Great Falls Historic District, in close proximity to the Great Falls of the Passaic River. Paterson is on I-80 in northern New Jersey. Call for directions.

RUTHERFORD

Museum

Meadowlands Museum
91 Crane Avenue
P.O. Box 3
Rutherford, NJ 07070
Phone: (201) 935-1175
Fax: (201) 935-9791
www.meadowlandsmuseum.com

Open: All year, 1:00 P.M.–4:00 P.M. Monday, Wednesday, and Saturday, 2:00 P.M.–4:00 P.M. Sunday. Call ahead to verify hours.

Info: Museum features changing displays of the rocks and minerals of northern New Jersey, and a collection of fluorescent minerals, about half of which are from the Franklin Mine in New Jersey. The museum also has a display showing the many types of quartz. Another display shows the three types of rock (igneous, sedimentary, and metamorphic), while still another display presents minerals from the Paterson area. The museum also displays about

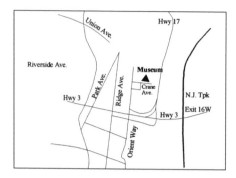

TRENTON

Museum

New Jersey State Museum
Natural History Office, P.O. Box 530
205 West State Street
Trenton, NJ 08625
Phone: (609) 292-6464
www.newjerseystatemuseum.org

20 rocks/minerals from Snake Hill (Laurel Hill) in Secaucus, New Jersey.

Admission: Donations appreciated.

Directions: South on Route 17: turn right at Service Road/Local Streets sign, then turn right at Crane Avenue.

North on Route 17: Make jug-handle turn at Highland Cross, then follow directions above.

East on Route 3: Take Ridge Road exit, then turn left on Orient Way at second traffic light. Drive 2 blocks into Rutherford, and turn right on Crane Avenue.

West on Route 3: Take Ridge Road exit, then turn left at the stop sign. Turn left at the traffic light onto Rutherford Avenue, then turn left at the next light onto Orient Way. Go 3 blocks to Crane Avenue, and turn right.

Open: 9:00 A.M.–4:45 P.M. Tuesday–Saturday, noon–5:00 P.M. Sunday. Closed on state holidays.

Info: The museum's geological collection contains minerals, rocks, sediments, and geological structures. The best mineral specimens are trap rock minerals and fluorescent Franklin/Sterling Hill samples. There is an extensive historic collection of magnetite ore samples from the old iron mines of New Jersey, many of which are closed or no longer exist.

Admission: Free. Parking is free.

Directions: The museum is located in two buildings on West State Street, which is reached by way of the Calhoun Street exit off Route 29.

SECTION 3: Special Events and Tourist Information

TOURIST INFORMATION

State Tourist Agency

New Jersey Division of Travel and Tourism

P.O. Box 460
20 West State Street
Trenton, NJ 08625
Phone: (800) VISITNJ
www.visitnj.org

NEW YORK

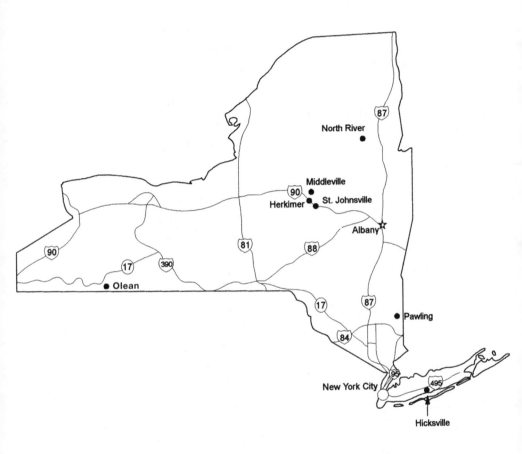

North River ●

⑧⑦

Middleville
⑨⓪ ●
St. Johnsville
Herkimer ● ●

Albany ☆

⑧① ⑧⑧

⑨⓪

⑰ ③⑨⓪

● Olean

⑰ ⑧⑦

● Pawling

⑧④

⑨⑤

New York City ⑷⑼⑸
●
Hicksville

State Gemstone: Garnet (1969)

HERKIMER / *Native • Easy to Difficult*

Dig for Herkimer "Diamonds" *T*

The following gems or minerals may be found:

• **"Herkimer diamonds" quartz crystals**

Mailing address:
Herkimer Diamond Mines and KOA
Kampground Corporate Office
800 Mohawk Street
Herkimer, NY 13350
Phone: (315) 717-0175

Physical address:
4601 State Route 28 North
Herkimer, NY 13350
www.herkimerdiamond.com

Open: April 15–October 31, weather permitting, 9:00 A.M.–5:00 P.M., 7 days/week.
Info: "Herkimer diamonds" are quartz crystals found in specific locations in New York.

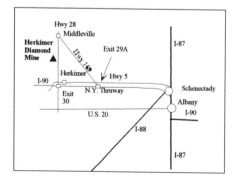

Upon admission you will be given a hammer. However, it's suggested that you come prepared with safety eye wear, gloves, and closed-toe shoes. For the aggressive digger, you may want chisels, screeners, small shovels, buckets, and other hammers (up to a 12-lb sledge). Dress for the weather and bring sunscreen if necessary. Follow all safety precautions. And don't forget to look for those loose "diamonds" on the ground!
Admission: Ages 13 and up, $10.00/person; ages 5–12 $8.00/person; 4 and under free.

Other services available: Picnic area, playground, mineral museum containing thousands of specimens, gift and mineral shop.

KOA Kampground has cabins, cottages, tent sites, and RV sites with water, sewer, and electrical hookups. Its New Solar Kolony is the world's first campground with 100% off-the-power-grid, solar-powered camping lodges packed with "green" technologies and products. Modern restrooms and showers, ice and firewood, fishing, tubing, swimming, miniature golf, playgrounds, and restaurant are available. Call for rates.
Directions: From the NYS Thruway, use exit 30 and take State Highway 28 north. Herkimer Diamond Mines is 7 miles north of Herkimer.

MIDDLEVILLE / *Native • Easy to Difficult*

Prospect for Herkimer "Diamonds"

The following gems or minerals may be found:

• Herkimer "diamonds," calcite crystals, dolomite crystals

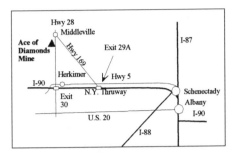

Ace of Diamonds Mine and Campground
P.O. Box 505
Middleville, NY 13406
Phone: (315) 891-3855
www.herkimerdiamonds.com

Open: April 1–October 31, 9:00 A.M.–5:00 P.M., 7 days/week.

Info: Bring your own tools or rent tools at the mine. Suggested tools include a small shovel, a pick, a garden rake or a trowel, a 2½-pound hammer, and a bucket. You may want to bring gloves or kneeling pad, and a screenbox.

To stake a claim, place a blue tarp or tools in your area, not to exceed 10 feet. You may pay in advance to keep your claim from day to day.

The mine's conservation rule is as follows: One pocket only per person or group. After cleaning out the pocket, the digger or group must leave the mine for 2 weeks, or a $75.00 trophy fee may be paid by the successful prospector or group in order to continue mining for a second pocket. If a second pocket is obtained, then the person or group must leave the mine for 2 weeks. The following activities are not allowed at any time:

Herkimer "Diamonds"

Herkimer "diamonds" are very brilliant, clear, quartz crystals, which are double-terminated (points on both ends) and six-sided. They appear to be faceted by nature, and many are used in jewelry. Rare ones are found with liquid bubble inclusions. They range in size from microscopic to several inches. They are found in a rock formation known as dolomite. The crystals are found mostly in pockets in the rock; many others, however, are found in the surrounding soil.

Also see listings under Lakeport, CA, for moon tears, or Lake County "diamonds," and Cape May, NJ, for Cape May "diamonds."

---

using sledgehammers over 12 pounds, using hydraulic jacks in the mining areas, rolling boulders down the slopes, and breaking rocks in the camping areas.

Admission: Adults $9.50, children (4–7) $4.50. Groups: Schoolchildren with adult supervision $7.00/student, college and adult groups $8.00/person. To rent long-handled tools at the mine, $1.00 each; sledgehammer, $4.00 each. Deposit or driver's license is required for tool rental. New tools are offered for sale.

Other services available: Picnic area, snack shop, rock shop, restrooms, camping right where you dig. Within walking distance: luncheonette, grocery store, post office, trout fishing.

Note: All collecting is done at your own risk. The mine is not responsible for injury or loss of personal property.

Campground: $15.00/night for each vehicle and two people, each additional person $1.00/night, $3.00/night for electrical hookup, free water hookup, bathrooms with coin-operated showers.

Directions: From the NY Thruway, use exit 30, and take State Highway 28 north. Ace of Diamonds Mines is 9 miles north of Herkimer.

NORTH RIVER / *Native • Moderate*

Collect Garnets in a Historic New York Garnet Mine

The following gems or minerals may be found:

- **Garnets**

The Barton Mines
P.O. Box 30
North River, NY 12856

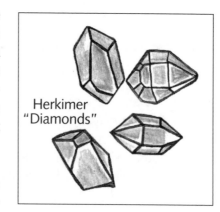

Herkimer "diamonds" can be found simply by walking around the prospecting area or using a screenbox to sift dirt in the prospecting area. The most popular method is breaking them out of the rock. A few rules must be followed:

Herkimer "Diamonds"

- Wear eye protection.
- Never break rocks close to someone else. Look in all directions before hammering.
- Keep a close eye on children. Never allow them on top of any high wall or cliff.

A 23-ton block of matrix rock from the Barton Garnet Mine has been cut and polished, and transported to Ground Zero at the World Trade Center in New York City. It will be the cornerstone of the new World Trade Center, and, until then, is on display.

Phone: (518) 251-2706
www.garnetminetours.com

Open: July–Labor Day, 9:30 A.M.–5:00 P.M. Monday–Saturday, 11:00 A.M.–5:00 P.M. Sunday. Labor Day–Columbus Day open on weekends only. Groups may arrange tours during the week.

Info: The Barton Mines on Gore Mountain has the hardest garnets on the planet. This garnet is the official New York State stone and gemstone. The admission fee includes a lecture on the history and geology while in the actual mine site, followed by a demonstration on how to easily find your own garnets. Hammers are not allowed in the mine due to the Barton Mines safety policy. Since the garnet is all over the ground, tools are not necessary.

Admission: Adults $11.75, children (7–14) $7.75, seniors (60+) $10.75

Other services available: Mineral shop, picnic tables.

Directions: From Interstate 87, take Exit 23 to Route 9. Follow Route 9 to Route 28, and take Route 28 for approximately 21 miles to North River. Turn left onto Barton Mines Road and drive approximately 5 miles to the Gore Mountain Mineral Shop, where the tours begin.

ST. JOHNSVILLE / *Native • Easy to Difficult*

Dig for Herkimer "Diamonds" 𝑇

The following gems or minerals may be found:

• Herkimer "diamonds"

Crystal Grove Diamond Mine and Campground
161 County Highway 114
St. Johnsville, NY 13452
Phone: (518) 568-2914;
(800) KRY-DIAM or (800) 579-3426
E-mail: fun@crystalgrove.com
www.crystalgrove.com

Open: 7 days/week, April 15–October 15, 9:00 A.M.–dusk; Memorial Day–Labor Day, 8:00 A.M.–8:00 P.M.

Info: Use a shovel, hammer and chisel, or small garden tool. If you would rather not break rocks, sifting the dirt through a screenbox will also reveal these gems. Bring your own tools, or some rental tools are available. Suggested tools include various-sized chisels, a 3-pound hammer, a pry bar, eye protection, and gloves. For the very aggressive digger, a sledgehammer may be useful.

Admission: Adults $10.00/day, children under 14 $8.00/day. Group rates available.

Other services available: Picnic area, playground, rock shop with mineral and rock specimens from all over the world. A wooded campground, located at the foothills of the beautiful Adirondacks, is adjacent to the mine. It has water and electrical sites, tent sites, dump station, modern restrooms and showers, ice and firewood, playground, horseshoe pit, volleyball, basketball, ping-pong. There are many nearby attractions. Rates: $25.00 to $32.00 per day (four people), extra charge for additional persons. Camping cabins for 4–6 people are also available. **Directions:** From the NY Thruway, use

exit 29 or exit 29A and go to St. Johnsville. Turn at traffic light (Division Street) and travel north ½ mile to a fork in the road. Take the right fork for 4 miles to the campsite. From the north, get on Route 29 to County Road 114. Take 114 south to the mine.

SECTION 2: Museums and Mine Tours

ALBANY

Museum 🏛

New York State Museum
Room 3023
Cultural Education Center
Albany, NY 12230
Phone: (518) 474-5877
www.nysm.nysed.gov

Open: All year, Monday–Saturday, 9:30 A.M.–5:00 P.M. Closed Sundays and Thanksgiving, Christmas, and New Year's Day.
Info: Exhibits include "Minerals of New York" and "Ancient Life of New York—a Billion Years of Earth History." The minerals in the "Minerals from New York" exhibit will be rotated periodically.

Admission: Free. Donations accepted at the door.
Directions: The museum is located in the Cultural Education Center of the Empire State Plaza in Albany, on Madison Avenue across the Plaza from the State Capitol Building. Parking is available at two lots adjacent to the museum; parking there is free after 3:00 P.M. and on weekends. GPS Address: 260 Madison Avenue.

HICKSVILLE

Museum 🏛

The Hicksville Gregory Museum
Long Island Earth Science Center
1 Heitz Place
Hicksville, NY 11801-3101

Phone: (516) 822-7505
Fax: (516) 822-3227
E-mail: mail@gregorymuseum.org
www.gregorymuseum.org

Open: All year, 9:30 A.M.–4:30 P.M. Tuesday–Friday; 1:00–5:00 P.M. Saturday and Sunday; closed Mondays and major holidays. Groups by appointment.

Info: The mineral collection has approximately 10,000 specimens. Only a small number are on display at any one time. The permanent display features a sampling that serves as an introduction to the major mineral groups. It includes many economically important minerals. Also on display are New Jersey zeolites, Herkimer "diamonds," and fluorescent minerals.

Admission: Adults $5.00, children (6–16) and seniors (65+) $3.00.

Special programs offered include school programs, teacher training, science and craft workshops, and merit badge programs for Girl Scouts and Boy Scouts.

Directions: Located at the Heitz Place Courthouse.

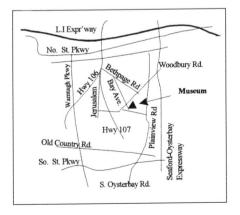

NEW YORK CITY

Museum

American Museum of Natural History
Central Park West at 79th Street
New York, NY 10024-5192
Phone: (212) 769-5100
www.amnh.org

Open: All year, 10:00 A.M.–5:45 P.M. daily, closed Thanksgiving and Christmas. Groups by appointment.

Info: The natural history of our planet and its species is revealed in more than 46 exhibit halls. The Morgan Memorial Hall of Gems features the Star of India, the world's largest and most famous blue star sapphire. Among other permanent halls is the Arthur Ross Hall of Meteorites, which features the 4½-billion-year-old Ahnighito, the largest meteorite ever retrieved from the earth's surface.

Admission (suggested): Adults $16.00, students and seniors $12.00, children (2–12) $9.00.

Other services available: Museum shops, restaurants, discovery room for children, theatre, and planetarium.

OLEAN

Rock Display and Museum

Rock City Park
505 Route 16 South
Olean, NY 14760
Phone: (716) 372-7790 or (866) 404-ROCK (866-404-7625)
www.rockcitypark.com

Open: May–October, 9:00 A.M.–6:00 P.M. Last trail tickets sold at 5:00 P.M.

Info: This former prehistoric ocean floor is the world's largest exposure of quartz conglomerate (also called ocean spar or puddingstone), and has gigantic boulders several stories high with huge crevices between them. The park has a three-quarter-mile natural trail that requires comfortable clothing and good walking shoes. There is also a museum with a virtual video room and a fluorescent mineral room.

Admission: Adults $4.50, seniors (62+) $3.75, children (6–12) $2.50, children 5 and under free. Group discount and annual passes are available.

Other services available: Museum shop, rock shop, picnic area, free parking.

Directions: Located on NY Route 16, 5½ miles south of Olean, NY.

PAWLING

Museum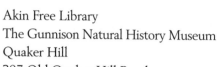

Akin Free Library
The Gunnison Natural History Museum
Quaker Hill
397 Old Quaker Hill Road
P.O. Box 345
Pawling, NY 12564
Phone: (914) 855-5099

Open: Call for days and times.

Info: This natural history museum was presented to the community by Olive Mason Gunnison, whose collection covers all phases of natural history. The mineral sections are outstanding, and complete information on each specimen is provided.

Admission: Adults $2.00, children $1.00.

Other services available: Historical museum, Akin Free Library.

Directions: Pawling is located on State Highway 22, 13 miles north of I-84, near the NY–CT border. The library can be reached by taking Quaker Hill Road 3 miles east from Pawling.

SECTION 3: Special Events and Tourist Information

TOURIST INFORMATION

State Tourist Agency

New York Division of Tourism
Phone: (800) CALL NYS
www.iloveny.com

OHIO

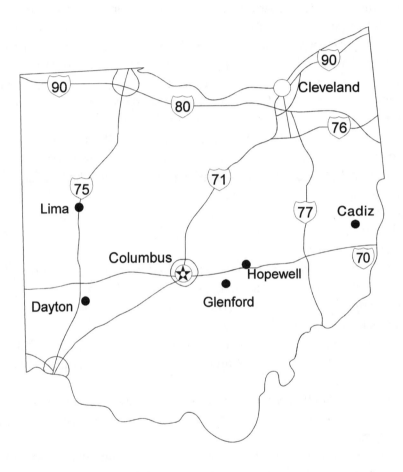

State Gemstone: Flint (1965)

Ohio Flint

Centuries ago, Native Americans from throughout the Midwest forged trails to a range of hills, about 10 miles long, located between the present cities of Newark and Zanesville, Ohio. They came to these hills to obtain flint, and the area came to be known as Flint Ridge. They used the flint to make implements to kill and skin game and to make weapons. The flint in this area occurs in shades of pink, gray, white, yellow, orange, black, and multicolored.

Quarrying for flint was hard work. The flint on the surface exposed to the elements cracked easily; below the surface, a layer of material between 1 and 10 feet deep was of high quality. Large hammerstones weighing up to 25 pounds were used to drive wedges into natural cracks in the flint layer to break large pieces off. Smaller stones were then used to break workable pieces of flint, which were finished as tools or weapons.

Extensive trading networks established by the Hopewell people spread items from Flint Ridge across the eastern half of the country in exchange for such things as copper from the upper Great Lakes and shells from the Gulf of Mexico.

White settlers in the area used the lower grade of weathered flint for making buhrstones for water-powered mills. Smaller pieces were used for hand grinding.

Today, Ohio flint, which is a form of chalcedony, is used by jewelry makers, who polish it and make it into items such as pendants and belt buckles.

For information on other Native American stone quarries, see listings in Newark, DE: jasper quarries (Vol. 4); Calumet and Copper Harbor, MI: copper (Vol. 4); Pipestone, MN: pipestone quarries (Vol.1); and Fritch, TX: flint quarries (Vol. 2).

HOPEWELL / *Native • Easy to Difficult*

Dig for Flint $\mathcal{T}$

The following gems or minerals may be found:

- Ohio flint

Hidden Springs Ranch
Gene Wyrick
9305 Hidden Springs Road
Hopewell, OH 43746
Phone: (740) 787-2060
E-mail: gwgenie@windstream.net

Open: By appointment in advance; limited to groups. 8:00 A.M.–8:00 P.M., 7 days/week.

Info: Dig for Ohio flint in a prehistoric Indian flint quarry. Flint occurs in a hard rock environment, so bring appropriate equipment, including safety goggles and gloves. Bring your own 5-gallon bucket! The ranch can accommodate a maximum of 35 people in a group.

Admission: $6.00/person and $6.00 per 5-gallon bucket of flint removed, $60.00

nonrefundable deposit required.

Other services available: Hay rides; outdoor barbecues; stocked fishing lake; outhouses; square dancing; wood for campfires; horseback trail ride; cross-country skiing; campground (primitive campsites for use by tents or campers, $5.00/night) with reservation.

Directions: Send a stamped self-addressed envelope for specific directions to the ranch.

HOPEWELL / *Native • Easy to Difficult*

Dig for Flint $\mathcal{T}$

The following gems or minerals may be found:

- Ohio flint

Nethers Flint
John Nethers
3680 Flint Ridge Road
Hopewell, OH 43746
Phone: (740) 787-2263

Open: All year, weather permitting, daylight hours.

Info: Dig or find your own flint in a wooded ancient quarry area across from the farmhouse. Remember, flint is very sharp. See the safety notes below.

Admission: $5.00/person. All flint taken is $0.50/pound. Bring your own tools and protective equipment.

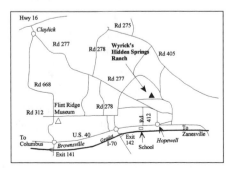

How to Dig for Flint

Today, one can obtain flint in much the same way those Native Americans did centuries ago. The only difference is that today you can use implements made of steel instead of stone.

Because most of the flint is several feet underground, the overlying soil must be removed to expose the flint. There is flint on the surface in some areas, but it is weathered and cracks easily. The normal method used to expose the flint is to dig a pit. (From the numerous ancient pits observable at the various sites, it is obvious that this is what the Native Americans did.) This exposed flint can then be chipped away.

Quarrying for flint is still hard work unless you go the easy route that the authors used and pick through pieces lying in the pits from previous quarrying. The authors collected 65 pounds of flint in varying colors of pink, orange, red, yellow, white, black, and gray. Many pieces contained quartz crystals; even some individual quartz crystals were found. They plan to make cabochons from some of the nice pieces!

Caution: There is a reason why flint was used by Native Americans to make weapons—it can be very sharp. Appropriate caution should be taken, especially if children are involved in the collection. Safety glasses or goggles, gloves, and hard-sided/hard-soled boots should be worn. Care should be taken when working in the "pits" to ensure that the earthen walls do not collapse. *Note:* The authors' daughter, Annie, 9 years old at the time, collected flint, did a little quarrying, and even tried to make an arrowhead, without a scratch.

Note: The Nethers allow flint collecting on their farm, but the collecting is at your own risk. No liability is assumed by the owners.

Directions: Going on I-70 to Brownsville-Gratiot, take Exit 141. Turn left on SR 668 to Route 40. Turn right on Route 40 to Hopewell School. Just past the school, turn left on County Line Road and travel about 3 miles to Mt. Olive Road, on the left, and Flint Ridge Road (ahead to left). Turn onto Flint Ridge Road and travel 1.2 miles; stop at the white two-story house on the right to pay. The collecting area is on the left. If coming from Zanesville on I-70, take exit 152 to Route 40; turn right on Route 40 West and travel approximately 9 miles to Hopewell School; turn right on County Line Road and follow the directions above.

CADIZ

Museum 🏛

History of Coal Museum
Puskarich Public Library
200 East Market Street
Cadiz, OH 43907
Phone: (740) 942-2623
www.harrison.lib.oh.us

Open: 9:00 A.M.–8:00 P.M. Monday–Thursday, 9:00 A.M.–5:00 P.M. Friday–Saturday.

Info: The museum offers a comprehensive look at both early-day and modern mining in Southeastern Ohio. A guided tour provides views of exhibits detailing the formation of coal, early mining tools, items from the company store, heavy machinery, a working scale model of a dragline, and a wealth of historic photographs.

Admission: Free.

Directions: On Route U.S. 250 in Cadiz.

CLEVELAND

Museum 🏛

The Cleveland Museum of Natural History
Wade Gallery of Gems and Jewels
1 Wade Oval Drive, University Circle
Cleveland, OH 44106-1767

Phone: (216) 231-4600; (800) 317-9155
Fax: (216) 231-5919
E-mail: info@cmnh.org
www.cmnh.org

Open: 10:00 A.M.–5:00 P.M. Monday–Saturday, 10:00 A.M.–10:00 P.M. Wednesday, noon–5:00 P.M. Sunday. Closed major holidays.

Info: The Wade Gallery of Gems and Jewels opened in 1998, showcasing more than 1,500 cut gemstones next to their natural crystals, historic and modern jewelry, and other treasures, including a moon rock. The collection is considered to be one of the top five institutionally owned collections in the United States. Most of the gems currently on display were donated in 1924 by Jeptha Homer Wade II, grandson of the founder of Western Union.

Wade Gallery displays more than 100

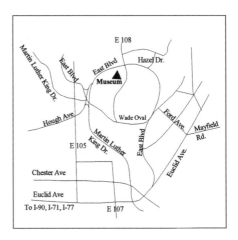

varieties of gemstones, with traditional rubies, sapphires, emeralds, pearls, opals, and jade, as well as rare demantoid, cat's eye chrysoberyl, and colored diamonds. The colored diamonds range from deep, clear green to pale orchid, pink, orange, brown, and blue. The collection also contains one of the largest groups of opals in the country, including black opal from Australia, fire opal from Mexico, and vibrant colored opals from Nevada's Virgin Valley. Also on view are a striking peridot necklace, a strand of jade beads, a Tiffany topaz and diamond necklace (ca. 1905), and some of the spectacular Davidson lapidary collection of polished stone eggs and cabochons.

Reinberger Hall of Earth & Planetary Exploration displays large crystals including meter-long selenite crystals from Cave of Swords, Mexico, and over 60 economically valuable minerals such as native gold, rutile, sphalerite, wulfenite, and a 70-lb. sheet of native copper from the White Pine Mine, Michigan. In the Planetarium Gallery there are over 3 dozen rare meteorites and tektites on display, as well as a video documenting the fall of the Peekskill meteorite.

Admission: Adults $10.00; youth (7–18), seniors (60+), and students $8.00; children (3–6) $7.00, children 2 and under free.

Other services available: Museum store, museum's Blue Planet Café.

Directions: Take Martin Luther King Blvd. south from I-90 for 2.5 miles.

COLUMBUS

Museum

Orton Geological Museum
Ohio State University
155 South Oval
Columbus, OH 43210
Phone: (614) 292-6896
www.geology.ohio-state.edu/facilities.php

Open: 9:00 A.M.–5:00 P.M. Monday–Friday. Weekend and evening hours by special request.

Info: The museum features geology of Ohio, showing rocks and minerals from the state. Also includes specimens from all over the world. Other exhibits include meteorites (including one that fell in Ohio), minerals, crystals, and fluorescent minerals.

Exhibits illustrate the fundamental concepts about minerals and their physical properties. From the clay tiles in the entrance hall to its wall and foundations, Orton Hall is built of 40 different Ohio building stones.

Admission: Free.

Other services: Free identification of rocks and minerals, museum store.

Directions: Located in Orton Hall on the campus of Ohio State University in Columbus.

DAYTON

Museum

Boonshoft Museum of Discovery
2600 DeWeese Parkway
Dayton, OH 45414
Phone: (937) 275-7431
Fax: (937) 275-5811
www.boonshoftmuseum.org

Open: 9:00 A.M.–5:00 P.M. Monday–Saturday, 12:00–5:00 P.M. Sunday.

Info: Many crystals and minerals are on display in the Bieser Discovery Center, a hands-on area of the museum.

Admission: Adults $8.50, seniors and children (2–12) $7.50, under 2 free.

Other services available: Zoo, children's play area, space theatre.

Directions: From I-75, take exit 57B (Wagner Ford–Siebenthaler exit). Go west on Wagner Ford Road to North Dixie Drive to Siebenthaler Avenue to Ridge Avenue to DeWeese Parkway. Watch for signs.

GLENFORD

Museum

Flint Ridge State Memorial
15300 Flint Ridge Road
Glenford, OH 43739
Phone: (740) 787-2476; (800) 283-8707
www.ohweb.ohiohistory.org

Open: Park open all year during daylight hours. Museum hours: May–October, 10:00 A.M.–5:00 P.M. Sunday.

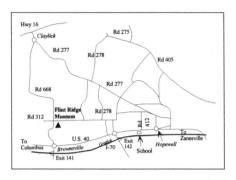

Info: In 1933, the Ohio Historical Society established the Flint Ridge State Memorial. In 1968, a museum was constructed over one of the original quarry pits (see discussion on Ohio flint at the beginning of this chapter). Exhibits present the geology and history of the site, and the location of other flint deposits in Ohio. In the ancient mining pit, a life-sized mannequin shows how flint was quarried. A short video shows how to knap flint into an arrowhead.

The museum displays a variety of objects made of flint. The shop features flint as a gemstone with hand-crafted jewelry. Also sold are books and gifts related to prehistoric Ohio.

A nature preserve with walking trails is located at the site with a new one opened in 2011. An asphalt road leads from the parking lot to the museum. Also provided are Braille and standard text signs.

Admission: Adults $3.00, AAA $2.00, students grade K–12 $1.00, children under 6, active military, and OHS members free.

Directions: Located at the intersection of County Road 312 (Flint Ridge Road) and County Road 668 (Brownsville Road), 3 miles north of Brownsville, Ohio, and 4 miles north of I-70.

LIMA

Museum

Allen County Museum
Allen County Historical Society
620 West Market Street
Lima, OH 45801
Phone: (419) 222-9426
E-mail: acmuseum@wcoil.com

www.allencountymuseum.org

Open: All year, 1:00 P.M.–5:00 P.M. Tuesday–Friday, 1:00 P.M.–4:00 P.M. Saturday–Sunday, closed Mondays and national holidays.

Info: The museum features an extensive rock and mineral collection, with an entire room solely for the mineral display.

Admission: Suggested donation: $5.00.

Other services available: Library, children's museum, garden, railroad, archives, and Victorian "MacDonell House."

Directions: Northwest of the intersection of State Highways 309 and 65 in Lima.

SECTION 3: Special Events and Tourist Information

ANNUAL EVENT

Flint Ridge Knap-In

Flint Ridge State Memorial
15300 Flint Ridge Road
Glenford, OH 43739
Phone: (740) 787-2476; (800) 283-8707

The Flint Ridge Knap-In is held Friday, Saturday, and Sunday of Labor Day Weekend. A few primitive campsites in the park are available for the event, and it is first-come, first-served. Watch accomplished crafters create items using the same chipping methods employed by Native Americans over 12,000 years ago. Witness demonstrations of primitive bows and atlatls. Many Native American vendors will be selling jewelry, clothes, instruments, leather goods, and flint. Admission fee charged.

TOURIST INFORMATION

State Tourist Agency

Ohio Division of Travel and Tourism
P.O. Box 1001
Columbus, OH 43216-1001
Phone: (800) BUCKEYE or
(800) 282-5393
www.ohiotourism.com

PENNSYLVANIA

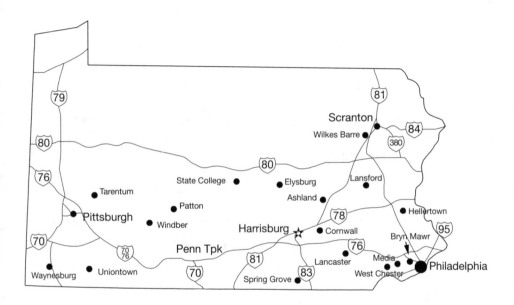

State Stone/Rock: None

SECTION 1: Fee Dig Sites and Guide Services

SPRING GROVE

Guide Services for Mineral Collecting *T*

The following gems or minerals may be found:

- Gold, various minerals

Jeri Jones
Jones Geological Services
2223 Stoverstown Road
Spring Grove, PA 17362

Phone: (717) 225-3744
E-mail: jonesgeo@comcast.net
www.jonesgeo.com

Open: By appointment.
Info: Mr. Jones offers a variety of field trips and collecting tours, which he can tailor to your needs. Also offered is a gold-panning program.
Rates: Call for rates.
Other services offered: A variety of publications on southeastern Pennsylvania geology are available on his website.

A free gold-panning program is presented at Spring Valley County Park on the last Saturday of July from 9:00 A.M.–2:00 P.M. Check it out at www.yorkcountyparks.org.

SECTION 2: Museums and Mine Tours

ASHLAND

Mine Tour

Pioneer Tunnel Coal Mine
Ashland Community Enterprises
19th and Oak Streets
Ashland, PA 17921
Phone: (570) 875-3850
www.pioneertunnel.com

Open: Memorial Day–Labor Day 10:00 A.M.–5:00 P.M. Last mine tour at 4:30 P.M.

Check website for off-season days/times.
Info: Visit an actual coal mine in the heart of Pennsylvania's anthracite region. Pioneer Tunnel is a horizontal drift mine, which runs 1,800 feet straight into the side of Mahanoy Mountain. Ride in open mine cars pulled by a battery-operated mine motor deep inside the mountain. The mine tour temperature averages 52°F throughout the tour, so bring your sweater or jacket (if necessary, one will be provided to you during the tour).

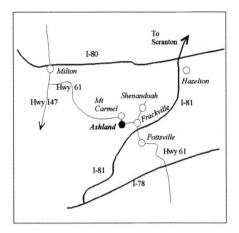

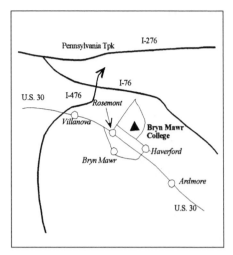

Admission: Mine tour: Adults $9.50, children (2–11) $6.50. Group rates available.

Other services available: Ride an old-fashioned narrow-gauge steam locomotive–powered mine train. See a strip mine, "bootleg" coal hole, and Ashland, a typical early 1900s mining town. Playground and picnic area, gift shop and snack bar. Train ride: Adults $7.50, children (2–11) $5.50, last ride at 5:00 P.M. Discount combo tickets available.

Directions: From I-80, take I-81 to exit 124B (Frackville exit). Take PA Route 61 north to Ashland. From I-78, take PA Route 61 north to Ashland.

BRYN MAWR

Museum

Department of Geology
Park Science Building
Bryn Mawr College

Phone: (610) 526-5111
E-mail: mcrawfor@brynmawr.edu
www.brynmawr.edu/geology/Minerals.htm

Open: September 1–May 15 (academic year), 9:00 A.M.–5:00 P.M. Other times of the year by appointment. Group or guided tours available by calling.

Info: View the 1,500 minerals on display in the halls (first and second floor of the Park Science Building). Approximately 23,500 additional specimens are in the storage rooms.

Admission: Free.

Directions: Bryn Mawr College is located just west of Philadelphia, just off U.S. 30. Park in the lower Science Center lot off New Gulph Road between Roberts Road and Morris Avenue. Morris Avenue intersects Montgomery Avenue near the Bryn Mawr train station. The lower parking lot, accessed by the entrance across from the Baptist church, has visitor parking spaces.

CORNWALL

Mine View and Museum

Cornwall Iron Furnace
Rexmont at Boyd Street
(94 Rexmont Road)
P.O. Box 251
Cornwall, PA 17016
Phone: (717) 272-9711
Fax: (717) 272-0450
www.cornwallironfurnace.org

Open: 9:00 A.M.–5:00 P.M. Thursday–Saturday, noon–5:00 P.M. Sunday; open Memorial Day, July 4, and Labor Day.

Info: Displays present the story of iron ore mining and iron production in the 1700s and 1800s. Cornwall Ore Banks was one of the world's greatest iron ore deposits, and more than 100 million tons were mined between 1730 and 1973. The pit depth reached five hundred feet below the surface. Digging and mineral collecting are not allowed on the property.

Admission: Adults $6.00; seniors $5.50, children (3–11) $4.00.

Directions: From Route U.S. 322, take PA 117 (Iron Master Road) east into Cornwall. Turn left onto Burd Coleman Road, then turn right onto Rexmont.

ELYSBURG

Anthracite Mining Museum

Knoebels Amusement Resort
Anthracite Mining Museum
391 Knoebels Blvd.
Elysburg, PA 17824

Phone: (800) 487-4386
www.knoebels.com

Open: Weekends, late April–May and September–October; every day June–August. Hours vary; check website or call for hours on a specific day.

Info: The Anthracite Mining Museum is located in the amusement park and is open to the public every day throughout the park season. The museum boasts the mining collection of Clarence "Mooch" Kashner, which was moved from the Anthracite Heritage Museum in Shamokin to the Knoebels Anthracite Mining Museum in 1988. The museum also contains artifacts ranging from a harness used in the Sheppton mine rescue to the tools and equipment used in the early mining days.

Admission: Admission to the resort is free.

Directions: On PA Route 487 between Elysburg and Catawissa, 3 miles north of PA 54, 5 miles north of PA 61, 6 miles south of PA 42, 10 miles south of U.S. 11, 13 miles south of I-80, 15 miles east of U.S. 15.

HARRISBURG

Museum

The State Museum of Pennsylvania
300 North Street
Harrisburg, PA 17120
Phone: (717) 787-4980
http://www.statemuseumpa.org

Open: 9:00 A.M.–5:00 P.M. Thursday–Saturday, noon–5:00 P.M. Sunday. Holiday hours subject to change.

Info: Exhibits and displays explain the basic concepts of geology. Visitors learn about practical applications of geology in displays that present information on materials extracted from rocks, and the everyday products that result.

Admission: Adults $5.00, children (1–12) and seniors (60+) $4.00. Free general admission on the third Saturday of every month.

Directions: At the corner of Third Street and North Street, in Harrisburg, at the capitol complex.

HELLERTOWN

Museum

The Gilman Museum
Lost River Caverns
726 Durham St.
P.O. Box M
Hellertown, PA 18055
Phone: (888) 529-1907; (610) 838-8767
www.lostcave.com

Open: Memorial Day–Labor Day: 9:00 A.M.–6:00 P.M.; Labor Day–Memorial Day: 9:00 A.M.–5:00 P.M., Closed Thanksgiving, Christmas, New Year's Day, and Easter.

Info: The museum contains unique minerals and gems. The price of admission includes a tour of Lost River Caverns.

Rates: Adults $11.00, children $7.00.

Directions: From PA Route 412 in Hellertown, take Penn Street, which turns into Durham Street for ½ mile.

LANCASTER

Museum

North Museum of Natural History & Science
400 College Avenue
Lancaster, PA 17603-3393
Phone: (717) 291-3941
E-mail: info@northmuseum.org
www.northmuseum.org

Open: 10:00 A.M.–5:00 P.M. Tuesday–Saturday, noon–5:00 P.M. Sunday. Closed Mondays and major holidays.

Info: The museum has an extensive geology collection with a large number of rocks and minerals on display. Other exhibits include Dinosaur Hall, discovery room, live animal room, birds, shells, insects, Native American, and more.

Admission: Adults $7.50, children (3–17) and seniors (65+) $6.50, children under 3 free.

Directions: In Lancaster, on the campus of Franklin and Marshall College, at the corner of College and Buchanan Avenues.

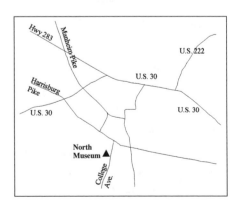

LANSFORD

Mine Tour/Museum

No. 9 Mine & Museum
9 Dock Street
P.O. Box 287
Lansford, PA 18232
Phone: (570) 645-7074
www.no9mine.com

Open: Call for dates and times.

Info: This anthracite coal mine operated from 1855 to 1972, and was reopened as a tour mine in 2002. Ride a tram 1600 feet into the mine and see how the miners worked. The museum exhibits chronicle nearly 200 years of mining in the Panther Valley.

Admission: Mine tour and museum, $8.00; museum only, $3.00.

Other services available: Picnic grove, gift shop.

Directions: Located in Lansford, just off U.S. Route 209 at the Lansford/Coaldale border.

MEDIA

Museum

Delaware County Institute of Science
11 Veterans Square
Media, PA 19063
Phone: (610) 566-5126
www.delcoscience.com

Open: 9:00 A.M.–noon Monday, Thursday, and most Saturdays, excluding holidays. Arrangements for group tours can be made by calling the institute.

Info: Display and research collection contains hundreds of minerals from around the world. Many minerals from famous localities in the area are included. The museum houses the original plate blocks used to print Dr. Samuel Gordon's 1922 *Mineralogy of Pennsylvania*. Specimens brought from the mineral prospects of the West by members of the Delaware County Institute of Science during the 1800s can be viewed and studied.

Admission: Free.

Directions: The institute is located in the center of Media near the county courthouse. Media is located west of Philadelphia, on old U.S. 1.

PATTON

Mine Tour/Museum

Seldom Seen Mine
P.O. Box 83
Patton, PA 16668
Phone: (814) 247-6305
Off-season/days closed: (814) 674-8939
www.seldomseenmine.com

Open: July and August: Thursday–Sunday; June: Saturday and Sunday, noon–5:00 P.M.; May, September, and October: scheduled tours for groups of 25 or more only. Check website or call for days and times.

Info: Tour an underground bituminous coal mine. Ride an electric mine train into the mine. During the tour, your

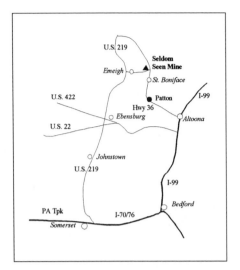

guide will discuss the past, present, and future of coal mining. Aboveground, view a theatre presentation or tour the museum to learn more about mining.

Admission: Adults $10.00, youth (4–12) $6.00.

Directions: Located on Route 36, 4 miles north of Patton.

PHILADELPHIA

Museum 🏛

Academy of Natural Sciences
1900 Benjamin Franklin Parkway
Philadelphia, PA 19103
Phone: (215) 299-1000
www.ansp.org

Open: All year, 10:00 A.M.–4:30 P.M. Monday–Friday, 10:00 A.M.–5:00 P.M. Saturdays, Sundays, and holidays; closed Thanksgiving, Christmas, and New Year's Day.

Info: The mineral collection recently has been restored and is newly housed in a research/collection area of the Academy. It is not on view to the public.

Admission: Adults $12.00; seniors (65+), children (3–12), military, and students $10.00; under 3 free.

Other services: Gift shop.

Directions: See website or call for directions.

PHILADELPHIA

Museum 🏛

Wagner Free Institute of Science
1700 West Montgomery Avenue
Philadelphia, PA 19121
Phone: (215) 763-6529
www.wagnerfreeinstitute.org

Open: 9:00 A.M.–4:00 P.M. Tuesday–Friday. Closed major holidays. Arrangements for group tours can be made by calling ahead.

Info: The institute houses an extensive collection of more than 100,000 natural history specimens, including rocks and minerals.

Admission: Free for all education programs. $8.00 suggested donation for museum visitors.

Directions: Take the Broad Street exit off I-676. Follow Broad Street north to Norris Street, and turn left at Norris. Go three blocks to 17th Street, turn left, and go one block to Montgomery Avenue.

PITTSBURGH

Museum

Carnegie Museum of Natural History
4400 Forbes Avenue
Pittsburgh, PA 15213
Phone: (412) 622-3131
E-mail: cmnhweb@carnegiemnh.org
www.carnegiemnh.org

Open: Year round; closed major holidays.
10:00 A.M.–5:00 P.M. Tuesday–Saturday
(10:00 A.M.–5:00 P.M. Monday between
July 4 and Labor Day, otherwise, closed
Mondays), 10:00 A.M.–8:00 P.M. Thursday,
noon–5:00 P.M. Sunday.

Info: The Hillman Hall of Minerals and
Gems contains many specimen displays,
including minerals from India and a display that features a massive calcite that
was shown during the 1893 World's
Columbian Exposition in Chicago. The
Wertz Galley of Gems and Jewelry
focuses on gems, crystals, and jewelry
made from precious stones, and includes
a permanent birthstone exhibit.

Some of the highlights at Hillman
Hall of Minerals and Gems, one of the
premier mineral halls in North America,
include displays on quartz, pseudomorphs, twins (crystals), fluorescent minerals, radioactive minerals, minerals as
natural art, minerals from the "Tin Isles,"
minerals from Bulgaria, Romania, and
the former Soviet Union, and a collection of Pennsylvania specimens, including
many from mines that quit producing

over 100 years ago. A "float" copper
exhibit allows hands-on investigations.

Admission: Adults $15.00, seniors (65+)
and students $12.00, children (3–18)
$11.00, children under 3 free.

Directions: Carnegie Museum of Natural History is located inside the city limits of Pittsburgh, on Forbes Avenue in the
Oakland section of the city. From the
north or west, take I-279 to I-376. Take
the Forbes Avenue exit, and stay on Forbes
to the Carnegie Museum and Library
complex. From the east, take I-376 to
the Bates Street exit. Stay on that street
until it ends, then turn left. Take the second right, and follow that road to the
Carnegie Museum and Library complex.

SCRANTON

Museums/Mine Tour

Anthracite Museum Complex
McDade Park
22 Bald Mountain Road
Scranton, PA 18504
Phone: (570) 963-4804
Fax: (570) 963-4194
www.anthracitemuseum.org

Info: Several mining or mining-related
attractions are found at or near McDade
Park, a reclaimed strip mine in Scranton, Pennsylvania. Some attractions are
free; others have admission fees.

Lackawanna Coal Mine Tour: Guided
tour 300 feet deep into an anthracite coal
mine. See how the "black diamonds"

were "harvested" from the earth. Mine temperature is 53°F, so jackets or sweatshirts may be needed. Site also has a gift shop and snack bar. Open April–November, 10:00 A.M.–3:00 P.M. Closed December–March. (800) 238-7245. Admission: Adults $10.00, children (3–12) $7.50, seniors (65+) $9.50. Located at McDade Park; take Keyser Avenue exit off the Scranton Expressway, travel 3 miles, and turn right at the sign.

Pennsylvania Anthracite Heritage Museum: Explore the history and heritage of the people who settled the anthracite region. Site also has a research library and a store. Open all year 9:00 A.M.–5:00 P.M. Monday–Saturday, noon–5:00 P.M. Sunday. Call for winter schedule; closed Mondays December–March. (570) 963-4804. Admission: Adults $6.00, youth (3–11) $4.00, seniors (65+) $5.50. Located at McDade Park; take Keyser Avenue exit off the Scranton Expressway, travel 3 miles, and turn right at the sign.

Scranton Iron Furnaces: Four stone blast furnace stacks symbolize Scranton's industrial heritage. At one time these furnaces were the second largest producers of iron in the nation, and they produced one sixth of the nation's rail output. Tours and events are offered. Parking lot opens to visitors on Memorial Day Weekend and is open each weekend of the summer, including Independence Day and Labor Day. (570) 963-4804. Free. Take exit 185 off I-81, Central Scranton

Expressway, to site.

Other related sites:
- Eckley Mining Village: Located in Hazelton; commemorates the history and heritage of the anthracite coal miners.

SCRANTON

Museum

Everhart Museum of Natural History, Science, and Art
1901 Mulberry Street
Scranton, PA 18510
Phone: (570) 346-7186
Fax: (570) 346-0652
E-mail: general.information@everhart-museum.org
www.everhart-museum.org

Open: Noon–4:00 P.M. Monday, Thursday, and Friday; 10:00 A.M.–5:00 P.M. Saturday; noon–5:00 P.M. Sunday; closed during the month of January.

Info: The Rocks & Minerals Gallery and the Fossil Gallery highlight selections from the Everhart Museum permanent collections.

Admission: Adults $5.00, seniors and students $3.00, children (6–12) $2.00, 5 and under free.

Other services available: Gift shop.

Directions: The museum is located in front of Nay Aug Park. Take exit 185 off I-81 (Central Scranton Expressway) and follow signs to Jefferson Avenue. Turn right onto Mulberry Street, and go straight to Nay Aug Park.

STATE COLLEGE

Museum

Earth and Mineral Sciences Museum
and Art Gallery
16 Deike Building
University Park, PA 16802-5000
Phone: (814) 865-6336
Fax: (814) 863-7708
E-mail: museum@ems.psu.edu
www.ems.psu.edu

Open: 9:30 A.M.–5:00 P.M. Monday–Friday. Closed weekends and legal holidays, including the university recess between Christmas and New Year. Call for special appointments.

Info: The main gallery has displays of minerals. The museum maintains collections of rocks, minerals, and fossils totaling more than 22,000 specimens as well as glasses, ceramics, metals, plastics, synthetic materials, old mining and scientific equipment, and archaeological artifacts. The country's most extensive collection of paintings and sculptures depicting mining and related industries is on display in the museum, which also houses the world's most extensive collection of mineral properties exhibits; there are push-button electro-mechanical exhibits demonstrating electrical, optical, and physical properties of minerals. Other displays include a collection of more than 100 mine safety lamps, scientific instruments, and specimens belonging to famous mineralogist Frederick Augustus Genth.

Admission: Free.

Directions: First floor of Deike Hall on the Penn State Campus.

TARENTUM

Museum/Mine Tour

Tour-Ed Mine
748 Bull Creek Road
Tarentum, PA 15084
Phone: (724) 224-4720
E-mail: info@tour-edmine.com
www.tour-edmine.com

Open: Memorial Day–Labor Day, daily (except Tuesday) 10:00 A.M.–4:00 P.M. Last tour at 3:20 P.M.

Info: Take an underground tour of a bituminous coal mine. Begin the tour by learning of past and present safety equipment, then board a mantrip car for your journey into the mine. Leave the car and follow your guide to learn about mining methods and machines. After the demonstrations, reboard the car, and return outside. Outside, view displays of surface mining equipment, see a working sawmill, and view a restored 1780s log cabin. The museum contains thousands of items showing what life was like in an

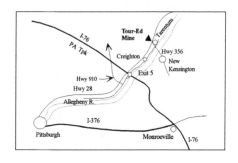

early 1900s mining community.
Admission: Adults $9.00, children 12 and under $7.50, group rates available.
Other services available: Gift shop.
Directions: Located at exit 14 (Tarentum) on Route 28 north from Pittsburgh; 25 minutes from downtown Pittsburgh. From the PA Turnpike, take State Highway 910 to State Highway 28.

UNIONTOWN

Museum

The Coal and Coke Heritage Center
Penn State Fayette, The Eberly Campus
One University Drive
P.O. Box 519
Uniontown, PA 15401
Phone: (724) 430-4158
Fax: (724) 430-4100
www.fayette.psu.edu/coalandcoke

Open: 10:00 A.M.–3:00 P.M. Monday–Friday and by appointment.
Info: The Coal and Coke Heritage Center captures and preserves the history and heritage of the Connellsville Coke Region during the 100-year span from 1870 to 1970. Located at the base of Chestnut Ridge in SW Pennsylvania, the Connellsville Coke Region is famous for the abundant, high-quality bituminous coal and the coke industries that resulted. During this period of phenomenal industrial growth in the U.S., the Region fueled the blast furnaces of the Pittsburgh steel industry. The collections held by the Center include mining and coking artifacts, literature, photographs, maps, blueprints, documents, and newspapers. Exhibits feature displays highlighting coals, coke, and communities.
Admission: Donations are appreciated.
Other services available: Lectures, tours, and a speaker's bureau.
Directions: The Center is located on the lower level of the campus library. The campus is located on US Route 119, 5 miles north of Uniontown, and 7 miles south of Connellsville.

WAYNESBURG

Museum

The Paul R. Stewart Museum
Waynesburg University
51 W. College Street
Waynesburg, PA 15370
Phone: (724) 852-3214
www.waynesburg.edu/depts/museum

Open: 9:00 A.M.–noon Monday–Friday during the school year. Special tours and summer hours by appointment.
Info: The museum has an outstanding mineral collection, with specimens from around the world. The museum was started in the 1920s by Prof. A. J. Waychoff, who would send back specimens from his travels. In addition, Prof. Waychoff collected many others locally. Other specimens were obtained as donations from alumni stationed all over the world during World War I and World War II.

Paul R. Stewart, Waychoff's nephew,

continued the collection when he served as president of the college for 42 years. Some specimens are from a geology field station Stewart set up in Colorado. His will named James "Fuzzy" Randolph, who had been helping with the museum, as curator. Prof. Randolph is always willing to share the many interesting facts and stories behind the collection of the Paul R. Stewart Museum.

The museum is one of the showcases of the Waynesburg College Campus today and could boast of having one of the finest college collections of geological specimens and Indian artifacts in the country. The fossil collection includes Permian flora from local coal mines. The museum collections also include early American glass and a great collection of salt glazed stoneware from early local factories. The collections are available for scholarly study.

Admission: Free.

Directions: Waynesburg is located on I-79, just north of the Pennsylvania–West Virginia border. Take exit 3 off I-79, and turn right onto State Highway 21 at the end of the ramp. Follow Highway 21 to the third traffic light, and turn right. Follow this road into town. At the fifth traffic light after the turn, turn right again (at the courthouse) onto Washington Street. Go two blocks to Miller Hall, which is the large red brick building on the left in the third block. Turn left into College Street in front of Miller Hall, go to the end of the block, and turn right onto Morris Street, then turn right into the parking lot. The museum is in Miller Hall.

WEST CHESTER

Museum

Geology Museum
West Chester University
Department of Geology and Astronomy
Merion Science Center 207
West Chester, PA 19383
Phone: (610) 436-2727
www.geology.wcupa.edu/geology_museum

Open: During school sessions.
Info: The museum has collections from several noted collectors. One collection focuses on specimens from Chester County, and another highlights fluorescent minerals.
Admission: Free.
Directions: On the campus of West Chester University, in the Schmucker Science Center Link.

WILKES-BARRE

Museum

Luzerne County Historical Society Museum
69 South Franklin Street
Wilkes-Barre, PA 18701
Phone: (570) 822-1727
Fax: (570) 823-9011
www.luzernehistory.org

Open: Call ahead for information.
Info: The museum has a display on anthracite coal mining, which includes a timbered coal mine gangway and its mine railway car.

Admission: Adults $5.00, children $2.00.

Other services available: Gift shop.

Directions: On South Franklin Street in the city of Wilkes-Barre.

WINDBER

Museum

Windber Coal Heritage Center
501 15th Street
Windber, PA 15963-1603
Phone: (814) 467-6680

Open: May–September, 11:00 A.M.–9:00 P.M. Monday–Saturday (call ahead to be sure); October by appointment.

Info: Housed in an old coal company headquarters building and featuring the mine rescue exhibit Quecreek, the Center uses high-tech exhibits, media presentations and archives to describe the everyday life of the coal miner and his family, the evolution of mining techniques, unionization, and the impact of the coal industry on small mining towns such as Windber.

Admission: Adults $6.00, seniors (62+) $4.50, students (17–21) $3.00, youth (7–16) $1.50, children under 6 free.

Directions: The Center is located at the corner of 15th Street and Graham Avenue (Route 160) in Windber, next to the Miner's Park.

Ringing Rocks

There are two locations in Eastern Pennsylvania where there are boulder fields of rocks, many of which ring with a tone when struck with a hammer or another rock. One is Ringing Rocks Park, Ringing Rock Rd., Upper Black Eddy, PA 18972 (Bucks County), the other is Ringing Hill Fire Company Park, on North Charlotte Street, (PA Rte 663), in Lower Pottsgrove Township, Montgomery County.

In June of 1890, Dr. J. J. Ott held the first-ever rock concert when he collected a number of rocks with different pitches and then, accompanied by a brass band, played several musical selections for the Buckwampum Historical Society. The tones are thought to occur due to high iron content in the mineral that makes up the boulders. The only other occurrence of ringing rocks in the U.S. is on Bureau of Land Management lands between Butte and Whitehall, MT.

SECTION 3: Special Events and Tourist Information

TOURIST INFORMATION

State Tourist Agency

Pennsylvania Tourism Office
400 North Street
4th Floor
Harrisburg, PA 17120-0225

Phone: (717) 787-5453; (800) VISITPA
or (800) 847-4872
www.visitpa.com

RHODE ISLAND

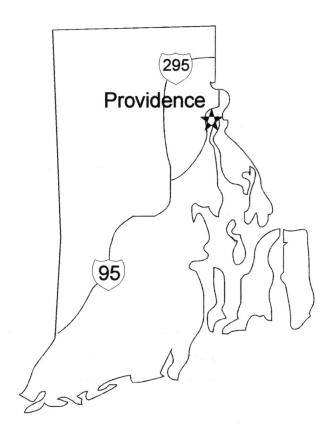

State Mineral: Bowenite (1966)
State Stone/Rock: Cumberlandite (1966)

SECTION 1: Fee Dig Sites and Guide Services

No information available.

SECTION 2: Museums and Mine Tours

PROVIDENCE

Museum

Museum of Natural History and
Planetarium
Roger Williams Park
1000 Elmwood Avenue
Providence, RI 02907
Phone: (401) 785-9457, ext. 221
www.providenceri.com/museum
Open: 10:00 A.M.–5:00 P.M. daily, except
holidays.
Info: Rhode Island's only natural history
museum has collections of minerals,
rocks, and fossils, assembled primarily by
local collectors. The museum has a mineral society and membership.
Admission: Adults $2.00, children (2–7)
$1.00.
Directions: From I-95 south, take exit
17, turn left at light, then turn left into
Roger Williams Park and follow signs to
the museum.

From I-95 North, take exit 16, bear
right, then turn left at the light onto
Elmwood Avenue. Turn right into Roger
Williams Park, and follow signs to the
museum.

SECTION 3: Special Events and Tourist Information

TOURIST INFORMATION

State Tourist Agency

Rhode Island Tourism Division
315 Iron Horse Way, Ste. 101
Providence, RI 02908

Phone: (800) 250-7384
Fax: (401) 273-8270
www.visitrhodeisland.com

VERMONT

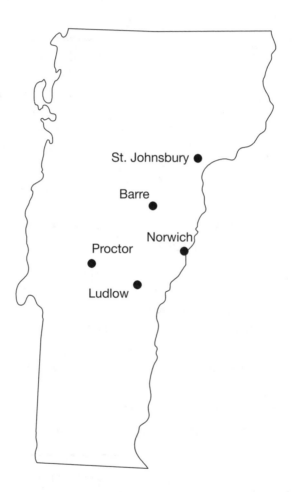

St. Johnsbury ●

Barre
●

Norwich
●

Proctor
●

Ludlow ●

State Gemstone: Grossular Garnet (1991)
State Mineral: Talc (1991)
State Stone/Rock: Granite, Marble, Slate (1991)

LUDLOW / *Native • Easy*

Pan for Gold *T*

The following gems or minerals may be found:

▪ Gold

Camp Plymouth State Park
2008 Scout Camp Road
Ludlow, VT 05149
Phone: (802) 228-2025

Open: Memorial Day–Labor Day, open for day use, 10:00 A.M.–9:00 P.M. or official sunset. Open for day use weekends through September.

Info: Buffalo Brook, which flows through the park, was the site of the Vermont gold rush, which lasted approximately 30 years. The site was a Boy Scout camp until it became a State Park in 1984.

Rates: Call for rates and reservations.

Other services available: Camping, recreational facilities. No pets are allowed in the Park.

Directions: From Highway 100 in Tyson: cross the concrete bridge, go 1 mile east uphill to crossroad and turn left, go 1 mile north on the east side of Echo Lake.

Vermont Gold Rush

In 1855, gold was discovered in the gravel of Buffalo Brook in Plymouth, Vermont. The brook soon got the name "Gold Brook" and had claims all along its length. Several mines were started, and a stamp mill was constructed to process gold ore. However, the gold rush was short lived, and had died out by the late 1880s.

BARRE

Museum/Quarry Tour

Rock of Ages Corporation
560 Graniteville Road

Graniteville, VT 05654
(866) 748-6877
www.rockofages.com

Open: Visitors' Center times vary throughout the year. See website or call for more information. Generally open mid-May–October.

Manufacturing facility tour open almost all year, 8:00 A.M.–3:30 P.M. Monday–Friday.

Upper E. L. Smith Quarry tour June–mid-October, 9:15 A.M.–3:35 P.M. Monday–Saturday and Sundays from September–mid-October.

Info: Watch granite being quarried, and view finished products being made. Watch videos on granite quarrying at the visitors center. Pick out a free granite sample from the grout box. Learn to sandblast your own granite souvenir. For a charge, take a narrated tour of the deepest granite quarry in the world. The visitors' center also displays mineral exhibits and geological information, and has a gift shop. There is also a small picnic area and a shop selling sandwiches and Vermont products, including maple syrup.

Manufacturing facility tour: Admission free.

Upper E. L. Smith tour charges: Adults $5.00, seniors (62+) $4.50, children (6–12) $2.50, children under 6 free.

Directions: Take Highway 63 (Exit 6) from I-89. Cross Highway 14 and continue up Middle Hill Road. Follow signs to the visitors center.

BARRE

Museum

Vermont Granite Museum and Stone Arts School

P.O. Box 282
7 Jones Bros. Way
Barre, VT 05641
Phone: (802) 476-4605
Fax: (802) 476-6866
E-mail: info@stoneartsschool.org
www.granitemuseum.org

Open: By appointment.

Info: The museum is located in an authentic turn-of-the-century granite manufacturing plant and has displays on the geology, technology, history, and art of Vermont's unique granite heritage of art and industry. The Stone Arts School is committed to creating an exciting environment where sculptors from around the world can explore traditional and modern stone carving techniques with working professionals, while promoting granite as a vital material for artistic expression.

Admission: Donation.

Directions: Call for directions.

PROCTOR

Mine Tour

Vermont Marble Museum
52 Main Street
P.O. Box 607
Proctor, VT 05765
Phone: (800) 427-1396; (802) 459-2948
www.vermont-marble.com

Open: Open 7 days/week, mid-May–end of October. Call for times.

Info: A theater presents "The Legacy of

Vermont Marble," a film showing how marble was formed over 400 million years ago. See the step-by-step process of marble quarrying. Watch a sculptor working.

Tour the Gallery of Presidents: life-sized white marble bas-relief busts of each of the past presidents. Tour the open-air marble market. View the exhibit "Earth Alive" and experience earth's geological history and its ongoing evolution.

Admission: Adults $7.00, seniors $5.00, teens $4.00, children free. (Get $1.00 off when you reserve ahead by phone.)

Directions: Take exit 6 from U.S. 4 in West Rutland. Turn east on Business Route 4 and then north on Vermont Route 3 to Proctor. Turn left over the marble bridge and bear right to the exhibit.

From the north, bear right on Vermont Route 3 from U.S. 7 in Pittsford to Proctor.

ST. JOHNSBURY

Museum 🏛

Fairbanks Museum and Planetarium
1302 Main Street
St. Johnsbury, VT 05819
Phone: (802) 748-2372
Fax: (802) 748-1893
www.fairbanksmuseum.org

Open: Summer hours, April–October: 9:00 A.M.–5:00 P.M. Monday– Saturday, 1:00 P.M.–5:00 P.M. Sunday. Closed Mondays November–March. Also closed New Year's Day, Easter, July 4, Thanksgiving, Christmas, and during the museum's Annual Winter Celebration Meeting in January.

Info: A variety of rocks and minerals from the Vermont Geological Collection are displayed in some of the balcony display cases.

Rates: Adults $8.00, seniors and children under 17 $6.00, children under 5 free. Family (immediate family members only) up to 2 adults, no limit on number of children: $20.00.

Directions: Take I-91 N (1/4 mile) to Exit 20. Bear right onto U.S. 5 N, take first left turn and proceed up hill to stop sign, then proceed 2 blocks to museum on the right.

SECTION 3: Special Events and Tourist Information

ANNUAL EVENT

Granite Festival, Barre, VT

Held on a Saturday in the summer or early fall. Contact the Vermont Granite Museum for information.

TOURIST INFORMATION

State Tourist Agency

Vermont Department of Tourism and Marketing
National Life Building, 6th Fl.
Montpelier, VT 05620
Phone: (800) VERMONT;
(800) 837-6668; (802) 828-3237
E-mail: info@vermontvacation.com
www.1-800-vermont.com

WISCONSIN

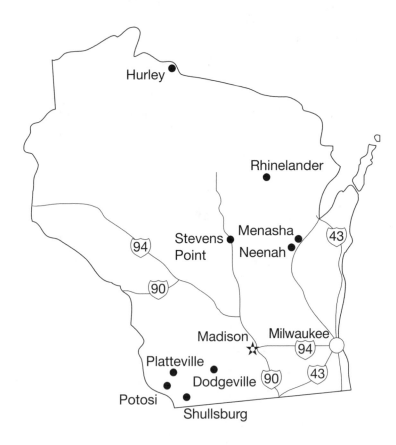

State Mineral: Galena (1971)
State Stone/Rock: Red Granite (1971)

RHINELANDER / *Native • Moderate*

Pan for Gold or Hunt for Rocks and Minerals *T*

The following gems or minerals may be found:

▪ Gold

Chequamegon-Nicolet National Forest
500 Hanson Lake Road
Rhinelander, WI 54501
Phone: (715) 362-1300
Fax: (715) 369-8859
E-mail: pswanson@fs.fed.us

Open: Daylight hours, weather permitting.

Info: The Chequamegon-Nicolet National Forest authorizes recreational mineral collecting, such as panning for gold or rock collecting, without a permit. Gold panning is only allowed with the use of small hand tools (pan, small shovel, and hand pick). Occasional recreation panning for an individual or group is limited to extremely small areas of stream disturbance; a few scattered areas of less than 1 square foot and totaling less than 40 square feet within a 500-foot segment of a stream. The National Forest does not issue permits for more substantial recreational collecting. The use of suction dredges, any type of motorized equipment, mercury or any kind of chemical, and sluice type devices is prohibited. Gold panning activity is not permitted in classified trout water before April 15 and after September 15. You must also avoid disturbing fish spawning nests.

Recreational rock collecting or "rock hounding" means the collecting of surface rock samples without digging tools or surface disturbance. Rock hammers or geo-picks are allowed for use in breaking off small hand samples from larger rock outcrops on surface boulders.

Digging for quartz crystals is prohibited at a specific historical quartzite crystal collecting area known as Quartz Hill, located in Oconto County, north of Townsend and ¼ mile east and northeast of the junction of FR 2123 and State Highway 32. You may collect small amounts of surface rock samples but may not do any kind of digging or other surface disturbance.

The Forest Service needs to know the locations and dates of your proposed recreational panning or rock collecting. In advance of this activity please contact Greg Knight, Forest Geologist, Medford-Park Falls Ranger Station, 850 N. 8th, Hwy. 13, Medford, WI 54451; (715) 748-4875, ext. 26 or e-mail gknight@fs.fed.us.

Rates: Free.

Directions: Contact the National Forest or check the website for directions.

SECTION 2: Museums and Mine Tours

DODGEVILLE

Museum

The Museum of Minerals and Crystals
4228 State Road 23 North
Dodgeville, WI 53533
Phone: (608) 935-5205

Open: April 1–Memorial Day, 9:00 A.M.–4:00 P.M. Memorial Day weekend–Labor Day weekend 9:00 A.M.–5:00 P.M., after Labor Day–October 31, 9:00 A.M.–4:00 P.M., closed Sundays. Call ahead.

Info: The museum has a collection of over 125 specimens of local crystals and minerals from deposits that are the reason the original settlers came to the area in the 1820s. The museum also contains thousands of geological specimens from around the world. Highlights of the collection include a 215-pound amethyst-filled geode, a 315-pound Brazilian agate, a single 90-pound quartz crystal from Arkansas, and a 160-pound specimen of fluorite. The museum also has a black light exhibit of fluorescent minerals, and a display of faceted lead crystals.

Admission: Adults $5.00, students $4.00.

Other services: Gift shop.

Directions: Located on State Highway 23, 4 miles north of Dodgeville, across from the entrance to Governor Dodge State Park, 5 miles south of House on the Rock.

HURLEY

Museum/Mine Exhibit

Iron County Historical Museum
303 Iron Street
Hurley, WI 54534
Phone: (715) 561-2244
www.ironcountymuseum.org

Open: 10:00 A.M.–2:00 P.M. Monday, Wednesday, Friday, and Saturday (except holidays). Winter hours: Closed Wednesday; open the rest of the week.

Info: This museum has exhibits on the area's mining history. Displays include iron ore and other local mineral samples.

Admission: Free. A recycling center for old fabric supports the museum. The fabric is transformed with looms into rag rugs, and these are sold to raise funds.

Directions: At the corner of Iron Street and 3rd Avenue in Hurley.

For a nearby related display, visit:
Plummer Mine Interpretive Park

Hwy 23
Mineral Museum ▲
State Park
Madison
U.S. 18
U.S. 18/151
Dodgeville
U.S. 151

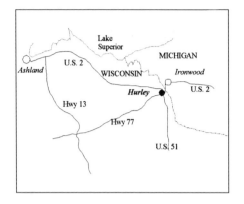

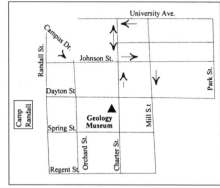

Located on State Highway 77 southwest from Hurley. This is the last remaining mine head frame in Wisconsin and is surrounded by an interpretive park that honors the area's miners.

MADISON

Museum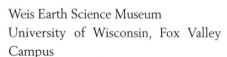

Geology Museum
Weeks Hall
University of Wisconsin–Madison
1215 West Dayton Street
Madison, WI 53706
Phone: (608) 262-2399
Fax: (608) 262-0693
www.geologymuseum.org

Open: All year except major holidays, 8:30 A.M.–4:30 P.M. Monday–Friday, 9:00 A.M.–1:00 P.M. Saturday.

Info: This museum has a rock and mineral collection, which includes a display of fluorescent minerals, meteorites, and gems. Touch a 1,300-lb. piece of copper and learn about Wisconsin's mining history. *Note:* Website contains a detailed discus-

sion on how to identify meteorites, including contact information should you have questions about a find.

Admission: Free.

Directions: In Weeks Hall on the college campus, at the corner of Charter and Dayton Streets. Note that on-street parking is extremely limited; however, most university parking lots in the vicinity are available on non-football Saturdays.

MENASHA

Museum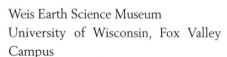

Weis Earth Science Museum
University of Wisconsin, Fox Valley Campus
1478 Midway Road
Menasha, WI 54952
Phone: (920) 832-2925
www.weismuseum.org

Open: Noon–4:00 P.M. Monday–Thursday, noon-7:00 P.M. Friday, 10:00 A.M.–5:00 P.M. Saturday, 1:00 P.M–5:00 P.M. Sunday; closed all national and campus holidays.

Info: The Weis Earth Science Museum is the official State Mineralogical Museum of Wisconsin. It is dedicated to the geology and mineral and mining heritage of Wisconsin with hands-on interactive displays. Walk through a lead mine tunnel, explore Wisconsin's mining history, discover how Native Americans mined copper, and learn how rocks and minerals are used.

Admission: Adults $2.00, seniors (65+) and juniors (13–17) $1.50, children (3–12) $1.00, children under 3 free.

Other services available: Gift shop; group tours and summer camps are also available.

Directions: In Menasha, near the intersections of Highways 47, 441, and 10. Check the website or call for detailed directions.

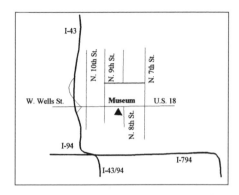

(60+), college students with ID, and teens (13–17) $11.00; children (3–12) $9.00; children under 3 free.

Other services available: Gift shop, theater, restaurant.

Directions: In downtown Milwaukee, take the West Wells Street/U.S. 18 exit off I-43, and drive 1½ blocks east. The museum is on the left.

MILWAUKEE

Museum

Milwaukee Public Museum
800 West Wells Street
Milwaukee, WI 53233
Phone: (414) 278-2702; (888)-700-9069 (toll free); if you have special access needs, call (414) 278-2728
www.mpm.edu

Open: 9:00 A.M.–5:00 P.M. daily (hours can vary seasonally, call for details).

Info: The museum displays some of its over half a million geological specimens from around the world.

Admission: Adults $12.50; seniors

PLATTEVILLE

Museum/Mine Tour 🏛

The Mining Museum
The 1845 Bevans Lead Mine
City of Platteville, Museum Department
405 E. Main, P.O. Box 780
Platteville, WI 53818-0780
Phone: (608) 348-3301
www.mining.jamison.museum/index.html

Open: May–October, 9:00 A.M.–5:00 P.M., 7 days/week. Self-guided exhibits open November–April, 9:00 A.M.–4:00 P.M. Monday–Friday. Closed major holidays. Group tours year round by appointment.

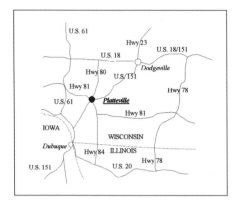

Info: Mining exhibits in the Mining Museum building are handicapped accessible.

The Mining Museum traces the development of lead and zinc mining in the upper Mississippi valley through models, dioramas, artifacts, and photographs. A guided tour includes a walk down into the Bevans Lead, an 1845 lead mine, which produced over 2 million pounds of lead ore in one year. It also includes a visit to a mine head frame where you can see how zinc ore was hoisted from a mine and hand sorted. A train ride around the museum grounds in ore cars pulled by a 1931 mine locomotive is also available.

The tour of the museum, the mine, and the train ride, along with a second museum tour (Rollo Jamison Museum displaying turn-of-the-century items), take approximately 1½ hours. Comfortable shoes and a light jacket are suggested. Rides on the mine train are included if weather permits.

Admission: May–October: Adults $9.00, seniors (65+) $7.50, children (5–15) $4.50, under 5 free. November–April: Adults and seniors $4.00, children $2.00. The museum does not accept credit cards.

Directions: Platteville is located at the intersection of Highway 80 and U.S. 151.

SHULLSBURG

Museum/Mine Tour

Badger Mine and Museum
279 W. Estey Street

The southwestern Wisconsin region had surface deposits of lead, zinc, and copper ore which were mined for centuries before European settlement. In the 1830s, however, a lead-mining craze brought miners flooding in, and the region boomed. By the 1830s, news of the "rush" had reached England, and miners from Cornwall and other regions immigrated and started digging deep mines in search of ore. In the late 1840s as the easy ores were dwindling, the news of the California Gold Rush drew many miners west, and the lead rush subsided. In the later part of the 1800s however, it was discovered that the waste material discarded during lead mining was a rich zinc ore, and zinc production boomed in the area, peaking in 1917 and ending in 1971.

Shullsburg, WI 53586
Phone: (608) 965-4860
www.shullsburgwisconsin.org
shullsburgbadgerminemuseum.htm

Open: Memorial Day–Labor Day, noon–4:00 P.M. Wednesday–Thursday, 11:00 A.M.–4:00 P.M. Friday–Sunday. Closed Mondays and Tuesdays, excluding holidays.

Info: Tour of a hand-dug nineteenth century lead mine, and displays of early lead mining equipment and techniques.

Admission: Museum and mine tour: Adults $5.00, seniors $4.00, children under 10 $3.00. Museum only: Adults $3.00, seniors $2.00, children under 10 $1.50.

Directions: From WI Route 11, turn onto W. Estey St., and follow to the mine and museum.

STEVENS POINT

Museum 🏛

UW–Stevens Point Museum of Natural History
900 Reserve Street
Stevens Point, WI 54481

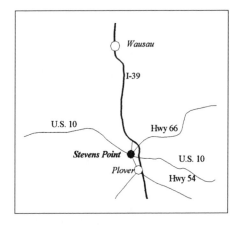

Phone: (715) 346-2858
http://www.uwsp.edu/museum

Open: The museum is open when the university library is open, during school hours. School year hours: 7:45 A.M.–12:00 A.M. Monday–Thursday, 7:45 A.M.–9:00 P.M. Friday, 9:00 A.M.–9:00 P.M. Saturday, 11:00 A.M.–1:00 A.M. Sunday. Please call for hours when school is not in session.

Info: A large collection of rocks and minerals is on display.

Admission: Free; donations appreciated.

Directions: Located on the University of Wisconsin–Stevens Point campus, at the intersection of Reserve Street and Portage Street.

ANNUAL EVENT

Quarry Quest

Info: Quarry Quest is a one-day event held in September at the Michels Materials Limestone Quarry in Neenah, WI. It has a wide variety of family activities at the quarry. More information can be found on the event website, www. QuarryQuest.com. Admission is charged, with all proceeds benefiting local charities. The mission of the event is to educate families in geology and construction through tours of a working quarry, chances to ride and explore giant excavation machinery, and hands-on educational activities.

TOURIST INFORMATION

State Tourist Agency

Wisconsin Department of Tourism
P.O. Box 8690
Madison, WI 53708-8690
Phone: (800) 432-TRIP;
(800) 432-8747 or (608) 206-2161
E-mail: tourinfo@travelwisconsin.com
www.travelwisconsin.com

Chamber of Commerce

Hurley Area Chamber of Commerce
316 Silver Street
Hurley, WI 54534
Phone: (715) 561-4334
www.hurleywi.com

Information on Hurley's historic mining area, one of the most famous mining towns of all time.

Iron County Heritage Days are from the last week in July to mid-August.

Index by State

ALABAMA

Fee Dig Mines and Guide Services

Cragford   Alabama Gold Camp—Pan, sluice, dredge, highbank and metal detect for gold

Trenton   Paint rock agate—Collecting trip

Museums and Mine Tours

Aldrich   Aldrich Coal Mine Museum—Mining history and simulated coal mine

Anniston   Anniston Museum of Natural History—Gemstones, meteorite, artificial indoor cave

Dora   Alabama Mining Museum—Focus on coal mining

McCalla   Tannehill Ironworks Historical State Park, Iron and Steel Museum of Alabama—Geology relevant to the iron industry

ALASKA

Fee Dig Mines and Guide Services

Anchorage   Alaska DNR—Pan, prospect, excavate, limited suction dredging for gold

Chicken   Chicken Gold Camp and Outpost—Pan or dig for gold

Chugach National Forest   Chugach National Forest—Pan for gold

Copper Center   Wrangell-St. Elias National Park and Preserve—Pan for gold, hunt for rocks and minerals (see exceptions in listing)

Fairbanks   El Dorado Gold Mine—Gold panning

Faith Creek Camp—Pan, sluice, dredge for gold

Girdwood   Crow Creek Mine—Pan, dredge, or use metal detectors for gold

Nome   Nome Beaches—Pan for gold

Skagway   Klondike Gold Dredge Tours—Pan for gold

Liarsville Gold Rush Trail Camp and Salmon Bake—Pan for gold

| **Talkeetna** | Clark/Wiltz Mining—Camp and prospect (with metal detectors) for gold |

Museums and Mine Tours

Anchorage	Alaska Museum of Natural History—Displays of rocks and minerals
Central	Circle Historical Museum—Mining equipment and gold display
Chicken	The Chicken Gold Camp & Outpost—Gold dredge tour
Copper Center	George Ashby Memorial Museum/Copper Valley Historical Society—Exhibits on gold and copper mining in the valley
Fairbanks	El Dorado Gold Mine—Gold mine tour and gold nugget display
	Gold Dredge No. 8—Gold dredge tour
	University of Alaska Museum—Minerals and gems from Alaska, Arctic Canada, and the Pacific Rim; includes gold and meteorites
Juneau	Juneau-Douglas City Museum—History of gold mining
	Last Chance Mining Museum—Hard-rock gold mining museum
Nome	The Carrie M. McLain Memorial Museum—History of area gold mining
Skagway	Klondike Gold Dredge Tour—Gold dredge tour
	Liarsville Gold Rush Trail Camp and Salmon Bake—Tour of gold rush camp
	Klondike Gold Rush National Historic Park—History of area gold mining
Wasilla	Independence Mine State Historical Park—Guided mine tour

ARIZONA

Fee Dig Mines and Guide Services

Apache Jct.	Apache Trail Tours—Gold panning jeep tours
Goldfield	Goldfield Ghost Town, Scenic Railroad, and Mine Tours—Gold panning
Prescott	Lynx Creek Mineral Withdrawal Area, Prescott National Forest—Pan for gold
Safford	Black Hills Rockhound Area—Dig for fire agates
	Round Mountain Rockhound Area—Search for fire agates, chalcedony, small geodes

Museums and Mine Tours

Apache Jct.	Superstition Mountain Museum—Geology, minerals, and mining
Bisbee	Bisbee Mining and Historical Museum—Displays on local mining
	Queen Mine Tour—Tour an underground copper mine

Flagstaff	Meteor Crater Enterprises, Inc.—View a meteor crater, museum of astrogeology
	Museum of Northern Arizona—History of Colorado Plateau, geologic models, mineral specimens
Goldfield	Goldfield Ghost Town, Scenic Railroad, and Mine Tours—Gold mine tour, museum, ghost town
Quartzsite	Quartzsite Historical Society—Displays of mining equipment
Sahuarita	ASARCO Mineral Discovery Center—Geology, mining, minerals, and tour of open-pit mine
Sun City	The Mineral Museum—2,000 rocks and minerals from the U.S. and the world, with emphasis on minerals from Arizona. Over 150 fluorescent rocks and minerals, most from Franklin and Sterling Hill, NJ
Tempe	R. S. Dietz Museum of Geology—Mineral displays, meteorites
Tombstone	Good Enough Mine—Silver mine tour
Tucson	Arizona-Sonora Desert Museum—Mineral collection from Sonora Desert region
	U. A. Science: Flandrau—Arizona minerals, meteorites, fluorescents, borate minerals
Wickenburg	Vulture Gold Mine—Self-guided mine tour

Annual Events

Quartzsite	Gem and Mineral Shows—Mid-January–mid-February
Tucson	Gem and Mineral Shows—End of January through mid-February
	Minerals of Arizona—Symposium one day in March/April

ARKANSAS

Fee Dig Mines and Guide Services

Jessieville	Ron Coleman Mining, Inc.—Dig for quartz crystals
	Colemans Rock Shop and Crystal Mines—Dig for quartz crystals
Mt. Ida	The Crystal Seen Trading Co.—Dig for quartz crystals, wavelite
	Fiddler's Ridge Rock Shop and Bear Mt. Crystal Mine—Dig for quartz crystals
	Judy's Crystals and Things—Dig for quartz crystals
	Ouachita National Forest, Crystal Vista Collecting Site—Collect quartz crystals on the ground, no digging permitted
	Wegner Quartz Crystal Mines—Dig, sluice, or pick through tailings for quartz crystals
Murfreesboro	Crater of Diamonds State Park—Dig and screen for diamonds, amethyst, agates, barite, calcite, jasper, quartz, other gems

Story   Gee and Dee Crystal—Dig for quartz crystals

Sweet Surrender Crystal Mine—Dig for quartz crystals

Museums and Mine Tours

Little Rock   Geology Learning Center—Arkansas gems, minerals, fossil fuels

Mt. Ida   Heritage House Museum of Montgomery County—Quartz and mineral exhibits

State University ASU Museum—Minerals, many from Arkansas

Annual Events

Mt. Ida   Quartz Crystal Festival and World Championship Dig—Second weekend in October

CALIFORNIA

Fee Dig Mines and Guide Services

Angels Camp   Angels Camp Museum and Carriage House—Pan native gold, quartz, and enriched soil for gems and minerals from around the world

Coalinga   Benitoite Gem Mine—Hunt for benitoite and other gems and minerals

Coloma   Marshall Gold Discovery State Historic Park—Gold panning

Columbia   Hidden Treasures Gold Mine—Pan for gold and garnets

Jackson   Kennedy Gold Mine—Gold panning

Jamestown   Gold Prospecting Adventures, LLC—Sluice, pan, and prospect with metal detectors for gold

Lucerne   Lake County Visitor Information Center—Rockhounding for Lake County "diamonds" or "moon tears"

Mariposa   Little Valley Inn—Gold panning

Mesa Grande Himalaya Tourmaline Mine, High Desert Gems and Minerals—Look for California tourmaline in mine tailings

Nevada City Malakoff Diggins State Historical Park—Gold panning

Pala   Oceanview Mine—Hunt for tourmaline (pink, green, bicolor), smoky crystals, garnets, book mica, cleavelandite, kunzite, morganite, gossanite (clear beryl), purple lepidolite, muscovite, aquamarine

Palo Verde   Fire Mountain Fire Agate Mine—Dig or screen for fire agate

Wiita Mining and Exploration—Guided gold hunting tours

Opal Hill Fire Agate Mine—Dig or screen for fire agate

Pine Grove   Roaring Camp Mining Company—Pan for gold, rockhound for quartz crystals, jade, jasper, and river rubies

Placerville   Hangtown's Gold Bug Park and Mine—Learn gold panning

Warner Springs Cryo-Genie Mine—Search mine dump for quartz crystals, tourmaline, beryl

Museums and Mine Tours

Alleghany	Underground Gold Miners Tours and Museum—Tour an active gold mine
Angels Camp	Angels Camp Museum and Carriage House—Museum features rocks and minerals, gold stamping mill, mining equipment
Avalon	Catalina Island Museum—Exhibits on mining on Catalina Island
Boron	Borax Visitor Center—Story of borax
	Boron Twenty Mule Team Museum—History of area borate mining
Coloma	Marshall Gold Discovery State Historic Park—Gold mining exhibit/museum
Death Valley	Furnace Creek Borax Museum—Rocks and minerals, featuring borate minerals
El Cajon	Heritage of the Americas Museum—Rocks, minerals, and meteorites
Fallbrook	Fallbrook Gem & Mineral Society Museum—Features of minerals from San Diego County
Grass Valley	Empire Mine State Historic Park—Hard-rock gold mine
Independence	Eastern California Museum—Regional gem and mineral collection
Jackson	Kennedy Gold Mine Tours—Surface tour of gold mine
Julian	Eagle and High Peak Gold Mine Tours—Hard-rock gold mine tour
	Julian Pioneer Museum—Rock and mineral display, gold mining tools and equipment displays
Lakeport	Historic Courthouse Museum—Minerals and gems found in Lake County
Los Angeles	Natural History Museum of Los Angeles County—150,000 specimens, minerals of California, native gold, gems, and minerals
Mariposa	California State Mining and Mineral Museum—Gold from California, gems and minerals from around the world
Needles	Needles Regional Museum—Collection of Needles blue agate, Colorado River pebble terrace stones
Nevada City	Malakoff Diggins Park Association—History of hydraulic gold mining
Pacific Grove	Pacific Grove Museum of Natural History—Monterey County rocks, fluorescent minerals
Paso Robles	Paso Robles Area Pioneer Museum—Display of local minerals
Placerville	Hangtown's Gold Bug Park and Mine—Tour hard-rock gold mine
Quincy	Plumas County Museum—Exhibits on gold and copper mining in Plumas County

Rancho Palos Verdes	Point Vicente Interpretive Center—Exhibits on area geology
Red Bluff	Gaumer's Mineral and Mining Museum—Minerals from around the world
Redlands	San Bernardino County Museum—45,000 rocks, minerals, and gems
Ridgecrest	Maturango Museum—Small but well-rounded regional gem and mineral collection
Riverside	Jurupa Mountains Discovery Center—Crestmore minerals display, minerals from around the world on display and for sale, family education programs
	World Museum of Natural History—Fluorescent minerals, meteorites, tektites, over 1,300 mineral spheres
San Diego	San Diego Natural History Museum—26,000 mineral specimens, includes minerals found in San Diego County mines
Santa Barbara	Department of Earth Science, UCSB—Gem and mineral collection, minerals and their tectonic settings
Shoshone	Shoshone Museum—Rock collection reflecting the geology of the area
Sierra City	Kentucky Mine and Museum—Exhibits of local gold mining
Sonora	Tuolumne County Museum—Gold from local mines
Sutter Creek	Sutter Gold Mine Tours—Hard-rock gold mine tour
Yreka	Siskiyou County Courthouse and Siskiyou County Museum—Gold exhibit
Yucca Valley	Hi-Desert Nature Museum—Rock and mineral collection, includes fluorescent minerals

Annual Events

Big Sur	Big Sur Jade Festival—Second weekend in October
Coloma	Marshall Gold Discovery State Historic Park: Gold Rush Live—Second week of October
Trona	Gem-O-Rama Searles Lake—Second weekend in October

COLORADO

Fee Dig Mines and Guide Services

Breckenridge	Country Boy Mine—Pan for gold
Idaho Springs	Argo Gold Mill—Pan for gold and gemstones
	Phoenix Mine—Pan for gold
Ouray	Bachelor-Syracuse Mine Tour—Learn to pan for gold
Silverton	Old Hundred Gold Mine Tours, Inc.—Pan for gold

Museums and Mine Tours

Breckenridge	Country Boy Mine—Hard-rock gold mine tour
Central City	Gilpin History Museum—Displays of local minerals
	Hidee Gold Mine—Gold mine tour and gold ore sample
Colorado Springs	Western Museum of Mining and Industry—Displays of mining and demonstrations on gold panning
Creede	Creede Underground Mining Museum—Displays of rocks, minerals, and mining equipment
Cripple Creek	Cripple Creek District Museum—Mineral displays
	Mollie Kathleen Gold Mine—Gold mine tour
Denver	Denver Museum of Nature and Science—Over 2,000 specimens; includes gold, topaz, aquamarine, amazonite, and other Colorado minerals
Georgetown	Lebanon Silver Mine—Ride a narrow-gauge train, then take a walking tour of the silver mine
Golden	Geology Museum, Colorado School of Mines—50,000 specimens, minerals from Colorado and from around the world, gemstones and precious metals
Idaho Springs	Argo Gold Mill—Historic gold mill, mining museum, Double Eagle Mine
	Edgar Experimental Mine—Tour an experimental mine (silver, gold, lead, copper)
	Phoenix Mine—See a working underground hard-rock mine (gold, silver)
Lake City	Hard Tack Mine—Gold mine tour
Leadville	Matchless Mine—Tour a symbol of the financial hazards of silver mining
	National Mining Hall of Fame and Museum—Story of the American mining industry from coal to gold
Ouray	Bachelor-Syracuse Mine Tour—Underground tour of gold and silver mine
	Ouray County Historical Society—Mineral and mining displays
Salida	Lost Mine Tour—Tour a closed manganese mine
Silverton	Mayflower Gold Mill—Tour a gold mill
	Old Hundred Gold Mine Tour, Inc.—Gold mine tour
	San Juan County Historical Society Museum—Minerals and gems from the Silverton area
Victor	Mine View—View of Colorado's largest open-pit gold mine

CONNECTICUT

Fee Dig Mines and Guide Services

Brookfield   Mother Earth Gallery and Mining Company—Hunt for minerals in a re-created mine, children's activity

Hartford   The Children's Museum—Sluice for gems, educational activity

Oakdale   The Dinosaur Place™ at Natures Art—Dig through gem dirt in a candlelit "silver mine," pan for gold, children's activities

Oneco   River Bend Campground—Hunt for gems in a re-created mine, children's activity

Roxbury   Green's Farm Garnet Mine—Search for garnets

Museums and Mine Tours

East Granby   Old New-Gate Prison and Copper Mine—Tour an old copper mine

Greenwich   Bruce Museum—Exhibits of minerals and rocks

Kent   Conn. Museum of Mining and Mineral Science—Local minerals

New Haven   Yale Peabody Museum of Natural History—Minerals of New England and the world

Special Events

Conn. DEP Educational Mineral Collecting—3 sites

DELAWARE

Fee Dig Mines and Guide Services

Wilmington   Woodlawn Quarry—Look through tailing piles for feldspar, quartz, mica, garnet, beryl

Museums and Mine Tours

Georgetown   Delaware Technical and Community College, Stephen J. Betze Library, Treasures of the Sea Exhibit—Jewels recovered from Spanish galleon Atocha

Newark   Iron Hill Museum—Natural history of Delaware, rock and mineral collections

University of Delaware, Mineralogical Museum—10,000 specimens (450 on display), crystals, gems, minerals

Special Events

Delaware Geological Survey—Geo Adventures

DISTRICT OF COLUMBIA

Fee Dig Mines and Guide Services
      None

Museums and Mine Tours
      Smithsonian Institution, National Museum of Natural History—Gems and minerals (over 375,000 specimens and a research collection)

FLORIDA

Fee Dig Mines and Guide Services

Ft. Drum   Ft. Drum Crystal Mine—Collect calcite encrusted fossil shells, micropyrite, iridescent marcasite

Museums and Mine Tours

Deland   Gillespie Museum, Stetson University—Minerals, gemstones, faceting equipment, replica mine, and a cave

Mulberry   Mulberry Phosphate Museum—Exhibits on the phosphate industry, dig for phosphate pebbles

Tampa   Ed and Bernadette Marcin Museum, University of Florida—Minerals and gemstones, mainly from Florida and the western U.S.

GEORGIA

Fee Dig Mines and Guide Services

Cleveland   Gold'n Gem Grubbin—Dig and pan for gold, sapphires, rubies, emeralds, amethyst, topaz

Dahlonega   Consolidated Gold Mines—Gold panning, gem sluicing
                    Crisson Gold Mine—Pan gold ore or enriched gemstone ore

Gainesville   Chattahoochee-Oconee National Forest—Gold panning, rockhounding (restrictions apply)

LaGrange   Hogg Mine—Collect star rose quartz, aquamarine, beryl, black tourmaline

Lincolnton   Graves Mountain—Search for lazulite, pyrophyllite, kyanite, hematite, pyrite, ilmenite, muscovite, fuchsite, barite, sulfur, blue quartz, quartz crystals, and microcrystals such as woodhouseite, variscite, strengite, phosphosiderite, cacoxenite, crandallite (collecting allowed on special dates only)

Tignall   Dixie Euhedrals—Hunt for amethyst crystals

Jacksons Crossroads Amethyst Mine—Hunt for amethyst crystals, druse quartz

Museums and Mine Tours

Atlanta   Fernbank Museum of Natural History—Joachim Gem Collection, mineral cave

Fernbank Science Center—Meteorite collection, outdoor rock and mineral walk

Cartersville Tellus Science Museum—Weinman Mineral Gallery

Dahlonega   Consolidated Gold Mines—Mine tour

Dahlonega Gold Museum—Tells the story of the Georgia gold rush

Elberton   Elberton Granite Museum & Exhibit—Granite quarry and products

Macon   Museum of Arts and Sciences—Display of gems and minerals

Statesboro   Georgia Southern University Museum—Natural history of Georgia's Coastal Plain

Tallapoosa   West Georgia Museum of Tallapoosa—Small collection of local minerals

Villa Rica   Pine Mountain Gold Museum at Stockmar Park—Story of gold mining in the Villa Rica area

Annual Events

Jasper   Pickens County Marble Festival—First weekend in October

Dahlonega   Gold Rush Days—Third full weekend in October

World Open Gold Panning Championship—Third Saturday in October, at the same time as Gold Rush Days

HAWAII

Fee Dig Mines and Guide Services
None

Museums and Mine Tours
Hawaii

National Park Thomas A. Jaggar Museum—Museum on vulcanology and seismology, tour of volcano

Hilo   Lyman Museum—Rocks, minerals, gems

IDAHO

Fee Dig Mines and Guide Services
Spencer   Spencer Opal Mines—Pick through a stockpile for opal

St. Maries   Emerald Creek Garnet Area—Screen for star garnets

Museums and Mine Tours

Boise	Museum of Mining and Geology—Exhibits on mining and geology
Caldwell	The Glen L. and Ruth M. Evans Gem and Mineral Collection, Orma J. Smith Museum of Natural History—Extensive collection of minerals, agate, jasper, other gemstones, 2,000 cabochons
Challis	Land of the Yankee Fork State Park—Museum exhibits, gold panning station
Cottonwood	The Historical Museum at St. Gertrude—Displays of gems and minerals from Idaho and around the world
Kellogg	Crystal Gold Mine—Mine tour
	Staff House Museum—Rocks, minerals, mining equipment
Pocatello	Idaho Museum of Natural History—Displays of specimens from Idaho and the Intermountain West
Wallace	Sierra Silver Mine Tour—Mine tour
	Wallace District Mining Museum—Story of mining in Northern Idaho

ILLINOIS

Fee Dig Mines and Guide Services

Hamilton	Jacobs Geodes—Hunt for geodes containing calcite, barite, quartz, kaolinite
	Nick's Geodes (aka Evans Property)—Dig for geodes
	Dennis Stevenson Geodes—Dig for geodes
Rosiclare	American Fluorite Museum—Dig for fluorite in mine ore

Museums and Mine Tours

Carbondale	University Museum—Over 26,000 geological specimens
Chicago	The Field Museum—Grainger Hall of Gems
	Museum of Science and Industry—Simulated coal mine
Elmhurst	Lizzadro Museum of Lapidary Art—1,300 pieces of cut and polished gems, fluorescent rocks, a birthstone display
Rockford	Burpee Museum of Natural History—Displays of rocks, minerals, and gems
Rock Island	Augustana Fryxell Geology Museum—Rock and mineral museum
Rosiclare	The American Fluorite Museum—Story of fluorospar industry
Shirley	The Funk Gem and Mineral Museum—Gem and mineral collection, petrified wood
Springfield	Illinois State Museum—Illinois specimens, rock collections, copper

Annual Events

Hamilton   Geode Fest—Last weekend in September

INDIANA

Fee Dig Mines and Guide Services

Knightstown   Yogi Bear's Jellystone Park Camping Resort—Midwestern gold
                    prospecting

Museums and Mine Tours

Bedford   Land of Limestone Exhibit—History of Indiana limestone industry

                    Lawrence County Museum of History—Exhibits on limestone, geo-
                    logical specimens from Lawrence County.

Fort Wayne   Indiana Purdue University Fort Wayne—Hallway displays of miner-
                    als, meteorites, and rocks

Indianapolis   Indiana State Museum—Indiana and regional minerals

Richmond   Joseph Moore Museum of Natural History, Earlham College—Geol-
                    ogy exhibit from local Ordovician limestone

IOWA

Fee Dig Mines and Guide Services

                    (See annual event—Geode Fest)

Museums and Mine Tours

Danville   Geode State Park—Display of geodes

Iowa City   University of Iowa—Displays on state geology

Sioux City   Sioux City Public Museum—Mineralogy exhibit

Waterloo   Grout Museum of History and Science—Displays of rocks and min-
                    erals

West Bend   Grotto of the Redemption—Grotto made of precious stones and
                    gems

Winterset   Madison County Historical Society—Rock and mineral collection

Annual Events

Keokuk   Geode Fest—Three-day weekend in September or October; field
                    trips for geodes

Keokuk   Holiday Inn Express—Display of Brevard Collection of Keokuk geo-
                    des found in the tri-state area

KANSAS

Fee Dig Mines and Guide Services
          None

Museums and Mine Tours
Ashland   Pioneer-Krier Museum—Mineral and gem exhibit
Emporia   Johnston Geology Museum—Tri-state mining display, geological specimens from Kansas
Galena   Galena Mining and Historical Museum—Focus on local lead mining and smelting industry
Greensburg Brenham Pallasite Meteorite at the Greensburg Chamber of Commerce—1,000-pound meteorite on display
Hays   Sternberg Museum of Natural History—Displays of gems and minerals
Hutchinson Kansas Underground Salt Mine Museum—Explains the underground mining of rock salt
McPherson   McPherson Museum—Meteorites, rocks, and minerals

KENTUCKY

Fee Dig Mines and Guide Services
Marion   The Ben E. Clement Mineral Museum—Fluorite and fluorescent mineral collecting

Museums and Mine Tours
Benham   Kentucky Coal Mine Museum—Displays on coal mining and formation of coal
Covington   Behringer-Crawford Museum—Periodic displays of gems and minerals
Lexington   Headley-Whitney Museum—Jewelry and mounted semi-precious stones
Lynch   Lynch Portal #31 Mine Tour—Mine tour
Marion   The Ben E. Clement Mineral Museum—Display of gems, minerals, mining artifacts
Olive Hill Northeastern Kentucky Museum—Displays of gems and minerals

LOUISIANA

Fee Dig Mines and Guide Services
          None

Museums and Mine Tours
Shreveport   Louisiana State Exhibit Museum—Displays on mining and salt domes

MAINE

Fee Dig Mines and Guide Services
Auburn   Mt. Apatite Quarry—Hunt for apatite, tourmaline, and quartz

Mt. Apatite Farm/Hatch Ledge—Hunt for tourmaline, garnet, graphic granite, clevelandite, autenite, mica, beryl, and more

Bethel   Maine Mineralogy Expeditions—Collect albite, almandine garnet, beryl, rose and other quartz, black tourmaline, biotite, autunite, zircon, and many others

Songo Pond Mine—Collect tourmaline and other Maine gems and minerals

Poland   Poland Mining Camps—Collect tourmaline and other Maine gems and minerals

West Paris   Perham's of West Paris—Collect tourmaline and other Maine gems and minerals

Woodstock   Maine Mineral Adventures—Screen mine material or go on a field trip to search for gems and minerals

Museums and Mine Tours
Augusta   Maine State Museum—Gems and minerals of Maine

Bethel   Maine Mineral Museum/Mt. Mann Jeweler's Gallery—Examples of gems from local and worldwide sources, crystal cave for kids

Caribou   Nylander Museum of Natural History—Minerals of Maine, lithic artifacts

Presque Isle   Northern Maine Museum of Science—Rotating displays of Maine minerals, fluorescent minerals, Maine slate

Annual Events
Augusta   Maine Mineral Symposium—Second full weekend in May

Poland   Maine Pegmatite Workshop—Week-long program at the end of May or beginning of June

MARYLAND

Fee Dig Mines and Guide Services
None

Museums and Mine Tours

Hancock   Hancock-Sideling Hill Museum—Exhibit on road cut geology

Potomac   Great Falls Geological Visitor's Center—Gold Mine Trail tours scheduled periodically

MASSACHUSETTS

Fee Dig Mines and Guide Services
>None

Museums and Mine Tours

Cambridge   Harvard Museum of Natural History—Gems, minerals, ores, meteorites

Gloucester   Cape Ann Historical Museum—Exhibits of local granite and the granite industry

Quincy   Quincy Historical Society Museum—Exhibits on granite industry in Quincy

Springfield   Springfield Science Museum—Minerals from around the world

MICHIGAN

Fee Dig Mines and Guide Services

Grand Marais   Woodland Park Campground—Search beaches for agates

Mohawk   Delaware Copper Mine—Search for souvenir copper

Ontonagon   Caledonia Copper Mine—Collect copper specimens, silver, epidote, calcite, datolite, quartz

Petoskey   Petoskey State Park—Hunt for Petoskey Stones

Museums and Mine Tours

Ann Arbor   Exhibit Museum of Natural History, University of Michigan—Exhibits of rocks and minerals

Battle Creek   Kingman Museum—Gem and mineral display

Bloomfield Hills   Cranbrook Institute of Science—5,000 minerals and crystals from around the world (including hiddenite, gold)

Calumet   Coppertown, U.S.A.—Exhibits on copper mining

Caspian   Iron County Museum and Park—Iron mining complex

Chelsea   Gerald E. Eddy Discovery Center—Michigan rocks, minerals, crystals, and mining

Copper Harbor	Fort Wilkins Historic State Park—History of copper mining in the area
Grand Marais	Gitche Gumee Agate and History Museum—Displays of agates, beach rocks, crystals, fluorescent rocks, historical displays on iron and copper mining
Greenland	Adventure Copper Mine—Tour underground copper mine
Hancock	The Quincy Mine Hoist Association—Tour an underground copper mine
Houghton	The A. E. Seaman Mineral Museum—Crystal collection, minerals from the Lake Superior copper district
Iron Mountain	Iron Mountain Iron Mine—Iron mine tour
	Iron Mining Museum and Gift Shop, Cornish Pumping Engine—Display of underground mining equipment
Ishpeming	Cliffs Shaft Mine Museum—Take guided tour of an iron mine, displays of rocks, gems and minerals
Lake Linden	Houghton County Historical Museum—Copper mining and refining equipment displays
Mohawk	Delaware Copper Mine—Mine tour
Mt. Pleasant	The Museum of Cultural and Natural History, Central Michigan University—Michigan rocks and minerals
Negaunee	Michigan Iron Industry Museum—Story of Michigan iron industry
Republic	Republic Iron Mine—Mine view
Shelby	Shelby Man-Made Gemstones—Visit a gemstone factory
South Range	The Copper Range Historical Museum—Exhibits on miners' lives and families

Annual Events

Eastport	Antrim County Petoskey Stone Festival—One day during early summer
Houghton	Copper Country Mineral Retreat—One week in August, sponsored by the A. E. Seaman Museum of Michigan Tech

MINNESOTA

Fee Dig Mines and Guide Services

Moose Lake	Moose Lake Chamber of Commerce—Hunt for Agates

Museums and Mine Tours

Calumet	Hill Annex Mine State Park—Tour an open-pit iron mine
Chisholm	Minnesota Discovery Center—Tour and mining displays
	The Minnesota Museum of Mining—Indoor and outdoor exhibits

	Taconite Mine Tours—Iron industry taconite mining tours
Hibbing	Hull-Rust Mahoning Mine—Observe an open-pit iron mine
Moose Lake	Minnesota Agate and Geological Interpretive Center—Showcases Minnesota's gemstone, the Lake Superior Agate
Pipestone	Pipestone National Monument—Tour a Native American pipestone quarry
Soudan	Soudan Underground Mine State Park—Tour an underground iron mine
Virginia	Mineview in the Sky—View an open-pit iron ore mine
	Iron Range Tourism Bureau—Information on mine view sites

Annual Events

Moose Lake	Agate Days—One weekend in July

MISSISSIPPI

Fee Dig Mines and Guide Services

None

Museums and Mine Tours

Starkville	Dunn-Seiler Museum—Mineral and rock collections

MISSOURI

Fee Dig Mines and Guide Services

Alexandria	Sheffler Rock Shop—Dig geodes lined with crystals
St Francisville	Hill Top Mud Bogg—Dig for geodes

Museums and Mine Tours

Golden	Golden Pioneer Museum—Large mineral exhibit
Joplin	Everett J. Richie Tri-State Mineral Museum—Story of area's lead and zinc mining
Kansas City	University of Missouri–Kansas City, Geosciences Museum—Local and regional specimens
Park Hills	Missouri Mines State Historic Site—1,100 specimens of minerals, ores, and rocks
Point Lookout	Ralph Foster Museum, College of the Ozarks—Area minerals, mineral spheres and fluorescent minerals
Rolla	Mineral Museum, Missouri University of Science and Technology— 3,500 specimens of minerals, ores, and rocks from 92 countries and 47 states

MONTANA

Fee Dig Mines and Guide Services

Alder Red Rock Mine and Garnet Gallery—Screen for garnets and corundum (some star)

Dillon Crystal Park Recreational Mineral Collecting Area—Dig for quartz and amethyst crystal

Hamilton Sapphire Studio—Purchase and wash bags of ore for sapphires

Helena Spokane Bar Sapphire Mine and Gold Fever Rock Shop—Dig and screen for sapphires and other gems and minerals

Libby Libby Creek Recreational Gold Panning Area—Pan for gold

Philipsburg Gem Mountain—Search for sapphires

Sapphire Gallery—Wash bags of gravel to look for sapphires

Museums and Mine Tours

Butte Anselmo Mine Yard—Tour of mining facilities and history of area mining

The Berkeley Pit—Observation point for closed open-pit copper mine

Butte-Silver Bow Visitor and Transportation Center—Presents information on area geology and its mining, including local gold and silver mining

Mineral Museum, Montana Tech of the University of Montana—Gold, fluorescent minerals, and minerals from Butte and MT

World Museum of Mining—Tour of underground mine

Ekalaka Carter County Museum—Fluorescent mineral display

Lewistown Central Montana Museum—Rocks, minerals, and Yogo sapphires

Philipsburg Granite County Museum and Cultural Center—Tells story of mining community and has a replica of an underground mine

NEBRASKA

Fee Dig Mines and Guide Services

None

Museums and Mine Tours

Chadron Eleanor Barbour Cook Museum of Geology—Displays of rocks and minerals

Crawford Trailside Museum of Natural History—Displays of western Nebraska geology

| Hastings | Hastings Museum of Natural and Cultural History—Minerals, rocks, fluorescent minerals, and translucent slabs |
| Lincoln | University of Nebraska State Museum—Displays of rocks, minerals, and fluorescent minerals |

Annual Events
| Crawford | Crawford Rock Swap—Labor Day weekend |

NEVADA

Fee Dig Mines and Guide Services
Denio	Bonanza Opal Mines, Inc.—Dig crystal, white and black fire opal
	Rainbow Ridge Opal Mine—Tailings digging for wood opal
	Royal Peacock Opal Mine, Inc.—Dig black and fire opal
Ely	Garnet Fields Rockhound Area—Hunt for almandine garnets
Reno	High Desert Gems and Minerals—Gem mine collecting tours
Tonopah	Otteson's Turquoise—Dig in mine tailings for turquoise

Museums and Mine Tours
Las Vegas	Nevada State Museum and Historical Society—Natural history of Nevada
Nelson	Eldorado Canyon Mine Tours, Inc.—Hard-rock gold mine tour
Reno	W. M. Keck Earth Science and Mineral Engineering Museum—Collection of minerals and ores
Virginia City	Chollar Mine—Underground mine tour (gold and silver)

NEW HAMPSHIRE

Fee Dig Mines and Guide Services
Conway	White Mountain National Forest—Collect gems and minerals
Grafton	Ruggles Mine—Collect up to 150 different minerals
Rumney	Polar Caves Park—Hunt for gems and minerals in a re-created mine or sluice for gems and minerals, children's activity

Museums and Mine Tours
| Contoocook | The Little Nature Museum—Rocks, minerals, and ores |
| Dover | The Woodman Institute—1,500 specimens including local rocks |

NEW JERSEY

Fee Dig Mines and Guide Services
| Cape May | Cape May Welcome Center—Hunt for Cape May "diamonds" |

Franklin	Franklin Mineral Museum and Buckwheat Dump—Tailings diggings for fluorescent minerals and franklinite
Ogdensburg	Sterling Hill Mining Museum—Collect fluorescent minerals

Museums and Mine Tours

Franklin	Franklin Mineral Museum—Minerals and rocks from local and world-wide sources, fluorescent room
Monroe Township	Displayworld's Stone Museum—Minerals, hands-on exhibits
Morristown	The Morris Museum—Specimens from five continents
New Brunswick	Rutgers Geology Museum—Minerals and geologic specimens that emphasize the geology of New Jersey and surrounding states
Ogdensburg	Sterling Hill Mining Museum—Underground mine tour
Paterson	The Paterson Museum—Specimens from local basalt flows and basalt flow in the Poona region of India, minerals from NJ and around the world
Rutherford	Meadowlands Museum—Fluorescent minerals, quartz, minerals from NJ
Trenton	New Jersey State Museum—Minerals and rocks, including fluorescents and magnetite ore

NEW MEXICO

Fee Dig Mines and Guide Services

Bingham	Blanchard Rock Shop—Collect over 84 different kinds of minerals in a former lead mine
Deming	Rockhound State Park—Collect a variety of semiprecious stones
Dixon	Harding Mine—Look for over 50 minerals
Gila	Casitas de Gila Guesthouses—Rockhound on 60 acres when lodging in the Guesthouses. Some of the minerals found are white and pink chalcedony, chalcedony roses, red, brown, and yellow jasper, jasper breccia, picture jasper, banded agate, zeolites, geodes, massive hematite, banded rhyolite, andesite, volcanic bombs, scoria, limonite and hematite-banded welded tuff. Pan for gold in the creek.

Museums and Mine Tours

Albuquerque	Geology Museum, University of New Mexico—Displays of New Mexico minerals and geology
	Institute of Meteoritics, University of New Mexico—Meteorites
	New Mexico Museum of Natural History and Science—3,400 specimens with a focus on New Mexico and the southwestern U.S.

The Turquoise Museum—Displays of turquoise
Grants   New Mexico Mining Museum—Uranium mining
Portales   Miles Mineral Museum—Displays of minerals, gems, and meteorites
Socorro   Mineralogical Museum, New Mexico Tech—15,000 specimens of minerals from New Mexico, the U.S., and the world

Annual Events
Socorro   New Mexico Mineral Symposium—Two days in November

NEW YORK

Fee Dig Mines and Guide Services
Herkimer   Herkimer Diamond Mines and KOA Kampground Corporate Office—Dig for "Herkimer diamonds" quartz crystals
Middleville Ace of Diamonds Mine and Campground—Prospect for Herkimer "diamonds," calcite crystals, and dolomite crystals
North River The Barton Mines—Hunt for garnets
St. Johnsville Crystal Grove Diamond Mine and Campground—Dig for Herkimer "diamonds"

Museums and Mine Tours
Albany   New York State Museum—Minerals of New York
Hicksville   The Hicksville Gregory Museum—10,000 specimens from the major mineral groups, also NJ zeolites, Herkimer "diamonds," fluorescent minerals
New York City American Museum of Natural History—Gems, meteorites, emphasis on exceptional specimens from the U.S.
Olean   Rock City Park—Museum with fluorescent mineral room
Pawling   The Gunnison Natural History Museum—Minerals

NORTH CAROLINA

Fee Dig Mines and Guide Services
Almond   Nantahala Gorge Ruby Mine—Sluice for rubies, sapphires, amethyst, topaz, garnet, citrine, smoky quartz, emeralds
Boone   Foggy Mountain Gem Mine—Screen for topaz, garnet, aquamarine, peridot, ruby, star sapphire, amethyst, citrine, smoky quartz, tourmaline, emerald
Canton   Old Pressley Sapphire Mine—Sluice for sapphires, zircon, garnet, mica
Cherokee   Smoky Mountain Gold & Ruby Mine—Sluice for gold and gems

Chimney Rock	Chimney Rock Gemstone Mine—Screen for aquamarine, emerald, ruby, peridot, garnet, quartz, agate, hematite, amethyst, sodalite, and more
Franklin	Cherokee Ruby and Sapphire mine—Sluice for rubies, sapphires, sillimanite, rutile, moonstone, rhodolite garnet, pyrope garnet
	Cowee Mountain Ruby Mine—Sluice for rubies, sapphires, garnets, tourmaline, smoky quartz, amethyst, citrine, moonstone, topaz
	Gold City Gem Mine—Sluice for rubies, sapphires, garnets, emeralds, tourmaline, smoky quartz, amethyst, citrine, moonstone, topaz, aquamarine, gold
	Cowee Gift Shop and Mason Mountain Mine, aka TJRocks—Sluice for rhodolite garnets, rubies, sapphires, kyanite, crystal quartz, smoky quartz, moonstones
	Mason's Ruby and Sapphire Mine—Dig and sluice for sapphires (all colors), pink and red rubies
	Rose Creek Mine and Rock Shop—Sluice for rubies, sapphires, garnets, moonstones, amethysts, smoky quartz, citrine, rose quartz, topaz, emerald
	Sheffield Mine—Sluice for native rubies and sapphires, or enriched material from around the world
Hendersonville	Elijah Mountain Gem Mine—Pan for a variety of gems and minerals
Hiddenite	Emerald Hollow Mine–Hiddenite Gems, Inc.—Sluice for rutile, sapphires, garnets, hiddenite, smoky quartz, tourmaline, clear quartz, aquamarine, sillimanite, and others
Highlands	Jackson Hole Gem Mine—Sluice for rubies, sapphires, garnets, tourmaline, smoky quartz, amethyst, citrine, moonstone, topaz
High Point	Kersey Valley Gem Dig—Educational family activity
Jamestown	Castle McCulloch Gold and Gem Panning—Pan for gold, emeralds, rubies, crystals, amethyst
Leicester	Randall Glen Gem Mine—Pan for a variety of gems and gold
Little Switzerland	Emerald Village—Sluice for 45 different rocks, minerals, and gems
Marion	Carolina Emerald Mine and Vein Mountain Gold Camp—Mine for gold, emerald, aquamarine, moonstone, feldspar crystals, garnets, smoky, rose, blue, and clear quartz, tourmaline
	The Lucky Strike—Sluice for gems and pan for gold
Marshall	Little Pine Garnet Mine—Dig for garnets; can take a horseback ride to the mine
Micaville	Rock Mine Tours—Dig for aquamarine, feldspar, garnets, olivine, moonstone, pink thulite, tourmaline (schorl), mica, and more
Midland	Reed Gold Mine State Historic Site—Gold panning

New London	Cotton Patch Gold Mine—Gold panning
	Mountain Creek Gold Mine—Gold panning
Spruce Pine	Gem Mountain Gemstone Mine—Sluice for sapphires, crabtree emeralds, rubies, Brushy Creek and Wiseman aquamarine, and more
	Rio Doce Gem Mine—Sluice for emeralds, rubies, aquamarine, tourmaline, topaz, garnets, amethysts, citrine, beryl, rose, clear, rutilated, and smoky quartz
	Spruce Pine Gem Mine—Sluice for local gems such as sapphires, emeralds, rubies, aquamarine, garnets, amethyst, moonstone, smoky quartz, crystal quartz
Union Mills	Thermal City Gold Mine—Gold and gemstone panning

Museums and Mine Tours

Asheville	Colburn Earth Science Museum—Collection of mineral specimens from NC and the world
Aurora	Aurora Fossil Museum—Geology of the NC Coastal Plain
Franklin	Franklin Gem and Mineral Museum—Specimens from NC and around the world
	Ruby City Gems and Minerals—Specimens from NC and around the world
Gastonia	Schiele Museum—North Carolina gems and minerals
Greensboro	Natural Science Center of Greensboro—Mineral specimens from NC
Hendersonville	Mineral and Lapidary Museum of Henderson County, Inc.—Minerals and lapidary arts
Jamestown	Castle McCulloch—Museum, gold mill tour
Linville	Grandfather Mountain Nature Museum—Specimens from NC
Little Switzerland	North Carolina Mining Museum and Mine Tour—Tour a closed feldspar mine
Midland	Reed Gold Mine State Historic Site—Gold mine tour
Spruce Pine	Museum of North Carolina Minerals—Specimens primarily from local mines

Annual Events

Franklin	Mother's Day Gemboree—Mother's Day weekend in May
	Macon County Gemboree—4 days in July
	"Leaf Looker" Gemboree—3 days in October
Spruce Pine	NC Mineral and Gem Festival—Four days at the end of July/beginning of August

NORTH DAKOTA

Fee Dig Mines and Guide Services
      None

Museums and Mine Tours
Beulah, Center,
Underwood   Tours at several area lignite strip mines
Dickinson   Dakota Dinosaur Museum—Displays of rocks and minerals including borax from CA, turquoise from AZ, fluorescent minerals, aurora crystals from AR
Parshall   Paul Broste Rock Museum—Displays of rocks from the area and around the world

OHIO

Fee Dig Mines and Guide Services
Hopewell   Hidden Springs Ranch—Dig for flint (groups only)
            Nethers Flint—Dig for flint

Museums and Mine Tours
Cadiz   History of Coal Museum—Look at history of coal mining to present
Cleveland   The Cleveland Museum of Natural History—The Wade Gallery of Gems and Minerals has over 1,500 gems and minerals
Columbus   Orton Geological Museum—Rocks and minerals from OH and the world
Dayton   Boonshoft Museum of Discovery—Minerals and crystals
Glenford   Flint Ridge State Memorial—Ancient flint quarrying
Lima   Allen County Museum—Rock and mineral exhibit

Annual Events
Glenford   Flint Ridge Knap-In—Learn how prehistoric Native Americans worked flint

OKLAHOMA

Fee Dig Mines and Guide Services
Kenton   Black Mesa Bed & Breakfast—Rockhounding on a working cattle ranch

Museums and Mine Tours
Coalgate   Coal County Mining and Historical Museum—Mining museum

Enid	The Midgley Museum—Rock and mineral collection predominantly from OK and the TX shoreline
Noble	Timberlake Rose Rock Museum—Displays of barite roses
Tulsa	Elsing Museum—Gems and minerals

OREGON

Fee Dig Mines and Guide Services

Federal lands	Baker City, Halfway Jacksonville, Medford, Salem, Unity—Pan for gold
Klamath Falls	Juniper Ridge Opal Mine—Hunt for fire opal
Madras	Richardson's Rock Ranch—Dig for thundereggs, agate
Mitchell	Lucky Strike Geodes—Dig for thundereggs (picture jasper)
Plush	Dust Devil Mining Co.—Dig for sunstones
	Double Eagle Mining Company—Dig for sunstones
	Spectrum Sunstone Mines—Dig for sunstones
Roseburg	Cow Creek Recreational Gold Panning Area—Pan for gold
Sweet Home	Holleywood Ranch—Collect petrified wood
Yachats	City of Yachats—Beachcombing for agates and jaspers

Museums and Mine Tours

Baker City	Branch of US Bank—Gold display, including Armstrong nugget
Central Point	Crater Rock Museum—Displays of minerals, thundereggs, fossils, geodes, cut and polished gemstones
Corvallis	Oregon State University Dept. of Earth, Ocean and Atmospheric Sciences—Mineral displays
Cottage Grove	Bohemia Gold Mining Museum—Memorial to gold mining era of the Bohemia District
Hillsboro	Rice Northwest Museum of Rocks and Minerals—Displays of minerals and crystals
Redmond	Petersen's Rock Garden—Unusual rock garden, fluorescent display
Sumpter	Sumpter Valley Dredge State Heritage Area—View a gold dredge, tour historic gold mine towns

Annual Events

Cottage Grove	Bohemia Mining Days—Four days in July, gold panning and exposition
Nyssa	Thunderegg Days—Mid-July
Prineville	Rockhound Pow-Wow—Mid-June

PENNSYLVANIA

Fee Dig Mines and Guide Services
Spring Grove   Jones Geological Services—Guide services for mineral collecting

Museums and Mine Tours
Ashland   Pioneer Tunnel Coal Mine—Tour an anthracite coal mine
Bryn Mawr   Museum, Department of Geology, Bryn Mawr College—Rotating display of 1,500 minerals from a collection of 23,500 specimens
Cornwall   Cornwall Iron Furnace—Displays of iron ore mining and iron production
Elysburg   Knoebels Amusement Resort, Anthracite Mining Museum—Early mining artifacts
Harrisburg   State Museum of Pennsylvania—Practical applications of geology
Hellertown   The Gilman Museum/Lost River Caverns—Display of minerals and gems, cavern tour
Lancaster   North Museum of Natural History and Science—Extensive geology collection
Lansford   No. 9 Mine and Museum—Coal mine tour
Media   Delaware County Institute of Science—Minerals from around the world
Patton   Seldom Seen Mine—Tour a bituminous coal mine
Philadelphia   Academy of Natural Sciences—Mineral collection for research only
                   Wagner Free Institute of Science—Rocks and minerals
Pittsburgh   Carnegie Museum of Natural History—One of the premier gem and mineral exhibits in the country
Scranton   Anthracite Museum Complex—Several anthracite coal-related attractions, including a mine tour and a museum
                   Everhart Museum of Natural History, Science, and Art—Displays of rocks and minerals
State College Earth and Mineral Sciences Museum and Art Gallery—Displays of minerals, mining equipment, scientific instruments
Tarentum   Tour-Ed Mine—Bituminous coal mine tour
Uniontown   Coal & Coke Heritage Center—Connellsville Coke Region
Waynesburg   Paul R. Stewart Museum, Waynesburg University—Outstanding mineral collection
West Chester   Geology Museum, West Chester University—Specimens from Chester County, fluorescent specimens
Wilkes-Barre   Luzerne County Historical Society—Display on anthracite coal mining

Windber   Windber Coal Heritage Center—Exhibits present the heritage of coal mining

RHODE ISLAND

Fee Dig Mines and Guide Services
        None

Museums and Mine Tours
Providence   Museum of Natural History and Planetarium—Collections of rocks and minerals

SOUTH CAROLINA

Fee Dig Mines and Guide Services
Antreville   Diamond Hill—Dig your own quartz
Greenville   Greenville Gemstone Mine—Sluice for gems and minerals from around the world

Museums and Mine Tours
Charleston   The Charleston Museum—Small display of gems and minerals
Clemson   Bob Campbell Geology Museum—Rocks, minerals, lapidary objects
Columbia   McKissick Museum, University of South Carolina campus—Exhibits on geology and gemstones
                 South Carolina State Museum—Displays of gems and minerals

SOUTH DAKOTA

Fee Dig Mines and Guide Services
Deadwood   Broken Boot Gold Mine—Pan for gold
Hill City   Wade's Gold Mill—Pan for gold
Keystone   Big Thunder Gold Mine—Pan for gold
Lead   Black Hills Mining Museum—Pan for gold
Wall   Buffalo Gap National Grassland—Hunt for agates

Museums and Mine Tours
Deadwood   Broken Boot Gold Mine—Gold mine tour
Hill City   Wade's Gold Mill—Guided tour and displays of mining equipment
Keystone   Big Thunder Gold Mine—Mine tour
Lead   Black Hills Mining Museum—Simulated underground mine tour
                 Homestake Visitor Center—Gold mining displays

Murdo	National Rockhound and Lapidary Hall of Fame—Gems and minerals
Rapid City	Journey Museum—Geology of the Black Hills
	South Dakota School of Mines and Technology—Local minerals

TENNESSEE

Fee Dig Mines and Guide Services

| **Ducktown** | Burra Burra Mine—Collection area on site; look for garnets, pyrite, chalcopyrite, pyrrhotite, actinolite |

Museums and Mine Tours

Ducktown	Ducktown Basin Museum—Copper mining heritage
Johnson City	Hands On! Regional Museum—Simulated coal mine
Knoxville	The Frank H. McClung Museum—Geology of Tennessee
Memphis	Memphis Pink Palace Museum—Geology and minerals from famous mid-South localities
Murfreesboro	Mineral, Gem, and Fossil Museum, Middle Tennessee State University—Minerals from every state, birthstones, fluorescent minerals

TEXAS

Fee Dig Mines and Guide Services

Alpine	Stillwell Ranch—Hunt for agate and jasper
	Woodward Ranch—Hunt for agate, labradorite, and others
Mason	Lindsay Ranch Guesthouses—Hunt for topaz and other minerals
	Seaquist Ranch—Hunt for topaz
Three Rivers	House's Mother Lode Ranch—Hunt for agate and petrified wood

Museums and Mine Tours

Alpine	Last Frontier Museum and Antelope Lodge—Display of rocks from West Texas
Austin	Texas Memorial Museum—Gems and minerals
Canyon	Panhandle-Plains Historical Museum—Gems and minerals from the Texas Panhandle
Fort Davis	Chihuahuan Desert Research Institute—Displays on area mining and minerals
Fort Stockton	Annie Riggs Memorial Museum—Rocks and minerals of Pecos County and the Big Bend area
Fritch	Alibates Flint Quarries—View ancient flint quarries
Houston	Houston Museum of Natural Science—Displays of gem and mineral specimens

Marble Falls	Granite Mountain—View marble mining operations
McKinney	The Heard Natural Science Museum and Wildlife Sanctuary—Rocks and minerals
Odessa	Odessa Meteor Crater—Meteorite crater and museum

UTAH

Fee Dig Mines and Guide Services
Dugway Mountains	Dugway Geode Beds—Dig for geodes
Kanab	Joe's Rock Shop—Dig for septarian nodules
Moab	Deep Desert Expeditions—Guided collecting tours, dig through mine tailings for azurite, malachite, geodes

Museums and Mine Tours
Bingham Canyon	Bingham Canyon Mine Visitors' Center—Overlook for open-pit copper mine
Eureka	Tintic Mining Museum—Mineral display and mining artifacts
Helper	Western Mining and Railroad Museum—Mining exhibits, simulated 1900 coal mine
Lehi	John Hutchings Museum of Natural History—Displays linked to mining districts, display of uncut gems
Salt Lake City	Utah Museum of Natural History—Utah ores and minerals

Place of Interest
| Moab | Moab Rock Shop—Information on rockhounding |

VERMONT

Fee Dig Mines and Guide Services
| Ludlow | Camp Plymouth State Park—Gold panning |

Museums and Mine Tours
Barre	Rock of Ages Corporation—Watch granite being quarried
	Vermont Granite Museum and Stone Arts School—Displays on geology, history, art of Vermont's granite heritage. Sculptors from around the world explore stone carving
Norwich	Montshire Museum of Science—Fluorescent minerals
St. Johnsbury	Fairbanks Museum and Planetarium—Display of rocks and minerals from Vermont

Annual Event

Barre   Granite Festival—One Saturday in summer or early fall

VIRGINIA

Fee Dig Mines and Guide Services

Amelia   Ligon Mine—Dig in mine tailings for beryl, amazonite, quartz, topaz, tourmaline and others

Morefield Gem Mine, Inc.—Dig and sluice for quartz, topaz, and many others

McKenney   Lucky Lake Gem and Mineral Mine of Virginia—Sluice for natural minerals and salted material

Stuart   Fairy Stone State Park—Hunt for staurolite crystals (fairy stones)

Museums and Mine Tours

Big Stone Gap   Harry W. Meador, Jr., Coal Museum—Exhibits and mining equipment

Blacksburg   Virginia Tech Geosciences Museum—Large display of Virginia minerals

Breaks   Breaks Interstate Park—Overlook and museum, explains geological features and science behind local coal industry

Goldvein   The Gold Mining Camp Museum, Monroe Park—Tour a mine camp, gold panning demonstrations

Harrisonburg   The James Madison University Mineral Museum—Minerals, gems, specimens from Virginia

Martinsville   Stone Cross Mountain Museum—A museum of staurolite crystals

Virginia Museum of Natural History—Rocks and minerals

Pocahontas   Pocahontas Exhibition Coal Mine and Museum—Coal mine tour

Richmond   University of Richmond Museums—Displays Virginia minerals and a 2,400-carat blue topaz

WASHINGTON

Fee Dig Mines and Guide Services

Ravensdale   Geology Adventures, Inc.—Field trips; collect quartz, garnets, and others

Museums and Mine Tours

Castle Rock   Mount St. Helens National Volcanic Monument—Focus on geology

Cle Elum   Coal Mines Trail—Historical walk through mining history

Ellensburg	Kittitas County Historical Museum—Polished rocks
Pullman	Washington State University—Petrified wood, minerals
Seattle	Burke Museum of Natural History and Culture—Rocks, minerals, the geology of Washington, and a walk-through volcano
	Klondike Gold Rush National Historical Park—Commemorates gold rush

WEST VIRGINIA

Fee Dig Mines and Guide Services
| Shady Spring | Someplace Special Gem Mine—Dig, screen, sluice and metal detect for various gems and gold |

Museums and Mine Tours
Beckley	The Beckley Exhibition Coal Mine—Tour a bituminous coal mine
Charleston	The Avampato Discovery Museum at the Clay Center—Exhibits show the story behind West Virginia's geology
Morgantown	Museum of Geology and Natural History; W. V. Geological and Economic Survey—Geology of West Virginia

WISCONSIN

Fee Dig Mines and Guide Services
| Rhinelander | Chequamegon-Nicolet National Forest—Pan for gold or collect rocks |

Museums and Mine Tours
Dodgeville	The Museum of Minerals and Crystals—Local mineral specimens, specimens from around the world
Hurley	Iron County Historical Museum—History of area mining, last remaining mine head frame in Wisconsin (nearby site)
Madison	Geology Museum, University of Wisconsin at Madison—Minerals, fluorescent minerals, meteorites
Menasha	Weis Earth Science Museum, University of Wisconsin, Fox Valley— Official state mineralogical museum of Wisconsin
Milwaukee	Milwaukee Public Museum—Displays of geological specimens
Platteville	The Mining Museum—Lead and zinc mining in the upper Mississippi Valley
Shullsburg	Badger Mine and Museum—Displays of lead mining equipment, tour a hand-dug mine
Stevens Point	UW–Stevens Point Museum of Natural History—Rock and mineral display

Annual Event

Neenah   Quarry Quest—Kid-oriented collecting activities, held in September and sponsored by many businesses in the local community

WYOMING

Fee Dig Mines and Guide Services

Shell   Trapper Galloway Ranch—Agate for sale

Museums and Mine Tours

Casper   Tate Geological Museum—Rocks and minerals, including Wyoming jade, and fluorescent minerals
Cheyenne   Wyoming State Museum—Minerals of Wyoming, coal "swamp"
Kemmerer   Fossil County Museum—Replica of underground coal mine
Laramie   Geological Museum, University of Wyoming—Rocks and minerals, fluorescent minerals from Wyoming
Rawlins   Rawlins Paint Mines—Geologic feature
Rock Springs Rock Springs Historical Museum—Coal mining exhibits
Saratoga   Saratoga Museum—Minerals from around the world, local geology
Worland   Washakie Museum—Geology of Big Horn Basin

Index by Gems and Minerals

This index lists all the gems and minerals that can be found at fee dig mines in the U.S., and shows the city and state where the mine is located. To use the index, look up the gem or mineral you are interested in, and note the states and cities where they are located. Then go to the state and city to find the name of the mine, and information about the mine.

The following notes provide additional information:

(#)   A number in parentheses is the number of mines in that town that have that gem or mineral.

(*)   Gem or mineral is found in the state, but the mine may also add material to the ore. Check with the individual mine for confirmation.

(FT) Field trip.

(GS) Guide service (location listed is the location of the guide service, not necessarily the location of the gems or minerals being collected).

(I)   Mineral has been identified at the mine site but may be difficult to find.

(M)   Museum that allows collection of one specimen as a souvenir.

(MM) Micromount (a very small crystal, which, when viewed under a microscope or magnifying glass, is found to be a high-quality crystal).

(O)   Available at mine but comes from other mines.

(R)   Can be found, but is rare.

(S)   Not the main gem or mineral for which the site is known.

(SA) "Salted" or enriched gem or mineral.

(U)   Unique to the site.

(Y)   Yearly collecting event.

Actinolite Tennessee: Ducktown

Agate Arkansas: Murfreesboro (S); Michigan: Grand Marais; Minnesota: Moose Lake; Montana: Helena (S); New Mexico: Deming; North Carolina: Chimney Rock; Oklahoma: Kenton (2); Oregon: Madras, Yachats; South Dakota: Wall; Texas: Three Rivers
> **Banded agate** Texas: Alpine; New Mexico: Gila
> **Fire agate** Arizona: Safford (2); California: Palo Verde (2); Nevada: Reno (GS)
> **Iris agate** Texas: Alpine
> **Ledge agate** Oregon: Madras
> **Moss agate** Oregon: Madras, Mitchell; Texas: Alpine (2); Wyoming: Shell
> **Paint rock agate** Alabama: Trenton
> **Polka-dot jasp-agate** Oregon: Madras
> **Pom pom agate** Texas: Alpine
> **Rainbow agate** Oregon: Madras
> **Red plume agate** Texas: Alpine

Albite Maine: Bethel, Poland (GS), West Paris; New Hampshire: Grafton (I); New Mexico: Dixon
> **Albite (cleavelandite var.)** Maine: Poland (GS)

Amazonite Virginia: Amelia (2)

Amber Texas: Mason (R); Washington: Ravensdale (GS)

Amethyst Arkansas: Mt. Ida (SA), Murfreesboro (S); Georgia: Cleveland, Dahlonega, Tignall (2); Maine: Bethel (R), West Paris; Montana: Dillon; Nevada: Reno (GS); New Hampshire: Conway, Grafton (I), Laconia; North Carolina (*): Almond, Boone, Cherokee, Chimney Rock, Franklin (3), Hendersonville, Highlands, Jamestown, Leicester, Spruce Pine (3); South Carolina: Antreville
> **Amethyst scepters** Nevada: Reno (GS)

Amblygonite Maine: West Paris

Amphibolite New Hampshire: Grafton (I)

Andesite New Mexico: Gila

Apatite Maine: Auburn, Bethel, Poland (GS), West Paris; New Hampshire: Grafton; New Mexico: Dixon; West Virginia: Shady Spring (SA)
> **Blue apatite** Maine: Auburn
> **Fluorapatite** Maine: Poland (GS); New Hampshire: Conway, Grafton
> **Hydroxylapatite** Maine: Poland (GS)
> **Purple apatite** Maine: West Paris

Aplite New Hampshire: Grafton (I)

Aquamarine California: Pala; Georgia: LaGrange; Maine: Bethel, Poland (GS), Woodstock; New Hampshire: Grafton (I); North Carolina (*): Boone, Chimney

Rock, Franklin, Hendersonville, Hiddenite, Little Switzerland, Marion, Micaville, Spruce Pine (2) (FT)

Brushy Creek aquamarine North Carolina: Spruce Pine (I) (FT)

Weisman aquamarine North Carolina: Spruce Pine (I) (FT)

Arsenopyrite Maine: Poland (GS)

Augelite Maine: Poland (GS)

Autunite Maine: Auburn, Bethel, Poland (GS); New Hampshire: Grafton (I)

Azurite Utah: Moab (GS)

Aventurine North Carolina: Hendersonville

Barite Arkansas: Murfreesboro (S); Georgia: Lincolnton; New Mexico: Bingham; Washington: Ravensdale (GS)

Benitoite California: Coalinga

Beraumite Maine: Poland (GS)

Bermanite Maine: Poland (GS)

Bertrandite Maine: Poland (GS), West Paris; New Hampshire: Conway, Grafton (I)

Beryl California: Warner Springs; Delaware: Wilmington; Georgia: LaGrange; Maine: Auburn, Bethel, Poland (GS), West Paris; New Hampshire: Grafton (I); New Mexico: Dixon; North Carolina (*): Little Switzerland, Spruce Pine (2); Virginia: Amelia (2)

Aqua beryl New Hampshire: Grafton (I)

Blue beryl (see also aquamarine) New Hampshire: Grafton (I)

Golden beryl Maine: Woodstock; North Carolina: Spruce Pine (FT); New Hampshire: Grafton (I)

Beryllonite Maine: Poland (GS)

Beta-uranophane New Hampshire: Grafton

Biotite Maine: Bethel; New Hampshire: Grafton (I)

Borate California: Boron (Y)

Bornite New Hampshire: Grafton (I)

Brazilianite Maine: Poland (GS)

Brochantite New Mexico: Bingham

Cacoxenite Georgia: Lincolnton

Calcite Arkansas: Murfreesboro (S); Florida: Ft. Drum; Michigan: Ontonagon; New Hampshire: Grafton; New Mexico: Bingham; New York: Middleville; North Carolina: Leicester; Texas: Mason; Virginia: Amelia

Cape May "Diamonds" See Quartz

Cassiterite Maine: Poland (GS); West Paris, Woodstock; Texas: Mason

Chalcedony Arizona: Safford; Nevada: Reno (GS); New Mexico: Deming

Blue Nevada: Reno (GS)

Pink New Mexico: Gila
Chalcedony roses New Mexico: Gila
White New Mexico: Gila

Chalcopyrite Tennessee: Ducktown

Childrenite Maine: Poland (GS)

Chrysoberyl New Hampshire: Grafton (I)

Citrine North Carolina (*): Almond, Boone, Cherokee, Franklin (3), Hendersonville, Highlands, Leicester, Spruce Pine (2); Virginia: McKenney

Clarkite New Hampshire: Grafton (I)

Cleavelandite California: Pala; Maine: Auburn, Poland (GS), West Paris; New Hampshire: Grafton (I); New Mexico: Dixon

Columbite Maine: Bethel, Poland (GS), West Paris; New Hampshire: Grafton (I)

Compotite New Hampshire: Grafton (I)

Cookeite Maine: West Paris

Copper, pure Michigan: Mohawk, Ontonagon

Copper minerals Michigan: Mohawk (M); New Mexico: Magdalena

Corundum Montana: Alder

Crandallite Georgia: Lincolnton

Cryolite New Hampshire: Grafton (I)

Cymatolite New Hampshire: Grafton (I)

Datolite Michigan: Ontonagon

Dendrite New Hampshire: Grafton (I)

Diadochite Maine: Poland (GS)

Diamond Arkansas: Murfreesboro

Dickinsonite Maine: Poland (GS)

Djurleite California: Coalinga

Dolomite crystals New York: Middleville

Earlshannonite Maine: Poland (GS)

Elabite See listing under Tourmaline

Emerald Arkansas: Mt. Ida (SA); Georgia: Cleveland (SA), Dahlonega (2); North Carolina (*): Almond, Boone, Cherokee, Chimney Rock, Franklin (2), Hendersonville, Hiddenite, Jamestown, Leicester, Little Switzerland, Marion; West Virginia: Shady Spring (SA)
Crabtree emerald North Carolina: Spruce Pine

Eosphorite Maine: Poland (GS)

Epidote Michigan: Ontonagon; Texas: Mason

Fairfieldite Maine: Poland (GS)

Fairy stones (See Staurolite crystals)

Feldspar Delaware: Wilmington; Maine: Poland; New Hampshire: Conway, Grafton (I); North Carolina: Marion, Micaville; Oregon: Plush; Virginia: Amelia
  Albite feldspar Maine: Bethel

Flint Ohio: Hopewell (2)

Fluoroapatite New Hampshire: Conway, Grafton (I)

Fluorescent minerals Kentucky: Marion; New Jersey: Franklin, Ogdensburg; North Carolina: Little Switzerland; Washington: Ravensdale (GS)

Fluorite Illinois: Rosiclare; Kentucky: Marion; New Mexico: Bingham; North Carolina: Hendersonville, Leicester; Virginia: Amelia; Washington: Ravensdale (GS)

Franklinite New Jersey: Franklin

Fuchsite Georgia: Lincolnton

Gahnite (spinel) Maine: Poland (GS), West Paris; New Hampshire, Conway

Gainsite Maine: Poland (GS)

Galena New Mexico: Bingham; Texas: Mason

Garnet Arizona: Apache Junction; California: Columbia, Pala; Connecticut: Roxbury; Delaware: Wilmington; Georgia: Dahlonega (2); Idaho: St. Maries; Maine: Auburn, Bethel (2), Poland (GS), West Paris; Montana: Alder, Helena (S); Nevada: Ely; New Hampshire: Conway, Grafton (I); New Mexico: Dixon; New York: North River; North Carolina (*): Almond, Boone, Canton, Cherokee, Chimney Rock, Franklin (4), Hendersonville, Hiddenite, Highlands, Leicester, Little Switzerland, Marion, Marshall, Micaville, Spruce Pine (3) (FT); South Dakota: Hill City; Tennessee: Ducktown; Texas: Mason; Virginia: McKenney; Washington: Ravensdale (GS)
  Almandine garnet Maine: Bethel, Poland (GS); Nevada: Ely
  Pyrope garnet North Carolina: Franklin
  Rhodolite garnet North Carolina: Franklin
  Star garnet Idaho: St. Maries

Geodes Arizona: Safford; Illinois: Hamilton (3); Missouri: Alexandria, St. Francisville; New Mexico: Deming, Gila; Utah: Dugway Mountains, Moab (GS)

Lined with:
  Agate, blue New Mexico: Deming
  Aragonite Illinois: Hamilton; Missouri: Alexandria
  Barite Illinois: Hamilton; Missouri: Alexandria
  Calcite Illinois: Hamilton; Missouri: Alexandria
  Chalcedony New Mexico: Deming
  Crystal Missouri: Alexandria; Washington: Ravensdale (GS)
  Dolomite Missouri: Alexandria
  Goethite Missouri: Alexandria

Hematite Missouri: Alexandria
Kaoline Missouri: Alexandria
Kaolinite Illinois: Hamilton
Opal, common New Mexico: Deming
Pyrite Illinois: Hamilton; Missouri: Alexandria
Quartz Illinois: Hamilton; New Mexico: Deming
Selenite needles Missouri: Alexandria
Sphalerite Missouri: Alexandria

Gold (*) Alabama: Cragford; Alaska: Anchorage, Chicken, Chugach, Copper Center, Fairbanks (2), Girdwood, Nome, Skagway (2),Talkeetna; Arizona: Apache Junction, Goldfield, Prescott; California: Angels Camp, Coloma, Columbia, Jackson, Jamestown, Mariposa, Nevada City, Palo Verde, Pine Grove; Colorado: Breckenridge, Idaho Springs (2), Ouray, Silverton; Georgia: Cleveland, Dahlonega (2), Gainesville; Indiana: Knightstown; Montana: Helena, Libby; New Hampshire: Conway; New Mexico: Gila; North Carolina: Cherokee, Franklin, Jamestown, Leicester, Marion (2), Midland, New London (2), Union Mills; Oregon: Baker City, Halfway, Jacksonville, Medford, Roseburg, Salem, Unity; Pennsylvania: Spring Grove (GS); South Dakota: Deadwood, Hill City, Keystone, Lead; Vermont: Ludlow; West Virginia: Shady Spring (SA); Wisconsin: Rhinelander

Gossanite (clear beryl) California: Pala

Goyazite Maine: Poland (GS)

Graftonite Maine: Poland (GS); New Hampshire: Grafton (I)

Granite, graphic Maine: Auburn

Gummite New Hampshire: Grafton (I)

Hematite Georgia: Lincolnton; Montana: Helena; North Carolina: Chimney Rock (SA)
 Banded welded tuff New Mexico: Gila
 Massive New Mexico: Gila

Herderite hydroxyl Maine: Bethel, Poland (GS), West Paris

Herkimer "diamonds" See Quartz

Heterosite Maine: Poland (GS)

Hiddenite (spodumene) California: Pala; North Carolina: Hiddenite

Hureaulite Maine: Poland (GS)

Ilmenite Georgia: Lincolnton

Iron ore Michigan: Iron Mountain (M)

Jade California: Pine Grove

Jadite Montana: Helena (S)

Jahnsite Maine: Poland (GS)

Jasper Arkansas: Murfreesboro (S); California: Pine Grove; Montana: Helena (S);

Oklahoma: Kenton; Oregon: Madras, Yachats; South Dakota: Hill City; Texas: Alpine

Brown jasper New Mexico: Deming, Gila

Chocolate jasper New Mexico: Deming

Jasper breccia New Mexico: Gila

Orange jasper New Mexico: Deming

Picture jasper New Mexico: Gila; Oregon: Mitchell

Pink jasper New Mexico: Deming

Red jasper New Mexico: Gila

Variegated jasper New Mexico: Deming

Yellow jasper New Mexico: Deming, Gila

Joaquinite California: Coalinga

Kaolinite Maine: Poland (GS)

Kasolite New Hampshire: Grafton (I)

Kosnarite Maine: Poland (GS)

Kunzite California: Pala

Kyanite Georgia: Lincolnton; North Carolina (*): Franklin, Leicester; West Virginia: Shady Spring (SA)

Labradorite Oregon: Plush; Texas: Alpine

Lake County "diamonds" See Quartz

Landsite Maine: Poland (GS)

Laueite Maine: Poland (GS)

Lazulite Georgia: Lincolnton

Lepidolite Maine: Poland (GS), West Paris, Woodstock; Nevada: Reno (GS); New Mexico: Dixon; North Carolina (*): Little Switzerland

Lemon yellow lepidolite New Hampshire: Grafton (I)

Purple lepidolite California: Pala

Lepidomelane New Hampshire: Grafton (I)

Limonite New Mexico: Gila

Linarite New Mexico: Bingham

Lithiophilite Maine: Poland (GS); New Hampshire: Grafton (I)

Lollingite Maine: Poland (GS), Woodstock

Ludlamite Maine: Poland (GS)

Magnesium oxide See Psilomellane

Malachite Utah: Moab

Manganapatite New Hampshire: Grafton (I)

Manganese minerals New Mexico: Deming

Manganese oxide minerals New Mexico: Deming

Marcasite Florida: Ft. Drum; New Hampshire: Grafton (I)

McCrillisite Maine: Poland (GS)

Mica Delaware: Wilmington; California: Pala; Maine: Auburn, Bethel (2), Poland (GS); New Hampshire: Grafton (I), Laconia; North Carolina: Canton, Micaville; Virginia: Amelia
  Biotite mica Maine: Bethel, Poland (GS)
  Book mica California: Pala
  Lepidolite mica Maine: Poland (GS)
  Muscovite mica California: Pala; Maine: Poland (GS); New Hampshire: Conway

Microcline Maine: Poland (GS)

Microlite New Mexico: Dixon

Mitridatite Maine: Poland (GS)

Molybdenite New Hampshire: Grafton (I)

Montebrasite Maine: Poland (GS), Woodstock

Montmorillonite Maine: Poland (GS), West Paris; New Hampshire: Grafton (I)

Monzaite Maine: Poland (GS)

Moonstone Georgia: Dahlonega; North Carolina (*): Franklin (5), Highlands, Leicester, Marion, Micaville, Spruce Pine (2)

Moraesite Maine: Poland (GS)

Morganite California: Pala; Maine: Poland (GS)

Muscovite California: Pala; Georgia: Lincolnton; New Hampshire: Grafton (I); New Mexico: Dixon

Natrolite California: Coalinga

Neptunite California: Coalinga

Olivine North Carolina: Micaville

Opal Nevada: Denio; North Carolina: Hendersonville (SA)
  Black opal Nevada: Denio
  Common opal New Mexico: Deming
  Fire opal Nevada: Denio (2); Oregon: Klamath Falls
  Hyalite opal Maine: Bethel
  Lemon opal Nevada: Reno (GS)
  Precious opal Idaho: Spencer
  Wood opal Nevada: Denio

Palm Wood Texas: Alpine, Three Rivers

Perhamite Maine: Poland (GS)

Peacock Ore Washington: Ravensdale (GS)

Petrified Wood Oregon: Sweet Home; Texas: Alpine, Three Rivers

Parsonite New Hampshire: Grafton (I)

Perlite (black to gray) New Mexico: Deming

Peridot Arkansas: Murfreesboro (S); North Carolina (*): Boone, Chimney Rock

Petalite Maine: Poland (GS), West Paris

Petoskey Stones Michigan: Petoskey

Phenakite New Hampshire: Conway; Virginia: Amelia

Phosphosiderite Georgia: Lincolnton; Maine: Poland (GS)

Phosphouranylite Maine: Poland (GS)

Phosphyanylite New Hampshire: Grafton (I)

Pitch Stone (with seams of red and brown) New Mexico: Deming

Pollucite Maine: Poland (GS), West Paris, Woodstock

Psilomelane New Hampshire: Grafton (I)

Purpurite Maine: Poland (GS); New Hampshire: Grafton (I)

Pseudomorphs South Carolina: Antreville

Pyrite Georgia: Lincolnton; Maine: Bethel, Poland (GS); New Hampshire: Grafton (I);
Tennessee: Ducktown; Virginia: Amelia; Washington: Ravensdale (GS)
> **Iron pyrite** Arizona: Apache Junction
> **Micropyrite** Florida: Ft. Drum

Pyrophyllite Georgia: Lincolnton

Pyrrhotite New Hampshire: Grafton (I); Tennessee: Ducktown

Quartz Arkansas: Jessieville (2), Mt. Ida (5) (Y), Murfreesboro (S), Story (2); California: Angels Camp, Pine Grove, Warner Springs; Delaware: Wilmington; Georgia: Dahlonega, Lincolnton; Maine: Auburn, Bethel, Poland (GS), West Paris, Woodstock; Michigan: Ontonagon; Montana: Dillon, Helena (S); Nevada: Reno (GS); New Hampshire: Conway, Laconia; New Mexico: Bingham, Deming, Dixon; North Carolina: Chimney Rock, Franklin, Hendersonville, Micaville, Spruce Pine; South Dakota: Hill City; Texas: Alpine, Mason; Virginia: Amelia (2); Washington: Ravensdale (GS)
> **Blue** Georgia: Lincolnton; North Carolina: Marion
> **Clear** Arkansas: Jessieville; Georgia: LaGrange; Maine: Woodstock; North Carolina (*): Hiddenite, Little Switzerland, Marion, Spruce Pine
> **Doubly Terminated Scepters** Washington: Ravensdale (GS)
> **Druse** Georgia: Tignall
> **Milky** Maine: Bethel; South Carolina: Antreville
> **Parallel growth** Maine: West Paris
> **Phantoms** Washington: Ravensdale (GS)
> **Pseudocubic crystals** Maine: West Paris
> **Rose** Maine: Bethel, Woodstock; New Hampshire: Grafton (I); North Carolina (*): Franklin, Leicester, Marion

Rutilated North Carolina (*): Little Switzerland, Spruce Pine
Skeletal quartz South Carolina: Antreville
Smoky Maine: Bethel, Woodstock; New Hampshire: Conway, Grafton, Laconia; North Carolina (*): Almond, Boone, Cherokee, Franklin (4), Hiddenite, Highlands, Leicester, Little Switzerland, Marion, Spruce Pine (2); South Carolina: Antreville; Virginia: McKenney
Star rose Georgia: LaGrange
White Arkansas: Jessieville; New Hampshire: Grafton
Quartz "diamonds"
Lake Co. "diamonds" (moon tears) California: Lucerne
Cape May "diamonds" New Jersey: Cape May
Herkimer "diamonds" New York: Herkimer, Middleville, St. Johnsville

Reddingite Maine: Poland (GS); New Hampshire: Grafton

Rhodochrosite Maine: Poland (GS)

Rhodolite (garnet) North Carolina: Franklin (2)

Rhyolite, banded New Mexico: Gila

Rochbridgeite Maine: Poland (GS)

Rose rocks See Barite

Rubalite Maine: Bethel

Ruby Arkansas: Mt. Ida (SA); California: Pine Grove; Georgia: Cleveland, Dahlonega (2); Montana: Helena; North Carolina (*): Almond, Boone, Cherokee, Chimney Rock, Franklin (7), Highlands, Hendersonville, Jamestown, Leicester, Little Switzerland, Spruce Pine (3); West Virginia: Shady Spring (SA)

Rutile Georgia: Lincolnton; Maine: Bethel, Poland (GS); North Carolina: Franklin, Hiddenite

Safflorite New Hampshire: Grafton (I)

Sapphire Georgia: Cleveland (SA), Dahlonega (2); Montana: Hamilton, Helena, Philipsburg (2); Nevada: Reno (GS); North Carolina (*): Almond, Cherokee, Franklin (7), Hendersonville, Hiddenite, Highlands, Leicester, Little Switzerland, Spruce Pine (2); West Virginia: Shady Spring (SA)

Sapphire, blue North Carolina: Canton
Sapphire, gray North Carolina: Canton
Sapphire, white North Carolina: Canton
Sapphire, bronze North Carolina: Canton
Sapphire, pink North Carolina: Canton
Star sapphire North Carolina: Boone (SA)

Scheelite Maine: West Paris

Scoria New Mexico: Gila

Selenite crystals New Mexico: Bingham

Septarian nodules Utah: Kanab

Serpentine Montana: Helena (S)

Siderite Maine: Bethel

Silica minerals New Mexico: Deming

Sillimanite New Hampshire: Grafton (I); North Carolina (*): Franklin, Hiddenite

Silver Michigan: Ontonagon; West Virginia: Shady Spring (SA)

Sodalite North Carolina: Chimney Rock (SA), Hendersonville (SA)

Soddylite New Hampshire: Grafton (I)

Spessartine New Mexico: Dixon

Spodumene Maine: Poland (GS), West Paris, Woodstock; New Mexico: Dixon
    Altered spodumene Maine: West Paris
    Hiddenite California: Pala

Staurolite New Hampshire: Grafton (I); Virginia: Stuart

Stewartite Maine: Poland (GS)

Strengite Georgia: Lincolnton

Strunzite Maine: Poland (GS)

Sulfur Georgia: Lincolnton

Sunstone Nevada: Reno (GS); Oregon: Plush (3)

Switzerite Maine: Poland (GS)

Tantalite-Columbite Virginia: Amelia

Thulite North Carolina: Micaville

Thundereggs Nevada: Reno (GS); New Mexico: Deming; Oregon: Madras, Mitchell

Tobernite New Hampshire: Grafton (I)

Topaz Georgia: Cleveland (SA), Dahlonega; Maine: Poland (GS); Montana: Helena; New Hampshire: Conway, Grafton (I); North Carolina (*): Almond, Boone, Cherokee, Franklin (3), Highlands, Leicester, Spruce Pine (2); Texas: Mason (2); Virginia: Amelia (2), McKenney

Torberite Maine: Poland (GS)

Tourmaline California: Mesa Grande, Warner Springs; Maine: Auburn (2), Poland (GS), West Paris, Woodstock; Nevada: Reno (GS); New Hampshire: Grafton (I); North Carolina (*): Boone, Franklin (2), Hiddenite, Highlands, Marion, Micaville, Spruce Pine (2); Texas: Mason; Virginia: Amelia (2), McKenney
    Bi-colored California: Pala
    Black tourmaline Georgia: LaGrange; Maine: Auburn, Bethel (2), Poland (GS), West Paris; New Hampshire: Grafton (I); North Carolina: Spruce Pine (FT)
    Gem tourmaline Maine: West Paris
    Green tourmaline California: Pala; Maine: West Paris

Pink tourmaline California: Pala

Triphyllite Maine: Poland (GS); New Hampshire: Grafton (I)

Triplite Maine: Poland (GS); New Hampshire, Conway

Turquoise Nevada: Reno (GS), Tonopah

Uralolite Maine: Poland (GS)

Uranite Maine: Poland (GS); New Hampshire: Conway, Grafton (I) (species with gummite, world-famous)

Uranium minerals New Hampshire: Grafton (I); North Carolina: Little Switzerland

Uranophane New Hampshire: Grafton (I)

Vandendriesscheite New Hampshire: Grafton (I)

Variscite Georgia: Lincolnton; Nevada: Reno (GS)

Vesuvianite Maine: West Paris (I)

Vivianite Maine: Poland (GS); New Hampshire: Conway, Grafton (I)

Voelerkenite New Hampshire: Grafton (I)

Volcanic Bombs New Mexico: Gila

Wardite Maine: Poland (GS)

Wavelite Arkansas: Mt. Ida

Whitlockite Maine: Poland (GS)

Whitmoreite Maine: Poland (GS)

Woodhouseite Georgia: Lincolnton

Wodginite Maine: Poland (GS)

Zeolite New Mexico: Gila

Zircon Maine: Bethel (2), Poland (GS), West Paris; New Hampshire: Conway, Grafton (I); North Carolina: Canton; Texas: Mason

Annual Events

JANUARY

Quartzite, AZ, Gem and Mineral Shows—Mid-January–mid-February

Tucson, AZ, Gem and Mineral Shows—End of January–mid-February

FEBRUARY

Quartzsite, AZ, Gem and Mineral Shows—Mid-January–mid-February

Tucson, AZ, Gem and Mineral Shows—End of January–mid-February

MARCH

Tucson, AZ, Minerals of Arizona—Symposium one day in March or April

APRIL

Tucson, AZ, Minerals of Arizona—Symposium one day in March or April

MAY

Augusta, ME, Maine Mineral Symposium—Second full weekend in May

Franklin, NC, Mother's Day Gemboree—Mother's Day weekend in May

Poland, ME, Maine Pegmatite Workshop—One week at the end of May or beginning
of June

JUNE

Poland, ME, Maine Pegmatite Workshop—One week at the end of May or beginning
of June

Prineville, OR, Rockhound Pow-Wow—Mid-June

JULY

Cottage Grove, OR, Bohemia Mining Days—Four days in July

Franklin, NC, Macon County Gemboree—Four days in July

Hurley, WI, Iron County Heritage Days—From the last week in July to mid-August

Moose Lake, MN, Agate Days—One weekend in July

Nyssa, OR, Thunderegg Days—Mid-July

Spruce Pine, NC, North Carolina Mineral and Gem Festival—Four days at the end of July and / or the beginning of August

AUGUST

Houghton, MI, Copper Country Mineral Retreat—August

Hurley, WI, Iron Country Heritage Days—From the last week in July to mid-August

Spruce Pine, NC, North Carolina Mineral and Gem Festival—Four days at the end of July and / or the beginning of August

SEPTEMBER

Crawford, NE, Crawford Rock Swap—Labor Day weekend

Glenford, OH, Flint Ridge Knap-In—First weekend in September

Hamilton, IL, Geode Fest—Last weekend in September

Keokuk, IA, Geode Fest—Held end of September or beginning of October

Neenah, WI, Quarry Quest—September

OCTOBER

Big Sur, CA, Big Sur Jade Festival—Second weekend in October

Coloma, CA, Marshall Gold Discovery State Historic Park: Gold Rush Live—Second week of October

Dahlonega, GA, Gold Rush Days—Third full weekend in October
World Open Gold Panning Championship, in October, at the same time as Gold Rush Days

Franklin, NC, "Leaf Looker" Gemboree—Three days in October

Jasper, GA, Pickens County Marble Festival—First weekend in October

Keokuk, IA, Geode Fest—Held end of September or beginning of October

Mt. Ida, AR, Quartz Crystal Festival and World Championship Dig—Second weekend in October

Trona, CA, Gem-O-Rama Searles Lake—Second weekend in October

NOVEMBER

Socorro, NM, New Mexico Mineral Symposium—Two days in November

DECEMBER

No information available.

OTHER

Barre, VT, Granite Festival—Held one Saturday in summer or early fall

Eastport, MI, Antrim County Petoskey Stone Festival—Held one day during early summer

State Gem and Mineral Symbols

STATE	GEMSTONE	MINERAL	STONE/ROCK
Alabama	Star Blue Quartz (1990)	Hematite (1967)	Marble (1969)
Alaska	Jade (1968)	Gold (1968)	
Arizona	Turquoise (1974)	Fire agate	Petrified Wood
Arkansas	Diamond (1967)	Quartz crystal (1967)	Bauxite (1967)
California	Benitoite (1985)	Gold (1965)	Serpentine (1965)
Colorado	Aquamarine (1971)	Rhodochrosite(2002)	Yule Marble (2004)
Connecticut	Garnet (1977)		
Delaware		Sillimanite (1977)	
Florida	Moonstone (1970)		Agatized coral (1979)
Georgia	Quartz (1976)	Staurolite (1976)	
Hawaii	Black Coral (1987)		Lava
Idaho	Star Garnet (1967)		
Illinois		Fluorite (1965)	
Indiana			Salem Limestone (1971)
Iowa			Geode (1967)
Kansas			
Kentucky	Freshwater Pearl (1986)	Coal (1998)	Kentucky Agate (2000)
Louisiana	Agate (1976)		Petrified Palm
Maine	Tourmaline (1971)		
Maryland	Patuxent River Stone (2004)		
Massachusetts	Rhodonite (1979)	Babingtonite (1971)	Plymouth Rock, Dighton Rock, Roxbury Conglomerate, Granite (1983)
Michigan	Isle Royal Greenstone (Chlorostrolite) (1973)		Petoskey Stone (1965)
Minnesota	Lake Superior Agate (1969)	Iron	

STATE	GEMSTONE	MINERAL	STONE/ROCK
Mississippi			Petrified Wood (1976)
Missouri		Galena (1967)	Mozarkite (1967)
Montana			Sapphire & Agate (1969)
Nebraska	Blue Agate (1967)		Prairie Agate (1967)
Nevada	Virgin Valley Black Fire Opal (1987) (Precious) Nevada Turquoise (1987) (Semiprecious)	Silver	Sandstone (1987)
New Hampshire	Smoky Quartz (1985)	Beryl (1985)	Granite (1985)
New Jersey			Stockton Sandstone
New Mexico	Turquoise (1967)		
New York	Garnet (1969)		
North Carolina	Emerald (1973)		Unakite/Granite (1979)
North Dakota			Teredo Wood
Ohio	Flint (1965)		
Oklahoma	Hourglass Selenite Crystals (2005)		Barite Rose (1968)
Oregon	Sunstone (1987)		Thunderegg (1965)
Pennsylvania			
Rhode Island		Bowenite (1966)	Cumberlandite (1966)
South Carolina	Amethyst (1969)		Blue Granite (1969)
South Dakota	Fairburn Agate (1966)	Rose Quartz (1966) (Mineral/Stone)	Black Hills Gold (1988) (official jewelry)
Tennessee	Tennessee River Pearls (1979)		Limestone (1979) and Tennessee Paint Rock Agate (2009)
Texas	Texas Blue Topaz (1969) Lone Star Cut (1977) (Gemstone Cut)	Silver (2007)	Petrified Palm Wood (1969)
Utah	Topaz (1991)	Copper (1994)	Coal (1991)
Vermont	Grossular Garnet (1991)	Talc (1991)	Granite, Marble, Slate (1991)

STATE	GEMSTONE	MINERAL	STONE/ROCK
Virginia			
Washington	Petrified Wood (1975)		
West Virginia	Mississippian Fossil Coral (*Lithostrotionella*) (1990)		Bituminous coal (2009)
Wisconsin		Galena (1971)	Red Granite (1971)
Wyoming	Nephrite Jade (1967)		

Finding Your Own Birthstone

Following is a listing of fee dig sites presented in this four-volume guide where you can find your birthstone! Refer to the individual mine listings for more information on individual mines.

Garnet (January Birthstone) Arizona: Apache Junction; California: Columbia, Pala; Connecticut: Roxbury; Delaware: Wilmington; Georgia: Dahlonega (2); Idaho: St. Maries; Maine: Auburn, Bethel (2), Poland (GS), West Paris; Montana: Alder, Helena (S); Nevada: Ely; New Hampshire: Conway, Grafton (I); New Mexico: Dixon; New York: North River; North Carolina (*): Almond, Boone, Canton, Cherokee, Chimney Rock, Franklin (4), Hiddenite, Highlands, Leicester, Little Switzerland, Marion, Marshall, Micaville, Spruce Pine (3) (FT); South Dakota: Hill City (S); Tennessee: Ducktown; Texas: Mason; Virginia: McKenney, Washington: Ravensdale (GS)
    Almandine garnet Maine: Bethel, Poland (GS); Nevada: Ely
    Pyrope garnet North Carolina: Franklin
    Rhodolite garnet North Carolina: Franklin
    Star garnet Idaho: St. Maries

Amethyst (February Birthstone) Arkansas: Mt. Ida (SA), Murfreesboro (S); Georgia: Cleveland, Dahlonega, Tignall (2); Maine: Bethel (R), West Paris; Montana: Dillon; Nevada: Reno; New Hampshire: Conway, Grafton (I), Laconia; North Carolina (*): Almond, Boone, Cherokee, Chimney Rock, Franklin (3), Highlands, Jamestown, Leicester, Spruce Pine (3); South Carolina: Antreville
    Amethyst scepters Nevada: Reno (GS)

Aquamarine or Bloodstone (March Birthstone)

Aquamarine California: Pala; Georgia: LaGrange; Maine: Bethel, Poland (GS), Woodstock; New Hampshire: Grafton (I); North Carolina (*): Boone, Chimney Rock, Franklin, Hendersonville, Hiddenite, Little Switzerland, Marion, Micaville, Spruce Pine (FT)
    Brushy Creek aquamarine North Carolina: Spruce Pine (I) (FT)
    Weisman aquamarine North Carolina: Spruce Pine (I) (FT)

Bloodstone No listing

Diamond (April Birthstone) Arkansas: Murfreesboro

Emerald (May Birthstone) Arkansas: Mt. Ida (SA); Georgia: Cleveland (SA), Dahlonega (2); North Carolina (*): Almond, Boone, Cherokee, Chimney Rock,

Franklin (2), Hiddenite, Jamestown, Leicester, Little Switzerland, Marion, Spruce Pine (2); West Virginia: Shady Spring (SA)

Crabtree emerald North Carolina: Spruce Pine

Moonstone or Pearl (June Birthstone)

Moonstone Georgia: Dahlonega; North Carolina (*): Franklin (5), Highlands, Leicester, Marion, Micaville, Spruce Pine (2)

Pearl No listing

Ruby (July Birthstone) Arkansas: Mt. Ida (SA); California: Pine Grove; Georgia: Cleveland, Dahlonega (2); Montana: Helena; North Carolina (*): Almond, Boone, Cherokee, Chimney Rock, Franklin (7), Hendersonville, Highlands, Jamestown, Leicester, Little Switzerland, Spruce Pine (3); West Virginia: Shady Spring (SA)

Peridot or Sardonyx (August Birthstone)

Peridot Arkansas: Murfreesboro (S); North Carolina (*): Boone, Chimney Rock

Sardonyx No listing

Sapphire (September Birthstone) Georgia: Cleveland (SA), Dahlonega (2); Montana: Hamilton, Helena, Philipsburg (2); Nevada: Reno (GS); North Carolina (*): Almond, Cherokee, Franklin (8), Hiddenite, Highlands, Leicester, Little Switzerland, Spruce Pine (2); West Virginia: Shady Spring (SA)

Sapphire, blue North Carolina: Canton
Sapphire, gray North Carolina: Canton
Sapphire, white North Carolina: Canton
Sapphire, bronze North Carolina: Canton
Sapphire, pink North Carolina: Canton
Star sapphire North Carolina: Boone (SA)

Opal or Tourmaline (October Birthstone)

Opal Nevada: Denio; North Carolina: Hendersonville (SA)
Black opal Nevada: Denio
Common opal New Mexico: Deming
Fire opal Nevada: Denio (2); Oregon: Klamath Falls
Hyalite opal Maine: Bethel
Lemon opal Nevada: Reno (GS)
Precious opal Idaho: Spencer
Wood opal Nevada: Denio

Tourmaline California: Mesa Grande, Warner Springs; Maine: Auburn (2), Poland (GS), West Paris, Woodstock; Nevada: Reno (GS); New Hampshire: Grafton (I); North Carolina (*): Boone, Franklin (2), Hiddenite, Highlands, Marion, Micaville, Spruce Pine (2); Texas: Mason; Virginia: Amelia

Bi-colored California: Pala
Black tourmaline Georgia: LaGrange; Maine: Auburn, Bethel (2), Poland (GS), West Paris; New Hampshire: Grafton (I); North Carolina: Spruce Pine (FT)

Gem tourmaline Maine: West Paris
Green tourmaline California: Pala; Maine: West Paris
Pink tourmaline California: Pala

Topaz (November Birthstone) Georgia: Cleveland (SA), Dahlonega; Maine: Poland (GS); Montana: Helena; New Hampshire: Conway, Grafton (I); North Carolina (*): Almond, Boone, Cherokee, Franklin (3), Highlands, Leicester, Spruce Pine (2); Texas: Mason (2); Virginia: Amelia, McKenney

Turquiose or Lapis Lazuli (December Birthstone)

Turquoise Nevada: Reno (GS), Tonopah

Lapis Lazuli No listing

The preceding list of birthstones is taken from a list adopted in 1912 by the American National Association of Jewelers ("The Evolution of Birthstones" from *Jewelry & Gems—The Buying Guide* by Antoinette Matlins and A. C. Bonanno; GemStone Press, 2009).

Finding Your Anniversary Stone

The following is a listing of fee dig sites contained in this four-volume guide where you can find the stone that is associated with a particular anniversary.

First: Gold (Jewelry) Alabama: Cragford; Alaska: Anchorage, Chicken, Chugach, Copper Center, Fairbanks (2), Girdwood, Nome, Skagway (2), Talkeetna; Arizona: Apache Junction, Goldfield, Prescott; California: Angels Camp, Coloma, Columbia, Jackson, Jamestown, Mariposa, Nevada City, Palo Verde, Pine Grove; Colorado: Breckenridge, Idaho Springs (2), Ouray, Silverton; Georgia: Cleveland, Dahlonega (2), Gainesville; Indiana: Knightstown; Montana: Helena (S), Libby; New Hampshire: Conway; New Mexico: Gila; North Carolina: Cherokee, Franklin, Jamestown, Leicester, Marion (2), Midland, New London (2), Union Mills; Oregon: Baker City, Halfway, Jacksonville, Medford, Roseburg, Salem, Unity; Pennsylvania: Spring Grove (GS); South Dakota: Deadwood, Hill City, Keystone, Lead; Vermont: Ludlow; West Virginia: Shady Spring (SA)

Second: Garnet Arizona: Apache Junction; California: Columbia, Pala; Connecticut: Roxbury; Delaware: Wilmington; Georgia: Dahlonega (2); Idaho: St. Maries; Maine: Auburn, Bethel (2), Poland (GS), West Paris; Montana: Alder, Helena (S); Nevada: Ely; New Hampshire: Conway, Grafton (I); New Mexico: Dixon; New York: North River; North Carolina (*): Almond, Boone, Canton, Cherokee, Chimney Rock, Franklin (4), Hendersonville, Hiddenite, Highlands, Leicester, Little Switzerland, Marion, Micaville, Marshall, Spruce Pine (3) (FT); South Dakota: Hill City (S); Tennessee: Ducktown; Texas: Mason; Virginia: McKenney; Washington: Ravensdale (GS)
   Almandine garnet Maine: Bethel, Poland (GS); Nevada: Ely
   Pyrope garnet North Carolina: Franklin
   Rhodolite garnet North Carolina: Franklin
   Star garnet Idaho: St. Maries

Third: Pearl No listing

Fourth: Blue topaz No listing

Fifth: Sapphire Georgia: Cleveland (2), Dahlonega (2); Montana: Hamilton, Helena, Philipsburg (2); Nevada: Reno (GS); North Carolina (*): Almond, Cherokee, Franklin (7), Hendersonville, Hiddenite, Highlands, Leicester, Little Switzerland, Spruce Pine (2); West Virginia: Shady Spring (SA)
   Sapphire, blue North Carolina: Canton
   Sapphire, gray North Carolina: Canton

Sapphire, white North Carolina: Canton
Sapphire, bronze North Carolina: Canton
Sapphire, pink North Carolina: Canton
Star sapphire North Carolina: Boone (SA)

Sixth: Amethyst Arkansas: Mt. Ida (SA), Murfreesboro (S); Georgia: Cleveland; Dahlonega, Tignall (2); Maine: Bethel (R), West Paris; Montana: Dillon; Nevada: Reno (GS); New Hampshire: Conway, Grafton (I), Laconia; North Carolina (*): Almond, Boone, Cherokee, Chimney Rock, Franklin (3), Highlands, Jamestown, Leicester, Spruce Pine (3); South Carolina: Antreville
Amethyst scepters Nevada: Reno(GS)

Seventh: Onyx No listing

Eighth: Tourmaline California: Mesa Grande, Warner Springs; Maine: Auburn (2), Poland (GS), West Paris, Woodstock; Nevada: Reno (GS); New Hampshire: Grafton (I); North Carolina (*): Boone, Franklin (2), Hiddenite, Highlands, Marion, Micaville, Spruce Pine (2); Texas: Mason; Virginia: Amelia, McKenney
Bi-colored California: Pala
Black tourmaline Georgia: LaGrange; Maine: Auburn, Bethel (2), Poland (GS), West Paris; New Hampshire: Grafton (I); North Carolina: Spruce Pine (FT)
Gem tourmaline Maine: West Paris
Green tourmaline California: Pala; Maine: West Paris
Pink tourmaline California: Pala

Ninth: Lapis Lazuli No listing

Tenth: Diamond (Jewelry) Arkansas: Murfreesboro

Eleventh: Turquoise Nevada: Reno (GS), Tonopah

Twelfth: Jade California: Pine Grove

Thirteenth: Citrine North Carolina (*): Almond, Boone, Cherokee, Franklin (3), Highlands, Leicester, Spruce Pine (2)

Fourteenth: Opal Nevada: Denio; North Carolina: Hendersonville (SA)
Black opal Nevada: Denio
Common opal New Mexico: Deming
Fire opal Nevada: Denio (2); Oregon: Klamath Falls
Hyalite opal Maine: Bethel
Lemon opal Nevada: Reno (GS)
Precious opal Idaho: Spencer
Wood opal Nevada: Denio

Fifteenth: Ruby Arkansas: Mt. Ida (SA); California: Pine Grove; Georgia: Cleveland, Dahlonega (2); Montana: Helena; North Carolina (*): Almond, Boone, Cherokee, Chimney Rock, Franklin (7), Hendersonville, Highlands, Jamestown, Leicester, Little Switzerland, Spruce Pine (3); West Virginia: Shady Spring (SA)

Twentieth: Emerald Arkansas: Mt. Ida (SA); Georgia: Cleveland (SA), Dahlonega (2);

North Carolina (*): Almond, Boone, Cherokee, Chimney Rock, Franklin (2), Hiddenite, Jamestown, Leicester, Little Switzerland, Marion, Spruce Pine (2); West Virginia: Shady Spring (SA)

Crabtree emerald North Carolina: Spruce Pine

Twenty-fifth: Silver Michigan: Ontonagon

Thirtieth: Pearl No listing

Thirty-fifth: Emerald Arkansas: Mt. Ida (SA); Georgia: Cleveland (SA), Dahlonega (2); North Carolina (*): Almond, Boone, Cherokee, Chimney Rock, Franklin (2), Hiddenite, Jamestown, Leicester, Little Switzerland, Marion, Spruce Pine (2); West Virginia: Shady Spring (SA)

Crabtree emerald North Carolina: Spruce Pine

Fortieth: Ruby Arkansas: Mt. Ida (SA); California: Pine Grove; Georgia: Cleveland, Dahlonega (2); Montana: Helena; North Carolina (*): Almond, Boone, Cherokee, Chimney Rock, Franklin (7), Hendersonville, Highlands, Jamestown, Leicester, Little Switzerland, Spruce Pine (3); West Virginia: Shady Spring (SA)

Forty-fifth: Sapphire Georgia: Cleveland (SA), Dahlonega (2); Montana: Hamilton, Helena, Philipsburg (2); Nevada: Reno (GS); North Carolina (*): Almond, Cherokee, Franklin (7), Hendersonville, Hiddenite, Highlands, Leicester, Little Switzerland, Spruce Pine (2); West Virginia: Shady Spring (SA)

Sapphire, blue North Carolina: Canton

Sapphire, gray North Carolina: Canton

Sapphire, white North Carolina: Canton

Sapphire, bronze North Carolina: Canton

Sapphire, pink North Carolina: Canton

Star sapphire North Carolina: Boone (SA)

Fiftieth: Gold (*) Alabama: Cragford; Alaska: Anchorage, Chicken, Chugach, Copper Center, Fairbanks (2), Girdwood, Nome, Skagway (2), Talkeetna; Arizona: Apache Junction, Goldfield, Prescott; California: Angels Camp, Coloma, Columbia, Jackson, Jamestown, Mariposa, Nevada City, Palo Verde, Pine Grove; Colorado: Breckenridge, Idaho Springs (2), Ouray, Silverton; Georgia: Cleveland, Dahlonega (2), Gainesville; Indiana: Knightstown; Montana: Helena (S), Libby; New Hampshire: Conway; New Mexico: Gila; North Carolina: Cherokee, Franklin, Jamestown, Leicester, Marion (2), Midland, New London (2), Union Mills; Pennsylvania: Spring Grove (GS); Oregon: Baker City, Halfway, Jacksonville, Medford, Roseburg, Salem, Unity; South Dakota: Deadwood, Hill City, Keystone, Lead; Vermont: Ludlow; West Virginia: Shady Spring (SA); Wisconsin: Rhinelander

Fifty-fifth: Alexandrite No listing

Sixtieth: Diamond Arkansas: Murfreesboro

Finding Your Zodiac Stone

The following is a listing of fee dig sites contained in this four-volume guide where you can find the stone that is associated with a particular zodiac sign. Refer to the individual mine listings for more information.

Aquarius (January 21–February 21) Garnet Arizona: Apache Junction; California: Columbia, Pala; Connecticut: Roxbury; Delaware: Wilmington; Georgia: Dahlonega (2); Idaho: St. Maries; Maine: Auburn, Bethel (2), Poland (GS), West Paris; Montana: Alder, Helena (S); Nevada: Ely; New Hampshire: Conway, Grafton (I); New Mexico: Dixon; New York: North River; North Carolina (*): Almond, Boone, Canton, Cherokee, Chimney Rock, Franklin (4), Hendersonville, Hiddenite, Highlands, Leicester, Little Switzerland, Marion, Marshall, Micaville, Spruce Pine (3) (FT); South Dakota: Hill City (S); Tennessee: Ducktown; Texas: Mason; Virginia: McKenney; Washington: Ravensdale (GS)
  Almandine garnet Maine: Bethel, Poland (GS); Nevada: Ely
  Pyrope garnet North Carolina: Franklin
  Rhodolite garnet North Carolina: Franklin
  Star garnet Idaho: St. Maries

Pisces (February 22–March 21) Amethyst Arkansas: Mt. Ida (SA), Murfreesboro (S); Georgia: Cleveland, Dahlonega, Tignall (2); Maine: Bethel (R), West Paris; Montana: Dillon; New Hampshire: Conway, Grafton (I), Laconia; North Carolina (*): Almond, Boone, Cherokee, Chimney Rock, Franklin (3), Highlands, Jamestown, Leicester, Spruce Pine (3); South Carolina: Antreville
  Amethyst scepters Nevada: Reno (GS)

Aries (March 22–April 20) Bloodstone (green chalcedony with red spots) No listing

Taurus (April 21–May 21) Sapphire Georgia: Cleveland (SA), Dahlonega (2); Montana: Hamilton, Helena, Philipsburg (2); Nevada: Reno (GS); North Carolina (*): Almond, Cherokee, Franklin (7), Hendersonville, Hiddenite, Highlands, Leicester, Little Switzerland, Spruce Pine (2); West Virginia: Shady Spring (SA)
  Sapphire, blue North Carolina: Canton
  Sapphire, gray North Carolina: Canton
  Sapphire, white North Carolina: Canton
  Sapphire, bronze North Carolina: Canton
  Sapphire, pink North Carolina: Canton
  Star sapphire North Carolina: Boone (SA)

Gemini (May 22–June 21) Agate Arkansas: Murfreesboro (S); Michigan: Grand Marais; Minnesota: Moose Lake; Montana: Helena (S); New Mexico: Deming; North Carolina: Chimney Rock; Oklahoma: Kenton (2); Oregon: Madras, Yachats; South Dakota: Wall; Texas: Three Rivers
Banded agate Texas: Alpine; New Mexico: Gila
Fire agate Arizona: Safford (2); California: Palo Verde (2); Nevada: Reno (GS); Wyoming: Shell
Iris agate Texas: Alpine
Ledge agate Oregon: Madras
Moss agate Oregon: Madras, Mitchell; Texas: Alpine (2); Wyoming: Shell
Paint rock agate Alabama: Trenton
Polka-dot jasp-agate Oregon: Madras
Pom pom agate Texas: Alpine
Rainbow agate Oregon: Madras
Red plume agate Texas: Alpine

Cancer (June 22–July 22) Emerald Arkansas: Mt. Ida (SA); Georgia: Cleveland (SA), Dahlonega (2); North Carolina (*): Almond, Boone, Cherokee, Chimney Rock, Franklin (2), Hiddenite, Jamestown, Leicester, Little Switzerland, Marion, Spruce Pine (2); West Virginia: Shady Spring (SA)
Crabtree emerald North Carolina: Spruce Pine

Leo (July 23–August 22) Onyx No listing

Virgo (August 23–September 22) Carnelian No listing

Libra (September 23–October 23) Chrysolite or Peridot

Chrysolite No listing

Peridot Arkansas: Murfreesboro (S); North Carolina (*): Boone, Chimney Rock

Scorpio (October 24–November 21) Beryl California: Warner Springs; Delaware: Wilmington; Georgia: LaGrange; Maine: Auburn, Bethel, Poland (GS), West Paris; New Hampshire: Grafton (I); New Mexico: Dixon; North Carolina (*): Little Switzerland, Spruce Pine (2); Virginia: Amelia (2)
Aqua beryl New Hampshire: Grafton (I)
Blue beryl (see also aquamarine) New Hampshire: Grafton (I)
Golden beryl North Carolina: Spruce Pine (FT); New Hampshire: Grafton (I)

Sagittarius (November 22–December 21) Topaz Georgia: Cleveland (SA), Dahlonega; Maine: Poland (GS); Montana: Helena; New Hampshire: Conway, Grafton (I); North Carolina (*): Almond, Boone, Cherokee, Franklin (3), Highlands, Leicester, Spruce Pine (2); Texas: Mason (2); Virginia: Amelia

Capricorn (December 22–January 21) Ruby Arkansas: Mt. Ida (SA); California: Pine Grove; Georgia: Cleveland, Dahlonega (2); Montana: Helena; North Carolina (*): Almond, Boone, Cherokee, Chimney Rock, Franklin (7), Hendersonville, Highlands, Jamestown, Leicester, Little Switzerland, Spruce Pine (3); West Virginia: Shady Spring (SA)

The preceding list of zodiacal stones has been passed on from an early Hindu legend (taken from *Jewelry & Gems—The Buying Guide* by Antoinette Matlins and A. C. Bonanno; GemStone Press, 2009).

The following is an old Spanish list, probably representing Arab traditions, which ascribes the following stones to various signs of the zodiac (taken from *Jewelry & Gems—The Buying Guide* by Antoinette Matlins and A. C. Bonanno; GemStone Press, 2009).

Aquarius (January 21–February 21) Amethyst Arkansas: Mt. Ida (SA), Murfreesboro (S); Georgia: Cleveland, Dahlonega, Tignall (2); Maine: Bethel (R), West Paris; Montana: Dillon; Nevada: Reno (GS); New Hampshire: Conway, Grafton (I), Laconia; North Carolina (*): Almond, Boone, Cherokee, Chimney Rock, Franklin (3), Highlands, Jamestown, Leicester, Spruce Pine (3); South Carolina: Antreville
Amethyst scepters Nevada: Reno (GS)

Pisces (February 22–March 21) Undistinguishable in original list

Aries (March 22–April 20) Quartz Arkansas: Jessieville (2), Mt. Ida (5) (Y), Murfreesboro (S), Story (2); California: Angels Camp, Pine Grove, Warner Springs; Delaware: Wilmington; Georgia: Dahlonega, Lincolnton; Illinois: Hamilton; Maine: Auburn, Bethel, Poland (GS), West Paris, Woodstock; Michigan: Ontonagon; Montana: Dillon, Helena (S); Nevada: Reno (GS); New Hampshire: Conway, Laconia; New Mexico: Bingham, Deming, Dixon; North Carolina: North Carolina: Chimney Rock, Franklin, Micaville, Spruce Pine; South Dakota: Hill City (S); Texas: Alpine, Mason; Virginia: Amelia; Washington: Ravensdale (GS)
Blue Georgia: Lincolnton; North Carolina: Marion
Clear Arkansas, Jessieville; Georgia: LaGrange; Maine: Woodstock; North Carolina (*): Hiddenite, Little Switzerland, Marion, Spruce Pine
Doubly Terminated Scepters Washington: Ravensdale (GS)
Druse Georgia: Tignall
Milky Maine: Bethel; South Carolina: Antreville
Parallel growth Maine: West Paris
Phantoms Washington: Ravensdale (GS)
Pseudocubic crystals Maine: West Paris
Rose Maine: Bethel, Woodstock; New Hampshire: Grafton (I); North Carolina (*): Franklin, Leicester, Marion
Rutilated North Carolina (*): Little Switzerland, Spruce Pine
Skeletal quartz South Carolina: Antreville
Smoky Maine: Bethel, Woodstock; New Hampshire: Conway, Grafton, Laconia; North Carolina (*): Almond, Boone, Cherokee, Franklin (4), Hiddenite, Highlands, Leicester, Little Switzerland, Marion, Spruce Pine (2); South Carolina: Antreville; Virginia: McKenney

White Arkansas: Jessieville; New Hampshire: Grafton

Quartz "diamonds"

Lake Co. "diamonds" (moon tears) California; Lucerne

Cape May "diamonds" New Jersey: Cape May

Herkimer "diamonds" New York: Herkimer, Middleville, St. Johnsville

Taurus (April 21–May 21) Ruby, Diamond

Ruby Arkansas: Mt. Ida (SA); California: Pine Grove; Georgia: Cleveland, Dahlonega (2); Montana: Helena; North Carolina (*): Almond, Boone, Cherokee, Chimney Rock, Franklin (7), Hendersonville, Highlands, Jamestown, Leicester, Little Switzerland, Spruce Pine (3); West Virginia: Shady Spring (SA)

Diamond Arkansas: Murfreesboro

Gemini (May 22–June 21) Sapphire

Georgia: Cleveland (SA), Dahlonega (2); Montana: Hamilton, Helena, Philipsburg (2); Nevada: Reno (GS); North Carolina (*): Almond, Cherokee, Franklin (7), Hendersonville, Hiddenite, Highlands, Leicester, Little Switzerland, Spruce Pine (2); West Virginia: Shady Spring (SA)

Sapphire, blue North Carolina: Canton

Sapphire, gray North Carolina: Canton

Sapphire, white North Carolina: Canton

Sapphire, bronze North Carolina: Canton

Sapphire, pink North Carolina: Canton

Star sapphire North Carolina: Boone (SA)

Cancer (June 22–July 22) Agate and Beryl

Agate Arkansas: Murfreesboro (S); Michigan: Grand Marais; Minnesota: Moose Lake; Montana: Helena (S); New Mexico: Deming; North Carolina: Chimney Rock; Oklahoma: Kenton (1); Oregon: Madras, Yachats; South Dakota: Wall; Texas: Three Rivers

Banded agate Texas: Alpine; New Mexico: Gila

Fire agate Arizona: Safford (2); California: Palo Verde (2); Nevada: Reno (GS)

Iris agate Texas: Alpine

Ledge agate Oregon: Madras

Moss agate Oregon: Madras, Mitchell; Texas: Alpine (2); Wyoming: Shell

Paint rock agate Alabama: Trenton

Polka-dot jasp-agate Oregon: Madras

Pom pom agate Texas: Alpine

Rainbow agate Oregon: Madras

Red plume agate Texas: Alpine

Beryl California: Warner Springs; Delaware: Wilmington; Georgia: LaGrange; Maine: Auburn, Bethel, Poland (GS), West Paris; New Hampshire: Grafton (I); New Mexico: Dixon; North Carolina (*): Little Switzerland, Spruce Pine (2); Virginia: Amelia (2)

Aqua beryl New Hampshire: Grafton (I)

Blue beryl (see also aquamarine) New Hampshire: Grafton (I)
Golden beryl Maine: Woodstock; North Carolina: Spruce Pine (FT); New Hampshire: Grafton (I)

Leo (July 23–August 22) Topaz Georgia: Cleveland (SA), Dahlonega; Maine: Poland (GS); Montana: Helena; New Hampshire: Conway, Grafton (I); North Carolina (*): Almond, Boone, Cherokee, Franklin (3) Highlands, Leicester, Spruce Pine (2); Texas: Mason (2); Virginia: Amelia

Virgo (August 23–September 22) Bloodstone (green chalcedony with red spots)
No listing

Libra (September 23–October 23) Jasper Arkansas: Murfreesboro (S); California: Pine Grove; Montana: Helena (S); Oklahoma: Kenton; Oregon: Madras, Yachats; South Dakota: Hill City; Texas: Alpine
Brown jasper New Mexico: Deming, Gila
Chocolate jasper New Mexico: Deming
Jasper braccia New Mexico: Gila
Orange jasper New Mexico: Deming
Picture jasper New Mexico: Gila; Oregon: Mitchell
Pink jasper New Mexico: Deming
Red jasper New Mexico: Gila
Variegated jasper New Mexico: Deming
Yellow jasper New Mexico: Deming, Gila

Scorpio (October 24–November 21) Garnet Arizona: Apache Junction; California: Columbia, Pala; Connecticut: Roxbury; Delaware: Wilmington; Georgia: Dahlonega (2); Idaho: St. Maries; Maine: Auburn, Bethel (2), Poland (GS), West Paris; Montana: Alder, Helena (S); Nevada: Ely; New Hampshire: Conway, Grafton (I); New Mexico: Dixon; New York: North River; North Carolina (*): Almond, Boone, Canton, Cherokee, Chimney Rock, Franklin (4), Hiddenite, Highlands, Leicester, Little Switzerland, Marion, Marshall, Micaville, Spruce Pine (3) (FT); South Dakota: Hill City (S); Tennessee: Ducktown; Texas: Mason; Virginia: McKenney; Washington: Ravensdale (GS)
Almandine garnet Maine: Bethel, Poland (GS); Nevada: Ely
Pyrope garnet North Carolina: Franklin
Rhodolite garnet North Carolina: Franklin
Star garnet Idaho: St Maries

Sagittarius (November 22–December 21) Emerald Arkansas: Mt. Ida (SA); Georgia: Cleveland (SA), Dahlonega (2); North Carolina (*): Almond, Boone, Cherokee, Chimney Rock, Franklin (2), Hiddenite, Jamestown, Leicester, Little Switzerland, Marion, Spruce Pine (2); West Virginia: Shady Spring (SA)
Crabtree emerald North Carolina: Spruce Pine

Capricorn (December 22–January 21) Chalcedony Arizona: Safford; Nevada: Reno (GS); New Mexico: Deming
Blue Nevada: Reno (GS)

Pink New Mexico: Gila
Chalcedony roses New Mexico: Gila
White New Mexico: Gila

Some Publications on Gems and Minerals

Lapidary Journal Jewelry Artist

P.O. Box 469004
Escondido, CA 92046-9105
(800) 676-4336, US and Canada
(760) 291-1531, other international
Fax: (760) 291-1567
www.jewelryartistmagazine.com
JewelryArtist@pcspublink.com

Rocks & Minerals

Taylor & Francis Group, LLC
325 Chestnut Street, Suite 800
Philadelphia, PA 19106
(800) 354-1420 press 4
www.rocksandminerals.org
customerservice@taylorandfrancis.com

Rock & Gem

c/o Miller Magazines, Inc.
290 Maple Court, Suite 232
Ventura, CA 93003
(805) 644-3824
Fax: (805) 644-3875
www.rockngem.com

Gold Prospectors Magazine

Gold Prospectors Association of America, Inc.
43445 Business Park Drive, Suite 113
Temecula, CA 92590

(800) 551-9707
www.goldprospectors.org

The Mineralogical Record

P.O. Box 35565
Tucson, AZ 85740
www.mineralogicalrecord.com

ICMJ's Prospecting and Mining Journal

California Mining Journal, Inc.
P.O. Box 2260
Aptos, CA 95001-2260
www.icmj.com

Other sources of information are local and regional rock, gem, and mineral clubs and federations, and rock, gem, and mineral shows. Many times clubs offer field trips and some shows have collecting trips associated with their annual event. Among these are The American Federation of Mineralogical Societies (www.amfed.org), which lists member clubs (many have yearly shows/swaps), and Bob's Rock Shop (www.rockhounds.com), which has a U.S. club directory (supplied information).

Send Us Your Feedback

Disclaimer

The authors have made every reasonable effort to obtain accurate information for this guide. However, much of the information in the book is based on material provided by the sites and has not been verified independently. The information given here does not represent recommendations, but merely a listing of information. The authors and publisher accept no liability for any accident or loss incurred when readers are patronizing the establishments listed herein. The authors and publisher accept no liability for errors or omissions. Since sites may shut down or change their hours of operations or fees without advance notice, please call the site before your visit for confirmation before planning your trip.

The authors would appreciate being informed of changes, additions, or deletions that should be made to this guide. To that end, a form is attached, which can be filled out and mailed to the authors for use in future editions of the guide.

Have We Missed Your Mine or Museum?

This is a project with a national scope, based on extensive literature search, phone and mail inquiry, and personal investigation. However, we are dealing with a business in which many owners are retiring or closing and selling their sites. In addition, many of the mines, guide services, and smaller museums have limited publicity, known more by word of mouth than by publication. Thus, it is possible that your operation or one you have visited was not included in this guide. Please let us know if you own or operate a mine, guide service, or museum, or have visited a mine, guide service, or museum that is not in the guide. It will be considered for inclusion in the next edition of the guide. Send updates to:

Treasure Hunter's Guides
GemStone Press
Route 4, Sunset Farm Offices
P.O. Box 237
Woodstock, VT 05091

Do You Have a Rockhounding Story to Share?

If you have a special story about a favorite dig site, send it in for consideration for use in the next edition of the guide.

A Request to Mines and Museums:

For sites already included in this guide, we request that you put us on your annual mailing list so that we may have an updated copy of your information.

Notes on Museums

In this guide we have included listings of museums with noteworthy gem, mineral, or rock collections. We particularly tried to find local museums displaying gems or minerals native to the area where they are located. This list is by no means complete, and if you feel we missed an important listing, let us know by completing the following form. Since these guides focus specifically on gems and minerals, only those exhibits have been recognized in the museum listings, and we generally do not mention any collection or exhibits of fossils. See our sequel on fossils for information on fossil collections.

READER'S CONTRIBUTION

I would like to supply the following information for possible inclusion in the next edition of *The Treasure Hunter's Guide*:

Type of entry: ☐ fee dig ☐ guide service ☐ museum ☐ mine tour
☐ annual event

This is a: ☐ new entry ☐ entry currently in the guide

Nature of info: ☐ addition ☐ change ☐ deletion

Please describe (brochure and additional info may be attached):

_____

_____

_____

_____

Please supply the following in case we need to contact you regarding your information:

Name: _____

Address: _____

_____

_____

Phone: ( ) _____

E-mail: _____

Date: _____

FIELD NOTES

FIELD NOTES

FIELD NOTES

FIELD NOTES

FIELD NOTES

FIELD NOTES

FIELD NOTES

FIELD NOTES

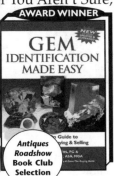
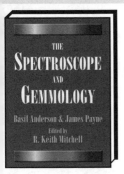

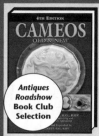
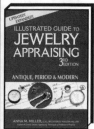
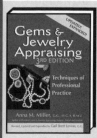

DIAMONDS, 3RD EDITION
THE ANTOINETTE MATLINS BUYING GUIDE
How to Select, Buy, Care for & Enjoy Diamonds with Confidence and Knowledge
by Antoinette Matlins, P.G.

Practical, comprehensive, and easy to understand, this book includes price guides for old and new cuts and for fancy-color, treated and synthetic diamonds. **Explains in detail** how to read diamond grading reports and offers important advice for after buying a diamond. **The "unofficial bible" for all diamond buyers who want to get the most for their money.**

6 x 9, 240 pp, 12 full-color pages, with over 150 color and b/w photos and illus.; index
Quality Paperback Original, 978-0-943763-73-6 **$18.99**

COLORED GEMSTONES, 3RD EDITION
THE ANTOINETTE MATLINS BUYING GUIDE
How to Select, Buy, Care for & Enjoy Sapphires, Emeralds, Rubies and Other Colored Gems with Confidence and Knowledge
by Antoinette Matlins, P.G.

This practical, comprehensive, easy-to-understand guide **provides in depth** all the information you need to buy colored gems with confidence. Includes price guides for popular gems, opals, and synthetic stones. Provides examples of gemstone grading reports and offers important advice for after buying a gemstone. **Shows anyone shopping for colored gemstones how to get the most for their money.**

6 x 9, 256 pp, 24 full-color pages, with over 200 color and b/w photos and illus.; index
Quality Paperback Original, 978-0-943763-72-9 **$18.99**

THE PEARL BOOK, 4TH EDITION
THE DEFINITIVE BUYING GUIDE
How to Select, Buy, Care for & Enjoy Pearls
by Antoinette Matlins, P.G.
COMPREHENSIVE • EASY TO READ • PRACTICAL

This comprehensive, authoritative guide tells readers everything they need to know about pearls to fully understand and appreciate them, and avoid any unexpected—and costly—disappointments, now and in future generations.

- A journey into the rich history and romance surrounding pearls.
- The five factors that determine pearl value & judging pearl quality.
- What to look for, what to look out for: How to spot fakes. Treatments.
- Differences between natural, cultured and imitation pearls, and ways to separate them.
- Comparisons of all types of pearls, in every size and color, from every pearl-producing country.

6 x 9, 248 pp, 16 full-color pages, with over 250 color and b/w photos and illus.; index
Quality Paperback, 978-0-943763-54-5 **$19.99**

The "Unofficial Bible" for the Gem & Jewelry Buyer

AWARD WINNER

Antiques Roadshow Book Club Selection

JEWELRY & GEMS
THE BUYING GUIDE, 7TH EDITION

Updated Retail Price Guides

How to Buy Diamonds, Pearls, Colored Gemstones, Gold & Jewelry with Confidence and Knowledge

by Antoinette Matlins, P.G., *and* A. C. Bonanno, F.G.A., A.S.A., M.G.A.

—over 400,000 copies in print—

Learn the tricks of the trade from *insiders:* How to buy diamonds, pearls, precious and other popular colored gems with confidence and knowledge. More than just a buying guide . . . discover what's available and what choices you have, what determines quality as well as cost, what questions to ask before you buy and what to get in writing. Easy to read and understand. Excellent for staff training.

6 x 9, 352 pp, 16 full-color pages, with over 200 color and b/w photos and illus.; index

Quality Paperback, 978-0-943763-71-2 **$19.99**

ENGAGEMENT & WEDDING RINGS, 3RD EDITION

by Antoinette Matlins, P.G., *and* A. C. Bonanno, F.G.A., A.S.A., M.G.A.

COMPREHENSIVE • EASY TO READ • PRACTICAL

Tells **everything you need to know to design, select, buy and enjoy that "perfect" ring** and to truly experience the wonder and excitement that should be part of it.

Updated, expanded, filled with valuable information.

Engagement & Wedding Rings, 3rd Ed., will help you make the *right* choice. You will discover romantic traditions behind engagement and wedding rings, how to select the right style and design for *you*, tricks to get what you want on a budget, ways to add new life to an "heirloom," what to do to protect yourself against fraud, and much more.

6 x 9, 320 pp, 16 full-color pages, with over 400 color and b/w photos and illus.; index

Quality Paperback Original, 978-0-943763-41-5 **$18.95**

JEWELRY & GEMS AT AUCTION

The Definitive Guide to Buying & Selling at the Auction House & on Internet Auction Sites

by Antoinette Matlins, P.G.

with contributions by Jill Newman

As buying and selling at auctions—both traditional auction houses and "virtual" Internet auctions—moves into the mainstream, **consumers need to know how to "play the game."** There are treasures to be had and money to be saved and made, but buying and selling at auction offers unique risks as well as unique opportunities. This book makes available—for the first time—detailed information on how to buy and sell jewelry and gems at auction without making costly mistakes.

6 x 9, 352 pp, 16 full-color pages, with over 150 color and b/w photos and illus.; index

Quality Paperback Original, 978-0-943763-29-3 **$19.95**

Buy Your *"Tools of the Trade"*...

Gem Identification Instruments Directly from *GemStone Press*

Whatever instrument you need, GemStone Press can help.
Use our convenient order form, or contact us directly for assistance.

Complete Pocket Instrument Set
SPECIAL SAVINGS!
BUY THIS ESSENTIAL TRIO AND SAVE 12%

Used together, you can identify 85% of all gems with these three
portable, pocket-sized instruments—the essential trio.
10X Triplet Loupe • Calcite Dichroscope • Chelsea Filter

Pocket Instrument Set:
Premium: With Bausch & Lomb 10X Loupe • RosGem Dichroscope • Chelsea Filter **only $197.95**
Deluxe: With Bausch & Lomb 10X Loupe • EZview Dichroscope • Chelsea Filter **only $179.95**

ITEM / QUANTITY	PRICE EA.*	TOTAL $
Pocket Instrument Sets		
_____ **Premium:** With Bausch & Lomb 10X Loupe • RosGem Dichroscope • Chelsea Filter	$197.95	$ _____
_____ **Deluxe:** With Bausch & Lomb 10X Loupe • EZview Dichroscope • Chelsea Filter	$179.95	_____
Loupes—Professional Jeweler's 10X Triplet Loupes		
_____ Bausch & Lomb 10X Triplet Loupe	$44.00	_____
_____ Standard 10X Triplet Loupe	$29.00	_____
_____ Dark-field Loupe	$58.95	_____
• Spot filled diamonds, identify inclusions in colored gemstones. Operates with Standard Mini Maglite (additional—see below).		
Analyzer		
_____ Gem Analyzer (RosGem)	$299.00	_____
• Combines Dark-field Loupe, Polariscope, and Immersion Cell. Operates with Standard Mini Maglite (additional—see below).		
Calcite Dichroscopes		
_____ Dichroscope (RosGem)	$135.00	_____
_____ Dichroscope (EZview)	$115.00	_____
Color Filters		
_____ Chelsea Filter	$44.95	_____
_____ Synthetic Emerald Filter Set (Hanneman)	$32.00	_____
_____ Tanzanite Filter (Hanneman)	$28.00	_____
_____ Bead Buyer's & Parcel Picker's Filter Set (Hanneman)	$24.00	_____
Diamond Testers and Tweezers		
_____ SSEF Blue Diamond Tester	$695.00	_____
_____ SSEF Diamond-Type Spotter	$150.00	_____
_____ DiamondNite Dual Tester	$269.00	_____
_____ Diamond Tweezers/Locking	$10.65	_____
_____ Diamond Tweezers/Non-Locking	$7.80	_____
Jewelry Cleaners		
_____ Speed Brite Ionic Jewelry Cleaner	$85.00	_____
_____ Ionic Solution—16 oz. bottle	$20.00	_____

Buy Your *"Tools of the Trade..."*
Gem Identification Instruments Directly from *GemStone Press*
Whatever instrument you need, GemStone Press can help.
Use our convenient order form, or contact us directly for assistance.

ITEM / QUANTITY	PRICE EA.*	TOTAL $
Lamps—Ultraviolet & High Intensity		
_____ UV-Blocking Goggles	$24.95	_____
• Recommended for use with all UV lamps.		
_____ Small Longwave/Shortwave (UVP)	$85.00	_____
_____ Large Longwave/Shortwave (UVP)	$237.00	_____
_____ Viewing Cabinet for Large Lamp (UVP)	$195.00	_____
_____ **Purchase Large Lamp & Cabinet together**	$385.95	_____
and save over $45.00		
_____ SSEF High-Intensity Shortwave Illuminator	$499.00	_____
• Operates with SSEF Diamond-Type Spotter (additional—see above).		
Other Light Sources		
_____ Solitaire Maglite	$11.00	_____
_____ Standard Mini Maglite	$15.00	_____
_____ Flex Light	$29.95	_____
Refractometers		
_____ Precision Pocket Refractometer (RosGem RFA 322)	$625.00	_____
• Operates with Solitaire Maglite (additional—see above).		
_____ Refractive Index Liquid 1.81—10 grams	$69.95	_____
Scale		
_____ GemPro50 Carat Scale	$174.95	_____
Spectroscopes		
_____ Spectroscope—Pocket-sized model (OPL)	$98.00	_____
_____ Spectroscope—Desk model w/stand (OPL)	$235.00	_____

Shipping/Insurance per order in the U.S.: **$7.95 first item,** SHIPPING/INS. $_____
$3.00 each add'l item; $10.95 total for pocket instrument set.

Outside the U.S.: Please specify *insured* shipping method you prefer
and provide a credit card number for payment. **TOTAL $ _____** **

Check enclosed for $ _____ (Payable to: GEMSTONE PRESS)
Charge my credit card: ❑ Visa ❑ MasterCard
Name on Card _____ Phone (____)_____
Cardholder Address: Street _____
City/State/Zip _____ E-mail _____
Credit Card # _____ Exp. Date _____
Signature _____ CID # _____
Please send to: ❑ Same as Above ❑ Address Below
Name _____
Street _____
City/State/Zip _____ Phone (____)_____

Phone, mail, fax, or e-mail orders to:
GEMSTONE PRESS, P.O. Box 237, Woodstock, VT 05091
Tel: **(802) 457-4000** • *Fax:* **(802) 457-4004**
Credit Card Orders: **(800) 962-4544** (8:30AM–5:30PM ET Monday–Friday)
sales@gemstonepress.com • www.gemstonepress.com
Generous Discounts on Quantity Orders

TOTAL SATISFACTION GUARANTEE
If for any reason you're not completely delighted
with your purchase, return it in resellable condition
within 30 days for a full refund.

*Prices, manufacturing specifications and term[...]
without notice. Orders accepted subject[...]

**All orders must be prepaid by credit card,[...]
in U.S. funds drawn on a U.S[...]

Please send me:

CAMEOS OLD & NEW, 4TH EDITION
_____ copies at $19.99 (Quality Paperback) *plus s/h**

COLORED GEMSTONES, 3RD EDITION: THE ANTOINETTE MATLINS BUYING GUIDE
_____ copies at $18.99 (Quality Paperback) *plus s/h**

DIAMONDS, 3RD EDITION: THE ANTOINETTE MATLINS BUYING GUIDE
_____ copies at $18.99 (Quality Paperback) *plus s/h**

ENGAGEMENT & WEDDING RINGS, 3RD EDITION: THE DEFINITIVE BUYING GUIDE
_____ copies at $18.95 (Quality Paperback) *plus s/h**

GEM IDENTIFICATION MADE EASY, 4TH EDITION:
A HANDS-ON GUIDE TO MORE CONFIDENT BUYING & SELLING
_____ copies at $36.99 (Hardcover) *plus s/h**

GEMS & JEWELRY APPRAISING, 3RD EDITION
_____ copies at $39.99 (Hardcover) *plus s/h**

ILLUSTRATED GUIDE TO JEWELRY APPRAISING, 3RD EDITION
_____ copies at $39.99 (Hardcover) *plus s/h**

JEWELRY & GEMS AT AUCTION: THE DEFINITIVE GUIDE TO BUYING & SELLING
AT THE AUCTION HOUSE & ON INTERNET AUCTION SITES
_____ copies at $19.95 (Quality Paperback) *plus s/h**

JEWELRY & GEMS, 7TH EDITION: THE BUYING GUIDE
_____ copies at $19.99 (Quality Paperback) *plus s/h**

THE PEARL BOOK, 4TH EDITION: THE DEFINITIVE BUYING GUIDE
_____ copies at $19.99 (Quality Paperback) *plus s/h**

THE SPECTROSCOPE AND GEMMOLOGY
_____ copies at $49.95 (Quality Paperback) *plus s/h**

TREASURE HUNTER'S GEM & MINERAL GUIDES TO THE U.S.A., 5TH EDITION:
WHERE & HOW TO DIG, PAN AND MINE YOUR OWN GEMS & MINERALS
IN 4 REGIONAL VOLUMES $14.99 per copy (Quality Paperback) *plus s/h**
_____ copies of NE States _____ copies of SE States _____ copies of NW States _____ copies of SW States

* In U.S.: Shipping/Handling: $3.95 for 1st book, $2.00 each additional book.
  Outside U.S.: Specify shipping method (insured) and provide a credit card number for payment.

Check enclosed for $_____ (Payable to: GEMSTONE Press)
Charge my credit card: ❑ Visa ❑ MasterCard
me on Card (PRINT) _____ Phone (_____)_____
holder Address: Street _____
te/Zip _____ E-mail _____
   # _____ Exp. Date _____
                                          _____ CID# _____
ame as Above ❑ Address Below
_____
_____
                                          Phone (_____)_____

Phone, mail, fax, or e-mail orders to:

STONE PRESS, Sunset Farm Offices,
P.O. Box 237, Woodstock, VT 05091
457-4000 • *Fax:* (802) 457-4004
  d Orders: (800) 962-4544
  30PM ET Monday–Friday)
  press.com • www.gemstonepress.com
  Discounts on Quantity Orders

Prices subject
to change

subject to change
availability
oney order or check
bank.

Your Bookstore First